# Breakfast
# with
# Tiffany

# Breakfast with Tiffany

## *A Memoir*

Edwin John Wintle

**THORNDIKE**
WINDSOR
PARAGON

This Large Print edition is published by Thorndike Press®, Waterville, Maine USA and by BBC Audiobooks Ltd, Bath, England.

Published in 2006 in the U.S. by arrangement with Miramax Books, a division of Miramax Film Corp.

Published in 2006 in the U.K. by arrangement with Simon & Schuster UK Ltd.

U.S.  Hardcover  0-7862-8216-9   (Biography)
U.K.  Hardcover  1-4056-1250-9   (Windsor Large Print)
U.K.  Softcover  1-4056-1251-7   (Paragon Large Print)

The text of this Large Print edition is unabridged.
Other aspects of the book may vary from the original edition.

Set in 16 pt. Plantin by Elena Picard.

Printed in the United States on permanent paper.

---

**British Library Cataloguing-in-Publication Data available**

---

**Library of Congress Cataloging-in-Publication Data**

Wintle, Edwin John.
    Breakfast with Tiffany : an uncle's memoir / by Edwin John Wintle.
        p. cm. — (Thorndike Press large print biography)
    ISBN 0-7862-8216-9 (lg. print : hc : alk. paper)
    1. Wintle, Edwin John.  2. Tiffany.  3. Teenage girls — New York (State) — New York — Biography.  4. Gay parents — New York (State) — New York — Biography.  5. New York (N.Y.) — Biography.  I. Title.  II. Series: Thorndike Press large print biography series.
CT275.W584747A3 2005
306.874'22092—dc22
    [B]                                            2005025777

In Loving Memory
of
Heather Ann Underwood
(1977–1997)

For the life of me, I cannot remember
what made us think that we were wise
and we'd never compromise.
For the life of me, I could not believe
we'd ever die for these sins . . .
We were merely freshmen.

> — The Verve Pipe
> "The Freshmen"
> (Tiffany's favorite song)

Me, I just say my prayers,
then I just light myself on fire,
and I walk out on the wire once again.

> — Counting Crows
> "Goodnight Elisabeth"
> (Uncle Eddy's favorite song)

# Author's Note:

The names and other identifying character-
istics of the persons included in this memoir
have been changed.

# Prologue

After breakfast I always walked Tiffany over to the F train at Sixth Avenue and Waverly Place. Sometimes we'd spend the ten-plus minutes in silence, sometimes not. I tried to follow her lead, as I figured there's nothing worse than forced conversation at seven thirty in the morning.

"I hate No Trespassing signs," she said one Tuesday morning, seemingly out of the blue. "They're so stupid."

"Oh, yeah? Why is that?"

"Because of course you're not supposed to trespass. It's illegal by definition. It's like putting a No Kidnapping sign in a playground."

"You know, you've got a point there."

"Yeah, the sign should say, Keep Out or Trespassers Will Be Persecuted."

"You mean 'prosecuted.' "

"Whatever."

I love the minds of thirteen-year-olds, I thought. They're always thinking about the stupidity of adults. How cute and clever.

"You know, Uncle Eddy, I had sex with Aleksi in the bathroom at the pizza place last Saturday," Tiffany said, looking straight ahead as she walked.

Oh, yeah, then there's this part. Dear Lord in heaven, I prayed, *please* let her be kidding.

# Part One

# Autumn

# Something's Coming

New Jersey Transit trains always manage to smell like someone just pissed on a ball of burning rubber and then doused the whole mess with liquid Lysol. I was trying to breathe through only my mouth — even though I know it's more sanitary to catch the stinky molecules in your nose hairs — when my cell phone rang. I was returning to New York City from Philadelphia, having attended the afternoon wedding of an old friend and, in one of my ridiculous attempts to save a few bucks, I wound up taking four local trains in both directions to complete a trip that takes only an hour and a half on Amtrak. I'd just switched trains at Trenton, where I'd gotten a third cup of coffee during a long layover, so I was now both wired *and* cursing myself for my "frugality." It had been a disgustingly humid mid-September day and this latest train was not only stench-ridden but airless as well.

Though the wedding had been adorably

eccentric — the groom cried hysterically every time he opened his mouth — the reception was held in the tiny, cramped backyard of a South Philly row house. I'd sat stoically for six hours, listening to folk music and dripping sweat into my couscous, all the while making pseudo artsy-fartsy conversation with strangers. I was in no mood to be on a hot, smelly train filled with noisy drunks (they seem to *live* on New Jersey Transit) and breaking out into my hundredth sweat of the day. The three cups of coffee were supposed to counteract the wine I'd imbibed, help me catch up on some work reading, and enable me to go out barhopping back in Manhattan to celebrate my unfettered singledom — something I always made it a point to do after weddings. But at the moment, the coffee was actually giving me minor heart palpitations.

After a few minutes of concentrated yogic breathing, I cracked open what promised to be another in a long line of bad screenplays. That's when my cell phone rang. Cell phones annoy everyone on all trains, but in this crowd they were still downright foreign. I answered it as quickly as possible and spoke in a stage whisper.

"Hello?"

"Hi, Eddy, it's me," my sister Megan said in the clipped way she spoke when extremely stressed, which was most of the time.

"What's wrong?"

"Tiffany, what else? I just don't think I can take it anymore. I really think I'm going to lose it." She started to sob. I hated to hear Megan cry, especially when she was sober. When she was drunk, her tears were filled with self-pity so I couldn't sympathize. But she'd kicked the booze a couple of months ago and was now facing her demons head-on. And one of them was her thirteen-year-old daughter, Tiffany. Now Megan's sadness pulled at my heart because her pain was real — and something she could no longer hide with the tough Irish-lass veneer she'd perfected.

"It's okay, Megan, take your time," I whispered. "Tell me what happened." Her sobs tapered off to small whimpers as she caught her breath.

"She's gone. It's ten o'clock on a Saturday night and she just walked right out the door after I told her not to." Megan inhaled deeply, and after she released her breath, her voice turned calm with resignation. "I can't keep her safe anymore, Eddy. I need you to take her." Megan had never spoken these words before.

A week or so earlier she had called me at work to report that she'd just smacked Tiffany around in front of two of her school friends. Apparently they'd argued about something, after which Tiffany marched into her bedroom where her friends were waiting, slammed the door, and called her mother a "fucking piece of shit." That's when Megan ran in and starting hitting her with both hands. Megan hadn't cried when she told me, nor was she contrite. "I'm not sorry I hit her," she'd announced. "She made me do it." It was as though she'd needed to immediately testify to what had happened, to have her version on record. She knew I'd probably hear from Tiffany within the hour, as I'd been attempting to mediate their fights long-distance for some time now. It wasn't working. I rarely got to Connecticut to see Tiffany face-to-face, and her calls were getting fewer and farther between. When we did speak, she either screamed about her mother or just responded to me with perfunctory, one-word answers. Tiffany was not only out of Megan's control but was slipping away from me as well.

Over the previous two summers Tiffany had spent a lot of time with me in Man-

16

hattan. Between seventh and eighth grade, when she was twelve, she took a six-week theater program at a well-known conservatory school on Pier 40 in Greenwich Village. Tiffany had shown some serious singing talent as a child, as well as an interest in dramatic writing — she wrote a thirty-page slasher movie when she was only ten — and I wanted to help foster those gifts. During seventh grade Tiffany's creative pursuits had begun taking a backseat to boys, partying, and hanging out. Her parents had finally divorced after years of fighting, my sister's drinking was escalating, and Tiffany found out that her father's extended "business trips" were really stints in the slammer for DUIs and driving with a suspended license. She'd found little comfort in her relationship with her younger sister, Sammy; the two girls fought like crazy, venting most of their rage on each other. It was as though Tiffany's family had driven her into the arms of her friends — friends who provided solace but weren't equipped to truly help her. I'd wanted to take her away from all that for a while, hoping that having her talents reinforced, along with getting to know some of my "girlfriends," would help her see through the muck to a brighter future. It seemed to work during the summer itself, when she spoke of attending college in the city and auditioning for Broadway, but things had gone downhill immediately upon her return to New Milford. Everything she'd learned seemed forgotten, and Tiffany completed eighth grade with Ds in math and science and Cs in everything else. The following summer — the one just before this muggy September day — she came down to the city again but was willing to leave her friends for only three weeks this time. Though our visit was brief, Tiffany seemed to relish it and, I thought, leave with her goals reestablished. But once she was back in Connecticut, things went from bad to worse. High school had just started and Tiffany was already labeled an "at-risk" student due to truancy. Megan said my niece had been hanging out with older guys, often taking off in cars with them. I was becoming frightened that Tiffany would end up a dropout, pregnant, or burnt out on drugs (or all three), so when Megan called and told me she'd gotten physically violent with her daughter again, I offered for Tiffany to come live with me in New York . . . permanently. I hadn't consciously planned to make that offer, but hearing just how horribly my sister and my niece were treating each other, it seemed the right thing to do — not only for them, but for Sammy too. To my relief, Megan had declined my offer then, but here she was now, less than two weeks later, taking me up on it. Without realizing it at the time, by having Tiffany visit New York City those two summers, I had somehow laid the foundation for what would be the biggest challenge of my life.

"Of course, Megan," I now whispered on the train. "We should get her down here as soon as possible. Let's plan on next weekend. This week I'll get ready for her and we'll figure out how to go about actually getting her to the city." The words were coming out automatically, as though I'd rehearsed them or something; I couldn't *really* be making this monumental a decision *and* expressing it in a rational fashion. Maybe a part of me believed this couldn't possibly come to pass — that I, Ed Wintle, would, in one week's time, be a single "parent" to a thirteen-year-old girl. But the words continued to pour out of my mouth. "You're doing the right thing, Megan. I don't see any other alternative at this point."

"Are *you* sure you're okay with this,

Eddy? It's going to completely change your life."

"Don't worry about me." I tried to sound reassuring. "I'll be fine. Let's just take it one step at a time. Call around and find out whose house Tiffany went to. Make sure she's safe for tonight."

When I closed the cell phone, my head shot back against the train seat and my eyes darted around wildly, looking for witnesses. Had this actually just happened? My mind sparked in a dozen different directions. What would I do about my roommate? Where would Tiffany go to school? Could I really afford to support a child? What if she runs away in New York City? Or worse, what if she's abducted? Hadn't they made a movie about that kid who disappeared in Soho back in the '80s — Etan something — starring JoBeth Williams and Daniel J. Travanti? And, even more frightening, would I have to throw away my porn collection? *What the hell have I gotten myself into?*

My head stayed glued to that seat back for the rest of the train ride and the script lay unread by my side. I'm sure I looked like an escapee from the asylum, with my rapid breathing and bugged-out Marty Feldman eyes.

What I felt more than anything, though — more than the fear, the self-doubt, more than the creeping nausea that comes with irrevocability — was excitement. Genuine, pure, adrenaline-fueled excitement. After all, I am a drama Queen (yes, with a capital Q) and I have always thrived on change. I adore endings and I love beginnings; it's the middles that I can do without. And I'd been in a "middle" for some time now, trudging through my days neither here nor there, neither up nor down. I was a single, forty-year-old man stuck in intermission, wondering when the next act would start. My life needed that proverbial shot in the arm. What it would get, though, would prove to be more like electroshock therapy.

# Uncle Mame

"Oh, you'll be just like Rosalind Russell in *Auntie Mame!*" Eugene's voice screamed through my headset. It was already the Thursday after I'd spoken to Megan and I was still scrambling to catch my best friends up on what was going on.

"You remember, don't you?" he chided. "Mame brings her young nephew to live with her in glamorous New York City and teaches him all about life. Oh, oh, oh!" Eugene was really working himself into a tizzy. "Can I be the Agnes Gooch character? She was a tragic, fat and ugly unwed mother who also sought refuge at Auntie Mame's."

I smiled to myself; everything was a movie to Eugene, but up to this point he had always been the star. Suggesting I be the leading lady was a huge concession for him.

"Peggy Cass played her, remember? She actually got an Oscar nomination for it, before going on to an illustrious career on tacky game shows. Real-life tragedy mimicking film tragedy — I love that!"

"And how exactly do you plan to play Agnes Gooch to my Auntie Mame?" I asked. "Are you going to show up in drag with a pregnancy pillow under your housedress?"

"No, silly," he laughed. "Agnes Gooch was the cautionary B story for young girls in the audience. With my own, real-life story, I can be the cautionary tale for your young charge."

Just then my assistant, Rob, announced that Gail from the school superintendent's office was on the line, responding to the fifteen messages I'd left for her in the last twenty-four hours.

"I gotta dash, Eugene. I'll invite you over to the set in a couple of weeks," I giggled, "but don't expect a double-wide all to yourself."

Eugene was one of my more colorful friends, with a past that was nothing short of psychedelic. He'd lived for sixteen years as Natalia (uncomfortably close to "genitalia" for a transsexual, in my opinion) and had just switched back to being a man before I'd met him about fifteen years earlier. His story was astonishing; he'd married a G.I. at twenty-one and lived as an army wife on a base in Germany. If the truth had been discovered by the soldiers there, he and his husband could easily have been

23

brutalized, if not murdered. When his marriage ended, he moved back to New York, where he worked as a model, actress, and nightclub performer. But eventually Natalia bottomed out on booze, pills, and prostitution, got sober, and decided to return to manhood. Luckily for him, as well as for his wallet, Eugene had kept his willy intact, so his partial gender re-reassignment hadn't been too complex an operation. Years later Eugene wrote and starred in an off-Broadway show about his life called *Switcheroo!* He'd received a rave review in the *New York Times* but the show failed to pull in the tourist crowds. It would be interesting to see Tiffany's reaction to Auntie Eugene, though I didn't quite see how he'd be a cautionary role model for her. To my knowledge, gender dysphoria was not on Tiffany's current list of problems.

My life had been insane since my phone conversation with Megan six days earlier. During every huge change that had taken place in my life — falling in love, breaking up, going back to school, graduating — I became what could probably be diagnosed as clinically manic. Indeed, from the moment I stepped off that New Jersey Transit train, I felt like there were sparks flying out of my head. Sure, I stuck with my plans to go out that night to revel in being single, but when I'd arrived at my idea of the city's premier nightspot — where gay men "of a certain age" still had a chance of getting lucky — there was no way I could engage in the usual moronic precoital banter. If anyone were to speak to me, I could just imagine the following exchange taking place:

HIM: "Hey. What's up? You're pretty hot."

ME: "Not much. So are you."

HIM: "What are you up to tonight?"

ME: "Listen, do you know how much additional iron a menstruating teenage girl needs in order to not get anemic?"

Sure, that'll guarantee you a hot tumble in the sack.

I'd managed a couple of laps around the smoky, cramped club, prying my way through hordes of shirtless, pumped men in predatory trances. But my heart just wasn't in it. Instead of feeling sexually charged, the whole scene just seemed empty and bleak. I was near to combusting and it was all I could do not to stand on the pool table and scream, *"So long, guys! These nights are over for me. I'm about to become a father!"* Instead I jumped into a cab and headed downtown, anxious to obsessively plan for the real rearrangement of the homestead.

My part-time roommate, a seven-foot-tall African-American pediatric eye surgeon from Pennsylvania, was first on my list. For five years Dr. Harland had been staying in my second bedroom once or twice a week, depending on how early his surgery appointments were the next morning. Occasionally too he'd stay the weekend, especially if there was a big leather or circuit party at one of the city's clubs. It would be a huge inconvenience for him to have to suddenly find another place, or a way to commute into Manhattan at 6 a.m. But I knew how desperately teenagers need their privacy — as well as their rest — so there was no way I was going to have Tiffany sleep on the sofa for even just two school nights each week. Plus, two gay men and a teenage girl would make for a fierce fracas when it came to my one bathroom. And it wasn't like Dr. Harland would be left homeless either, with his gorgeous nineteenth-century farmhouse, barn, built-in pool, and beaucoup acreage out in the hinterlands. Thus I assuaged my guilt about kicking out someone who'd begun as merely a regular presence in my life but who, with time, had become a dear friend.

I approached Dr. Harland nervously when he arrived that Sunday night with his tremendous bag of takeout from Monster Sushi. As he meticulously laid out his meal on three of my largest dinner plates, I explained the situation and the decision I'd made.

"Oh my!" Dr. Harland's eyes lit up as he spoke, his Boston terrier smile stretching clear from ear to ear. "This is an incredible thing you're doing. Come here." He opened his endless arms wider than I'd thought humanly possible, and I obeyed. My nose snuggled below his Adam's apple and he squeezed me hard.

"Children are the most important thing in the world," he whispered into my hair. "They're all we have left." His giant hands rubbed my back as I nuzzled his soft corduroy shirt. Sure, Dr. Harland could be as hedonistic and decadent as the next fifty-five-year-old gay man stuck in perpetual adolescence, but he had a wellspring of kindness and a heart as big as all the "clothing optional" resorts in Palm Springs put together.

★ ★ ★

All week my work hours had been spent almost entirely on the phone, and *not* negotiating book-to-film deals, my primary professional function for the last seven years. Instead I was talking with either Megan or some official from New York City's Byzantine public school system. Fearing Tiffany would run away if we told her six days ahead that on Sunday she'd be moving to New York City, Megan and I decided to wait until Friday to break the news. We thought it would be too cruel to not let her know before the weekend and effectively prevent her from saying goodbye to her friends. Tiffany regularly threw tantrums, so Megan was actually frightened to tell her even a mere two days ahead, as there was no telling how bonkers she might go. Another option was for me to show up at Megan's under the guise of taking Tiffany to the mall or something, only to gun it onto the highway and deploy the child locks when she started screaming. As that scenario was simply too melodramatic, we ultimately chose to take our chances with Tiffany's reaction; we'd tell her together on Friday.

Megan made the requisite call to Tiffany's dad, Tony, and he was all for the

28

idea. I was a bit surprised, as there was no love lost between Tony and me. We were always perfectly cordial to each other, but he was extremely conservative — some might even say redneck — in his views. He was a staunch Republican, and little things Tiffany and Sammy said led me to believe he was homophobic too. From the look of things, Tony probably just wanted Tiffany and her problems out of his hair. Besides being freshly out of jail and shacked up with a younger woman, Tony lived in a town ten miles away and was forbidden by law to drive. He claimed to be worried about Tiffany's behavior, but he'd basically fallen out of her life, usually surfacing when Megan called him to intervene, which he did by screaming and threatening. And Tiffany certainly wouldn't be asking to live with him anytime soon; she'd refused to speak with him for weeks now and had referred to him over the summer as "the crackhead." So, with Tony's blessing, Megan and I were now all set as far as the logistics went; we'd tell Tiffany on Friday, I'd spend the weekend by Megan's side, and we'd drive Tiffany down to the city together on Sunday.

To figure out the school issue, I started knocking on neighbors' doors. The few families I knew in my apartment complex who had children near Tiffany's age provided me with my school district number, an old catalogue of NYC high schools, some recommendations, and much-needed moral support. But I quickly realized that their children were attending schools that would be impossible for Tiffany to get into with her poor junior high transcript, and the performing arts high schools only took students who'd auditioned the year before. I started to worry that Tiffany would end up in a twenty-first-century version of *The Blackboard Jungle*, where girls were raped in bathrooms and teachers were hung out classroom windows. In that case the danger quotient might be greater than in New Milford, so, if anything happened to my niece, it would be entirely my fault.

It was during an insomnia-driven laundry session late that Tuesday night that my academic guardian angel arrived. She took the form of a cherubic fifty-something redhead named Patti who was up to her neck in whites. We'd said hello to one another in the past but had never had a conversation. That night, for some reason, she asked me how I was.

"Mythirteenyearoldnieceismovinginwith meinfivedaysandIhavenoideawhereshe'sgoing togotoschool," I blurted out in one breath. Deflated, I added, "The school system is impenetrable." I knew whereof I spoke as I'd spent my lunch hour that day trekking up to the high school general admissions office in the east thirties. Not only did I fail to get into the building that housed the office; the snake of a line was so long that I didn't get within a block of it. At its tail end two administrators informed me, "You have to come back with your kid and wait. Then it's a crapshoot. You get what you get." Wonderful, I thought. I wanted an American *To Sir, with Love* but I was going to end up with *Up the Down Staircase.*

"I've got just the person for you to speak with," Patti said, her kind eyes smiling. "Her name is Gail and she's the head of admissions at the superintendent's office. I'll be right back with her phone number, and you tell her I sent you." I was being sent right to the top; no more lines, no more endless bureaucracy. Between Dr. Harland's reaction, Tony's cooperation, and now Patti-Angel, it seemed the stars were aligning to help make this crazy plan actually happen. When Patti returned and said, "I promise Gail will take care of your niece," I hugged her in gratitude. I bounced up the four flights to my apartment, anxious to put the laundry away and begin bagging up Dr. Harland's five years' worth of *Honcho* magazines.

The next morning, after I'd caught up with Eugene (a.k.a. Agnes Gooch) and made an appointment for Tiffany and me to see Gail the following week, Rob announced that Megan was on the phone.

"Those goddamned assholes at Tiffany's school!" she shrieked through her tears. "They called her down to the principal's office this morning and told her that I'd withdrawn her from school and that she'd have to leave the premises! Can you friggin' believe it?"

"Oh, shit" was all I could say.

"She apparently screamed at the principal in front of the office staff and ran out of the building crying. They said she headed for the woods and disappeared. I have no idea *where* she is, Eddy."

"Sit tight, Meg," I said, knowing she was pacing around her living room, ready to jump out of her skin. "I'll take the next train out of Grand Central and be there within two hours."

How does that stupid saying go? I thought as I pulled off my headset. That's right: if you want to hear God laugh, make plans. Oh, how fucking true.

# Closing the Deal

"I'm not just blowing smoke up your ass," Rachel Goldstein said as I stared out my office window at the spectacular Cooper Union building on Astor and Bowery. Will Tiffany get a degree in architecture there one day? Who do I have to know — or blow — to get her in?

"I know we can get this movie set up in just a couple of weeks," she continued. "We're already talking with Sandy Bullock's people."

Sandra Bullock is going to play a sixty-year-old lesbian bounty hunter? The smoke was so far up my ass it was coming out my ears.

"Be that as it may, Rachel," I responded calmly into my headset, "there are a lot of producers interested in this story, so Cynthia is going to have to cough up some cash to get an exclusive option on my client's rights." Cynthia was a hot Hollywood producer — meaning her last film had made some money — and Rachel was her

New York VP of development, also known as a D-girl.

"Oh, come on, Ed," Rachel pleaded, "you know our discretionary fund is depleted. And there's bounty hunter roadkill all over town. J. Lo had one, Angelina had one, and they're all dead in the water."

This may've all been true, but Rachel would say anything to get an exclusive on material that Cynthia wanted, and for as little money as possible. Her job depended on it, and development jobs were hard to come by in New York.

"What am I supposed to go back to my client with? Zero dollars?" I'd had this conversation hundreds of times and I was bored to tears. Is Tiffany going to insist on painting her room purple?

"We're going to have to think outside the box on this one, Ed, because at the end of the day, this project has got to have Cynthia's name on it."

Rachel had just uttered the two movie business expressions of the month that I hated most — the "box" nonsense and "at the end of the day" — so the conversation had to end or I would throw myself out the window. Plus, it was Friday afternoon and all I could think about was Tiffany's arrival in thirty-six hours.

"Look, Rachel, let's pick this up next week. In the meantime, can you recommend a good gynecologist?"

"Sure I can," she answered with a combination of amusement and surprise. "And this would be for whom, may I ask?"

"Well, I'm sort of going to be a father," I said, not wanting to go into detail.

"Mazel tov, Ed," Rachel chuckled. "But baby girls need pediatricians, not gynecologists."

"It's a long story. I'll give you a holler on Monday," I said as I shut down my computer and tore off my headset.

Here we go, I thought. Let the countdown begin.

My trip to New Milford that Thursday morning had been aborted when my cell phone rang at Grand Central Station.

"She's home," Megan announced. "I found her over at Tommy Dash's house."

"Is she hysterical?" I pictured Tiffany trashing Megan's house while frothing at the mouth.

"No. She'd obviously been crying for a couple of hours, but she's strangely calm now." I went down the wide ramp next to Vanderbilt Hall and found a quiet corner near the entrance to the Oyster Bar.

"Why 'strangely'?" I asked. "Do you think she's on something?"

"No, I just think she really gets it, which I didn't expect. When I told her that she was moving in with you in the city, she didn't scream or yell about it. She just said, 'I understand,' like somehow she'd expected it or something."

"Well, that's a good start," I said, relieved. "Unless you think it's a cover for a plan to run away or something. Is she that diabolical?"

"Yes, of course she is. Why do you think I'm getting rid of her?" Megan laughed sardonically. "No, I'm only kidding. Sort of. But I don't think she's up to anything."

"Good," I said, hoping she was right. "Are we revising our plan now?"

"Yeah. I spoke to Mom and she's going to drive Tiffany down on Sunday, if that's okay with you. That way you don't have to come up here and I can spend the day with Sammy. I'm kind of worried about how this will affect her. First her father and I split, and now Tiffany leaves. We'll have gone from a family of four to a family of two in just a couple of years. And I think there's going to be some jealousy too."

"Reassure her that Tiffany is still part of the family," I said. "Tell her to think of it like Tiffany's away at boarding school. And it's nothing to be jealous of; it's going to be like boot camp for Tiffany. I'll be running a damned tight ship."

"She won't get that, Eddy. She's only eight years old."

"Hey, how ya doin', handsome?" a deep voice suddenly interrupted, speaking directly into my ear. Startled, I swung around to see who'd come so close, but no one was behind me. Then I realized what had happened and quickly moved away from the corner in embarrassment.

"Oh my God, Megan, I think I just got cruised by the Whispering Wall!" I stealthily looked across the underground plaza and saw an average-looking, tourist-type guy smiling at me from across the way. In my haste to find a quiet place to talk, I'd forgotten that this little plaza featured that architectural and acoustical oddity where people in opposite corners can whisper messages to each other via the smoothly arched stone ceiling — like in Brunelleschi's duomo in Florence.

"What are you talking about, Eddy?"

"Never mind," I said, walking quickly away from the wall. "Okay, so we have a new plan. There's one more thing I've been meaning to speak to you about, though."

"What?" Megan asked impatiently.

"Eric," I said. "You need to get rid of him, Megan. I don't think he's helped the Tiffany situation any, and you know Sammy doesn't like him at all." Eric was a lowlife whom Megan had met while she was still drinking, and they'd been seeing each other for over a year now. "Surely in sobriety you can see that he's not appropriate for you."

I was trying to be tactful but Eric gave me the creeps, plain and simple. Sure, he could be goofily amusing in a freak show sort of way, and I knew Megan put his much younger, fairly buff body to good use. But Eric was a loser, sad as it was to say; he'd been dealt a bad hand and hadn't done a thing to change it — except maybe to find Megan. Uneducated and virtually unemployable, Eric lived with his mother and grandmother, earning just enough money with the odd handyman job to keep his old jalopy running. I'd recently learned that his brother was in jail for murdering his girlfriend's mother and that Eric's father had shot himself in the face at the dinner table when the boys were teenagers. Exactly the kind of guy you want your sister dating and exposing your nieces to, I'd thought over and over again for months. Besides the fact that Eric's dopey grin couldn't disguise the crazy look behind his eyes, Tiffany had told me things Eric had done at Megan's that made my nose hairs curl.

"Yeah, I know, Eddy," Megan sighed. "It's so hard, you know? He's so nice, and I'm afraid to be alone." *Nice?* I wanted to scream, *He's out of his fucking mind! Talking to him makes less sense than talking to a fish. And I don't want him around Sammy!* I hadn't confronted Megan with the things I knew, as it wasn't necessary; she knew them as well, so in her heart, she had to know that I was right.

"Just promise me you'll try your best," I pleaded. "Please?"

"Okay, okay." I could tell Megan wanted to end the call.

"It's all going to work out." I tried to sound convincing. "Let me know if you need me to come up over the weekend," I offered halfheartedly, knowing I really needed more time to prepare. "Tiffany and I have an appointment on Monday with a bigwig in the superintendent's office, so I think the school thing is going to resolve itself quickly." She was silent. "I love you, Megan."

"I love you too," she replied, but the love

was hard to detect in her voice. "Good-bye, Eddy."

For as far back as I can remember, Megan and I have had a volatile relationship. Though we were less than two years apart in age, with me trailing her in school by only one grade, we didn't really get close until high school. (Our older sister, Kathleen, had a full five years on me, so she would remain an enigma well into adulthood.) As teenagers and young adults, though, we continued to have terrible fights. (The only fistfight I've ever had was with Megan, and we were in our early twenties when it took place.) Of course I have sweet memories of her from early childhood — building forts in the den on rainy afternoons and lying in her bed at night pretending we were boating through dark tunnels — but mostly we were antagonistic toward each other. From around eight to ten years old, I was the classic bratty little brother who tattled when I caught her smoking and who resented being told to get lost. She, in turn, beat me up easily and often, pinning my arms down with her knees so she could slap me or spit in my face. Our rows at the dinner table became so intolerable that, despite the family's having moved so my dad's commute would be shorter and he could make it home in time for supper, my parents extended their cocktail hour and ate after us.

Just as I was beginning tenth grade, Kathleen, who was nineteen, got pregnant and married (in that order) and moved out. Being the only kids left in the house pushed Megan and me together, but our real common ground was our mutual love of drinking and taking recreational drugs. I was a small, skinny kid who was picked on for the first three years of high school — often called a "faggot" by groups of boys and some of the younger girls — while Megan was tall and pretty and had a great body. She was popular and probably could have helped put a stop to some of my torment, but I was too ashamed to tell her about it. Though I took honors classes, kept my grades up to a B+ average, and began to emerge as one of my class's top artists, I found real acceptance (and thus solace) by becoming a partier. Getting stoned gave my social life a focus, something it badly needed, since I wasn't much interested in sex with girls, my high school had no drama club, and, except for skiing, sports were not an option. High, I discovered I could make people laugh and easily fell into the role of entertainer by being goofy and outrageous. Despite our parents' being aware of Megan's and my proclivities, in typical '70s fashion they left us alone when they went off on cruises or to visit friends. Megan's and my parties became legendary in our high school, and we bonded by dealing with police visits, complaining neighbors, and unruly guests. As we meticulously scrubbed the house from top to bottom the mornings after, hiding all evidence of our crimes, we'd swap stories of the night before and howl with laughter.

While I was away at college, Megan became close to several of my friends back home, which kept our social circles entwined well into our twenties. After I graduated and moved to Manhattan, one of our mutual friends came to the city to live with me, which brought Megan down regularly for visits. During the years I'd been away, though, Megan's relationship with the man she still calls the love of her life had ended, and the tenor of her partying had begun to change for the worse. Nights in Manhattan usually wound up with Megan blacking out and refusing to stay in the apartment, not wanting the "good time" to end. In that state she often cried about her life, calling herself a loser and wishing she were dead. Though I was a real party boy too — the moniker of "Crazy Eddy" had been given to me in college and definitely applied for a few years afterward — I was often nervous during a night out with Megan, fearful of how it would end. It wasn't that I was embarrassed by her behavior; I was deeply saddened by it, knowing that her drinking would only reaffirm her terrible feelings about herself. She had a bad case of middle child syndrome and would occasionally turn on me, spewing resentment about my having gone to college and being "Mommy's little boy." Frustrated, I began to pull away, limiting our social contact. As our twenties progressed, Megan became determined to get married and have children — something she was sure would "fix" things — and at twenty-seven she met Tony. Within a year they were married and three weeks later Tiffany was born.

Besides maybe Megan herself, no one was more hopeful than I that starting a family would prove to be the panacea she sought. It didn't.

Since I didn't have to go to New Milford for the weekend, I now had an extra couple of days before Tiffany's arrival, and I was determined to put them to good use. It would give me the chance to say a proper good-bye to my assortment of porn magazines and videotapes. It was not a grand collection, by any means, but I'd had some of the mags for more than twenty years and the guys in them felt sort of like old friends. They'd been there for me during the wacky days of college madness, the dark times of chasing an acting career in New York City, and later through the endlessly lonely hours of study during law school. But, alas, it was time to part, so I double-bagged it all in an effort to avoid finding it spread all over the sidewalk the next morning when I went out to get breakfast. Besides hating litter, I was sure everyone from my building would know I was the pervert to whom the collection had belonged. Of course I packed up the best videos for my friend Steven to keep for me, along with the ten-plus diaries I'd filled with my crackpot ramblings over the years.

Dr. Harland had finished clearing out his things, so I could now clean out closets for Tiffany, do her windows, and give the room a thorough scouring. But throughout the course of all this cleaning and organizing, what I did most was think. And worry.

Will I really be able to handle this? Up till now, I thought, Tiffany and I have been friends more than anything. Though I know she respects me, I'm hardly an authority figure to her. How am I going to get her to obey me? She's always been perfectly polite with me and behaved like a poised young lady around all of my friends, but I've heard her in the background screaming when I've been on the phone with Megan. The difference is night and day, like Regan in *The Exorcist*. Is she going to treat me that way? Can I deal with our relationship changing into something completely different? Is my ego strong enough to do battle with a raging teenager, especially considering how incredibly cruel they can be? How am I going to cope with the loss of my freedom? For my entire adult life, I've come and gone as I pleased: if there's a snowfall, I take off to Vermont for snowboarding; if there's a sale on tickets to Europe, I'm there. I go to the gym when I feel like it, catch a movie whenever, and generally have as much sex as humanly possible. Can I really give all of that up?

I broke out into a cold sweat.

While cleaning out the miscellaneous paperwork that had accumulated in Tiffany's soon-to-be closet, I found a copy of a letter I'd written to her a month earlier. Desperate to do something, anything, to help Megan and Tiffany's downward spiraling situation, Kathleen, Mom, Dad, and I all decided to write letters to Tiffany. Trying a somewhat creative approach in order to avoid being another lecturer, I wrote Tiffany two stories, each one about a young woman. The tales started out identical, describing sad childhoods for both girls in households filled with fighting, physical violence, and substance abuse. But the two stories veered in different directions when the girls became teenagers. In one, the young woman was determined to break out of the cycle and find a bigger life for herself; in the other, the girl sought refuge in drugs, alcohol, and boys and wound up becoming just like her mother, with an estranged teenaged daughter of her own. At the end I asked Tiffany which girl she was going to be and let her know that the choice was hers. "We are, each of us, writing the narratives of our lives every day that we live," I'd written. "You need only to decide which story you're going to tell."

Now, as I read my corny prose, I realized

that I had to stop worrying about myself. Whether I could withstand Tiffany's wrath, whether we became mortal enemies, or whether I would crack under the pressure and deprivation and wind up in a psych ward were all beside the point. This wasn't about me; it was about Tiffany. Maybe forcing her to move to New York City was *us* changing her narrative *for* her, but, once she was here, I would do whatever it took to help her write a different story. Newly determined, I tossed my copy of the letter in the Hefty bag, said one last good-bye to my naked old friends, and happily marched the whole shebang down to the trash.

"I had to pull over twice so Tiffany could throw up," my mother said when I opened my apartment door, "and I have to use the little girl's room." She gave me a quick hug and dashed down the hall.

"I'll go down and help Tiffany unload," I yelled after her, and headed down the stairs.

I hadn't seen Tiffany in about six weeks and what I saw now on the Washington Street sidewalk startled me. She was as pale as snow, probably from the terrible hangover she was nursing. But she seemed tiny and frail to me as well. The painted-on jeans she was wearing made her legs look like blue pipe cleaners and, with her sleeveless tank, her arms seemed thinner and longer than they had two months earlier. Her long, dark hair was piled high into a loose bun, and her little round head seemed precariously perched on an impossibly small neck. Could this delicate creature really be at the center of so much commotion? I pulled her into my arms and attempted to hold her tight.

"Okay, okay, Uncle Eddy," she said wanly. "I'm not feeling so good." She reached up and gave me a cursory peck on the cheek.

"Rough night?" I asked, trying not to sound sarcastic.

"Whatever," she replied, avoiding eye contact.

"So," I sighed, "here we are." I was unsure of what to say to this child who was being forced to live with me. It was ground I hadn't covered before. "Welcome" seemed completely inappropriate, dangerous even. "Well, let's get you moved in." I headed toward the back end of my mom's Subaru.

"Uncle Eddy, is this really happening?" Tiffany asked as a whirl of leaves danced around her ankles. "I mean, is it *really* happening?"

"Look, Tiffany," I said, pointing at the dervish, "it's autumn in New York, a magical time to be here." The trace of a smile may have crossed her lips, but I couldn't be sure.

"You're really wonderful to do this, Ed," my mother said after we'd both ordered our chicken Caesars and iced teas. "Thank God you and Tiffany have the relationship you do."

Since she'd agreed to drive my niece down to the city despite the fact that it was her birthday, I'd presented her with a huge wooden bucket of mums and insisted on taking her to lunch. We left Tiffany back at the apartment to start unpacking and to take a much-needed nap. Sitting now at an outdoor café on Hudson Street, we basked in the afternoon sun, which highlighted my mom's latest shade of red.

"Thanks, but I didn't want to see Megan put Tiffany into the system without at least trying this first." Megan had recently called the Department of Children and Families to find out if Connecticut had a version of New York's PINS ("Person In Need of Supervision") petition, which entailed bringing a child before a judge who'd issue an order setting out the rules to be followed. If the child violated them a certain number of times, she'd be sent to a home for juvies. Once a PINS was filed, the petitioning party could not change her mind. This seemed drastic to me, and I feared it would only make Tiffany's situation worse; I saw it as a last resort.

"It's a shame Kathleen and Tyler couldn't take her," Mom said. "I'm sure Tyler would whip her into shape." We both laughed. Kathleen was still with her high school sweetheart, a tough Texas cowboy who'd joined the military just after they were married. Discharged long ago, Tyler was now a manager at Home Depot who kept fit, still had his army buzz cut, and retained an unmistakable air of authority. "But with losing Heather only five years ago," she continued, "it would just be too strange for them to suddenly have a teenager around again."

My eldest niece, who was born when I was fifteen, had died suddenly of a brain aneurysm when she was twenty. There was no illness, no warning; on a beautiful Thursday in May 1997 she was simply taken from us. Heather was Kathleen's and Tyler's only child and, though my sister was only forty when Heather died, they'd decided against having another. They were doing fairly well now, considering, and their marriage seemed to have grown stronger as a result of their tragedy.

"Yeah, I don't think it was even mentioned, which I understand," I said. "And they don't have a very close relationship with Tiffany anyway." I paused to rearrange the salt and pepper shakers. "The way I see it is I've lost one niece already and I'm not going to lose another."

"Well, I applaud you," Mom replied, dabbing behind her sunglasses with the point of her paper napkin. "Your father is against this arrangement, I'm sorry to say. He thinks either Tiffany's going to make your life miserable too, or you're not going to be able to handle the stress of it."

"Well, that's typical, isn't it? Murphy's law. 'Anything that can go wrong will go wrong.' I've heard that my whole life, though it's a little harder to take seriously these days from a man who's had respiratory problems since September eleventh because he saw it on television."

"Oh, you're wicked!" Mom squeaked, trying unsuccessfully to stifle her high-pitched cackle behind her napkin. My mother has the loudest, most infectious laugh on the planet; at tables around us smiling heads swiveled to locate its source.

Our laughter was tinged with guilt, though, as my father always accused my mother and me of conspiring against him. While his allegations used to be unfounded, now that he'd gotten even gloomier in his old age it wasn't unusual for us to compare notes.

"And Tiffany's not *making* anyone's life miserable," I said. "Megan's *always* been miserable, which is the problem. It's ironic how Dad's always feeling sorry for Megan and taking her side when she thinks he doesn't even love her. I think Dad's just terrified of ever acknowledging that parents can screw up their kids in any way."

"Well, I have to say I come down somewhere in the middle on that one, Ed," Mom said as she elegantly lifted her iced tea to lipsticked lips. "Tiffany has got to start taking responsibility for her actions at some point. I've seen the way she and Sammy treat their mother, and honestly, I can't blame Megan for wanting to wallop them once in a while. It's all I can do to not sock them myself sometimes."

"Yeah, well that's why no one asked you and Daddy to take in Tiffany," I teased. In actuality, it was because neither of them had the energy or patience to deal full-time with a teenager, and because my father was on way too short a fuse these days. "No, but really, Megan should have begun disciplining the girls years ago. You can't suddenly start at this point, when the children have no respect for the parent, let alone a healthy fear of her."

"You're probably right, Ed, but there's got to be some way to get them to behave better. I hope you figure it out with Tiffany." My mother looked me in the eyes and smiled knowingly. "You'll certainly have more of an understanding of what it's like to be a parent very soon," she said.

Tiffany slept for fourteen hours that first night in New York City. She'd blasted Green Day the entire time she was unpacking and setting up her room, breaking only for a few bites of moo shu pork. Few words were spoken. While she slept, I tried to do some reading for work, but every other minute I found myself staring at the wall between our bedrooms. I couldn't believe it, but it was true: it had been done. In just eight days, everything had changed completely. As I've said, I thrive on change, and this one was a doozy. The mother of all changes, it seemed to me. I lay there wondering what the next year had in store for Tiffany and me, my mother's words swirling around in my mind. Like any arm-chair quarterback, I had found it easy to sit in judgment of my sister's parenting. I'd wanted badly to be a dad in my early thirties, and I'd watched carefully from the sidelines as Megan and Tony made their mistakes. Why didn't they enforce bedtime? Didn't they realize that if you gave in to a screaming child, the child would learn to scream more? I pictured myself as a loving but strict father, one who would limit television viewing and enforce structured reading time. I'd be involved in every aspect of my child's education and would, through encouragement and example, teach them how to explore and engage the world. This all sounds great in theory, I thought, but would I really have done any better? Wouldn't my low self-esteem and overcompensating perfectionism have totally screwed my children up, no matter what my intentions? Though I'd probably never know, I at least had a shot at making a difference in my niece's life. Indeed, I'd spent a lot of time over the last week thinking of ways to curb Tiffany's bad habits and foster better ones. But there was no telling how it would go. For all I knew, the boys she ran with in Connecticut would show up on Tuesday while I was at work and take her away. But for now, I could only pray that this arrangement would work out and try to rest assured that, at least for this one night, Tiffany was safe.

"Where it at? Where it at?" the large receptionist screamed over and over, standing on her chair with a look of terror in her eyes. Apparently, a mouse was on the loose in the office of the schools' superintendent. Yvonne, which we'd learned was the frightened gal's name, was refusing to come down until someone presented her with a trapped or dead rodent. Tiffany could not stop giggling at this preposterous scene, and I delighted in seeing her smile.

I'd insisted that we look spiffed up for our appointment with Gail Cohen, as a lot was riding on it; Tiffany was now officially without a school. Since all she owned were low-slung jeans and skintight half tops, Tiffany was wearing her single dressy outfit. She sat now with her legs crossed, attempting to cover the thigh-high slit in her long black skirt. Her purple velvet blouse ballooned down to cinched wrists, with matching slits running the length of each arm, and her black platform sandal high heels had to be at least three inches. It was the outfit of an eighteen-year-old attending a holiday dinner, not that of a thirteen-year-old freshman being interviewed for placement in the New York City public school system. But it was all we could come up with and, to be honest, there was no denying that Tiffany looked beautiful.

Gail was a tiny woman with short, graying hair and a thick New York accent. She came out to the waiting room, shot Yvonne a withering look, and led us into a small conference room. After maybe ten minutes of chitchat, during which Tiffany deflected the blame for her grades and relocation toward her chaotic home life, as planned, Gail said, "I know just the place for you, Tiffany." She proceeded to describe a small high school on the Lower East Side that had been founded just four years previously, in partnership with a major university. The university's professors had designed the curriculum, and graduate education students were available daily to tutor students in every subject. It was a challenging school, Gail said, but an academically nurturing environment that was perfect for a bright student who'd been faltering but was now determined to do well. It sounded too good to be true.

"I'm going to call down there right now,"

Gail said, picking up the telephone. "Hello, this is Gail Cohen from the superintendent's office," she announced, "and I have the most lovely little family sitting here right now with a young woman who will be a terrific addition to your freshman class." Tiffany and I glanced conspiratorially at each other and I smiled, realizing for the first time that we were indeed a family now, and that I was proud of us. "Perfect," Gail continued, "Tiffany Adeletta will be there tomorrow morning at eight a.m., vaccination documents, birth certificate, and proof of address in hand. Thank you." She hung up the phone and stood up to shake our hands. That was it, a fait accompli. Though I suspected it, I'd later confirm that Tiffany's new high school was one of the most difficult to get into in our district. Thank the Lord Jesus that I don't have a washer and dryer in the apartment, was all I could think as I said good luck to Yvonne, who was still perched high atop her chair.

# Liquid Eyeliner

"That's impossible, Tiffany, you can't be a size zero," I snipped. "No one is a size zero. It's like saying you don't exist, like you don't take up any space."

"I'm telling you, Uncle Eddy, I *am* a zero," Tiffany pleaded.

*Yikes!* Her self-image is worse than I thought.

"The zeroes are right over there," a sassy young salesgirl interrupted, pointing an impossibly long, curled fingernail depicting what appeared to be a beach at sunset, palm trees and all.

"Thank you." I offered her a tight-lipped smile and marched toward the zero rack with Tiffany in tow. Oh great, I thought, a target size for anorectics.

Tiffany had started school that Tuesday morning and had come home with the news that there was a strictly enforced dress code: no jeans, collared blouses only, and no belly or sleeveless shirts. Having no clue where thirteen-year-old Manhattanites shop, I figured we'd start with Daffy's on Fifth Avenue. Now we were swimming in the middle of a sea of velour, velvet, and lamé — heaven, maybe, for girls from Europe or even the Five Towns on Long Island, but hell for a girl who spent her waking life in hip-hugging jeans and half shirts. There were slacks and tops in orange, purple, gold, silver, and chartreuse, as well as psychedelic patterns that would put Joseph and his tacky Technicolor dreamcoat to shame. Nothing was without a fringe or a chain or a gold glitter butterfly appliqué.

"These are the butt-ugliest clothes I've ever seen!" Tiffany announced to everyone in the Karen Carpenter aisle, a clear edge of hysteria in her tone. "And this dress code sucks."

"Yeah, I agree with you there," I said calmly in the face of a teenage crisis. "I think it's time we headed down to the East Village." I handed her a tube of liquid eyeliner from a nearby counter, which soothed her as only liquid eyeliner can.

Getting up at six fifteen that first morning was excruciating, though I'm not sure who suffered more, me or Tiffany. I'd tossed and turned all night with anxiety dreams, but I was still operating with increased adrenaline. Tiffany, on the other hand, had to get out of bed to face the unknown.

"Rise and shine," I said cheerily as I turned on the light next to her bed. My mom had said that every morning when I was a kid. I watched as Tiffany opened her sleepy eyes and remembered where she was.

"I'm awake, I'm awake." She propped herself up on her elbows and squinted. "Can you turn on the light over there from now on, instead of this one? It hurts my eyes."

"Whatever you say, Your Heinie-ness," I joked, kind of. "Anything I can do to help make your reentry into the world more pleasant." I detected a smile. "Why don't you get into the shower while I start breakfast?"

One of Megan's biggest complaints had been that Tiffany wouldn't get up for school on time and was constantly missing the bus. If Megan wouldn't drive her, Tiffany would simply skip school. When I asked her why she didn't drag Tiffany out of bed if she had to, Megan replied that she herself didn't get up until it was time to wake Sammy, which was later. I don't remember ever getting up for school without Mom there to help, I thought, but I didn't say anything, especially since I was sure Megan wouldn't remember it that way. It often seemed like Megan and I grew up in completely different households. In any event, I was going to do my best to be up with Tiffany every day at that ungodly hour.

The sight and smell of scrambled eggs cooking that early made me want to hurl. The radio I'd set up in the kitchen to distract my senses wasn't doing the job, and it only got worse when Tiffany doused her portion liberally with ketchup. But I wanted to sit down to a proper breakfast with Tiffany every morning, like a regular family. During my high school years, I'd had a cup of tea, a Carnation Instant Breakfast, and a glass of Tang every morning. I'd thought that was normal and nutritious, but people seem horrified to this day when I happen to mention it. We ate in silence and managed to leave at the target time of seven thirty.

"Now try and pay attention to the way we're going," I said as we stepped out into the cool, late-September morning. "You're going to have to walk home from the subway on your own."

"I am going to get *so* lost, Uncle Eddy.

61

There's no way I'll ever figure out my way around this city." Tiffany had gelled her long hair into the wavy, wet look and had put on some makeup. She looks sort of Latina, I thought, and that's probably a good thing. She wore the standard tight jeans, sneakers, and a snug, light blue V-neck sweater that was a little too revealing for my comfort. And that's probably a bad thing, I thought, but you have to pick and choose your battles carefully.

"Oh, come on," I chided. "You know your way around this neighborhood pretty well. You lived here for *only* a total of nine weeks over the last two summers. And don't worry, we'll take it slow when it comes to your traveling to different sections of town without me." I had no idea how much of a sense of direction thirteen-year-olds were supposed to have developed, or how much freedom to navigate was appropriate in a place like New York City. I'd have to get some advice.

It was a good ten-minute walk to the West Fourth Street subway station on Sixth Avenue. Then we had to descend into what seemed like the bowels of hell to find the platform for the downtown F train.

"So, when you get off the train this afternoon, walk along the platform in the direction the train was going, all the way to the end, and then go up as many flights of stairs as it takes to reach the street. Then cross Sixth Avenue and walk along Waverly Place until you get to Sheridan Square, which you'll recognize." Tiffany looked shell-shocked sitting next to me on that orange plastic train seat, staring straight ahead, careful to avoid eye contact with the other passengers.

"Whatever you say, Uncle Eddy." Tiffany had never ridden public transportation by herself before and I knew the idea made her nervous. Her current anxiety, though, was probably more about being the new girl in a New York City public school than about riding the train home later.

"It's going to be okay," I whispered, and squeezed her knee. I wondered if she knew that I was speaking as much to myself as I was to her.

We emerged from the depths on an avenue called East Broadway. It was wide and busy, and I'd never heard of it. In fact, in my nineteen years of living on the island of Manhattan, I'd neither seen nor heard of this entire section of town. Gail Cohen had called it the Lower East Side, but it wasn't the Lower East Side of Clinton,

Ludlow, and Rivington Streets — the newly trendy neighborhood that had been established by Jewish immigrants early last century. This place was southeast of that area, east of Chinatown, and north of the South Street Seaport. It was an in-between, no-man's-land of tall, austere red-brick apartment buildings, built in clumps and at odd angles to each other. So this is where the projects are, I thought. The names were distantly familiar to me, like Knickerbocker, Rutgers, and LaGuardia, but they were names I didn't associate with happy events. *Oh, Jesus, what have I gotten my niece into?*

"Be sure to always walk on this busy avenue," I warned. "Don't take shortcuts through those buildings or hang out there before or after school. Those places can be very dangerous."

"You worry too much, Uncle Eddy," Tiffany responded. "And listen, you can't walk me all the way to school. That would be the worst possible thing you could do. Tell me when we're about two blocks away and point me in the right direction." *In your dreams*, I thought, but pretended to agree.

After five more minutes of walking along the bleak, bodega-lined avenue, I gave Tiffany a peck on the cheek and told her to make a right on Gouverneur Street and that the school would be on her right after she made the turn. I watched as she crossed the avenue, alone amid small groups of kids sporting large knapsacks and brightly colored sneakers. At the first corner Tiffany turned right, not paying attention to the street signs. I whistled as loud as I could and she turned around. I gave her a double-armed direction wave, like the guys do on the airport tarmac, and she smiled and righted her course. Then I proceeded to run from phone booth to kiosk to bus stop, seeking cover as I followed her the rest of the way.

Tiffany turned down the correct street this time and became engulfed by the United Colors of Benetton. Literally. Sure, there was a dazzling array of snappy Tommy Hilfiger apparel on display, but it was the diversity of the kids themselves that caught my attention. They were a sea of Asians, Hispanics, and African Americans, with Tiffany one of the few Caucasians mixed in. I watched as she walked — without skipping a beat — right up the steps past the security guards and into the handsome, newly renovated little building with bars on its windows. I couldn't believe this young girl's bravery. Tiffany was only thirteen, yet there had been no crying, no pleading, no begging to turn back. I don't think that I could have done it.

"It was pretty good," she responded on the phone later, when I asked her how it went. "The kids, like, crowded around my desk and introduced themselves. That doesn't happen in Connecticut." I laughed, giddy with relief that she'd gotten through it so well *and* found her way back to the apartment.

That night, though, after folding Tiffany's new sweaters (still clingy but with collars) and skin-tight corduroys, Tiffany asked to sleep on the floor next to my bed — something she'd done sometimes during our summers together, but only if she had nightmares. As much as I wanted to oblige, I had to say no. I could tell she was as exhausted as I was, so we'd both need the best possible rest we could get. After all, as the plan stood now, we'd be getting up together at the crack of dawn for the next four years.

# Smitten

I had my first night off the Friday after Tiffany moved in. Though the mania was beginning to wane and I was beyond exhausted, it was a friend's long-planned fortieth birthday party, so my presence was required. Maybe some adult chitchat, a few good laughs, and a hearty dose of wine would help me blow off some steam and rediscover a good night's sleep. Plus, I could tell that Tiffany would be happy — maybe even relieved — to have an evening to herself.

The party was held at a cozy French restaurant on the edge of the Meatpacking District, just up the street from our apartment, and I found myself squeezed in next to an old friend who taught at one of Manhattan's most exclusive private schools. He'd heard about my newfound guardianship and asked how it was going.

"I'm smitten with her," I told him. "Absolutely head over heels in love."

A huge smile swept across his face. "You

have to be," he said. "It's the only way we can do it."

A wave of relief washed over me. See, you're not *really* falling in love with your niece, silly. Adults come under the spell of children all the time. I mean, I wasn't afraid that I might have *actually* been in love with her but, boy, did my feelings resemble a powerful crush. Tiffany was like an exotic creature that had suddenly dropped from the sky into my boring, humdrum world. She was endlessly fascinating to me.

I loved to simply look at her, and I'd hunt for ways to do so without getting caught and making her self-conscious. When we watched movies at home, I'd be sure to sit on the sofa furthest from the television so that I could observe, undetected, her watching the film. And it wasn't just because Tiffany is beautiful, which is undeniable. It was because I wanted to see her reactions to things, to watch them imprint her mind, even if only a little. Like that moment in *Harold and Maude* when it's absolutely clear that Ruth Gordon and Bud Cort actually consummated their relationship. "Gross!" Tiffany had gasped. But from my vantage point I could see a look of delighted surprise cross her face. She'd seen something new, something she'd never before contemplated — that love could be found between a twenty-one-year-old boy and a seventy-nine-year-old woman. And I had the privilege of being there to see Tiffany discover this.

Her every movement captivated me. Sure, the way she imitated Britney Spears when she pranced around the living room charmed me, but that was to be expected from a girl Tiffany's age. What I'd forgotten was the way teenagers can find the strangest positions in which to perform mundane activities, like when Tiffany talked on the phone lying on her back on the floor with her legs stretched up the wall, ankles crossed. Or the illogical way she'd choose to do her homework on her stomach in our narrow hallway with her papers spread all around, making it all but impossible for me to pass by unhindered. (Seeing Tiffany like this reminded me of a photo my mom had taken of me doing my homework; I was propped up on my elbows on the living room carpet with Gidget, the family cat, sound asleep in the small of my back.) And I quickly learned that the only way to make a proper ponytail was to lie on the bed and hang your head upside down over the edge.

I'd also forgotten how seductive the teenage Teflon method of working through things — forgetting immediately and moving on — could be. The day before my friend's party was a perfect example. It had been a good morning. Tiffany was chatty and we hadn't butted heads back at the apartment while trying to get out on time. But then, on our way to the subway, we had the following exchange:

ME: "I want you to go to tutoring today, for math help."

HER: "I don't want to stay late."

ME: "It's not a question of 'want.' I don't want to go to work. In fact, the thought of sitting at my desk this morning makes me want to puke. But I'm going."

HER: (up a tone) "Well, you're not helping me any, always telling me that I'm going to fail. 'You're going to fail math. You're going to fail Spanish.' How am I supposed to have any faith in myself?"

ME: "That's not true. You know I'm trying to prevent you from failing."

But we were already across from the subway entrance. We had quickly established a routine where I'd give her a kiss and say, "Have a good day," before I'd watch her cross the street and disappear down the stairs. It gave me a chance to observe her for a moment, going off into the New York City world by herself. Plus, I could yell out things to embarrass her as she crossed, like "Don't *forget* to go to gym!" or "Lose the gum!" But on this morning when I went to kiss her, she turned her cheek just shy of my lips and never turned back. A terse "Bye" was my punishment.

Anger buzzed at the back of my brain all day. It wasn't true. I was building her confidence, not tearing it down. But she was so casual about everything to do with school. Her eighth grade Ds "weren't that bad." Failure was a real possibility here, and it would be healthy and motivating to fear it, wouldn't it? But now I stood accused.

She unchained the apartment door that evening with a bright smile and a "How was your day?" The phone was attached to her head, naturally, so I didn't have to answer. (In fact, it would soon seem that I'd *never* get to speak with her until we sat down for dinner.) Today she was decidedly upbeat, chatting away while IMing on

AOL. It would be so easy to let the morning's conversation disappear into the currents of our short history together.

Between bites of overcooked meat loaf, I took a deep mental breath and dove in.

"I want to talk about this morning for a minute."

"Oh, I'd forgotten all about it."

"Well, I felt kind of angry all day. I don't think it was fair of you to turn my trying to help you into my sabotaging you. Do you really feel that way?"

"No, I was just being cranky and looking for something to complain about."

End of story, processed and done with. Teenage Teflon.

When I returned home from my friend's birthday party, a bit tipsy from all the toasts, Tiffany was asleep on the sofa in front of the television. I took a moment to watch her breathing softly through her perfect lips, her angel face at peace. After guiding her gently into her room, tucking her in, and closing her door behind me, I sat on my bed and cried. The love was so big it hurt, and I knew just how lonely I'd been before Tiffany arrived.

# Obsessive-Compulsive Disorder

"Omigod, Uncle Eddy! Do you have OCD?" Tiffany practically yelled, waving a white piece of paper around, a big smile on her face. I was standing at the sink in our tiny galley kitchen, washing the Sunday morning breakfast dishes.

"Yes, as a matter of fact, I do," I answered, placing the dripping frying pan on the counter with a yellow Playtex Living Glove–covered hand. "What's that you've got there?" I asked, deciding not to tell her how impressed I was that she knew what OCD meant.

"Wait, do you take medicine for it?" she asked. Tiffany had often seen me taking handfuls of pills, so maybe she was trying to ferret out my various maladies by process of elimination.

"No, I wouldn't want to treat my OCD because I find that it works for me," I said as I washed the omelette whisk one metal wire at a time, which I enjoyed. "It helps keep me organized and detail-oriented and makes me feel like I have things under control. So, what's on the piece of paper?"

"Well," Tiffany began with a mischievous smile. "I keep finding these strange lists all over the apartment. I don't remember seeing these over the summer, so I think you were trying to hide your compulsive list-making from me."

"I wasn't hiding anything," I lied. "Lists are very helpful and not necessarily a sign of OCD. When I cross an item off a list, I feel a sense of accomplishment, no matter how small. So the list-making actually contributes to a healthy feeling of success."

"Oh, *really?*" she asked theatrically.

I began to worry just which list she might have found. I hoped it wasn't my "Things About My Body That I'd Like to Change, by Plastic Surgery or Otherwise" list. That would be tough to explain to a teenager you're desperately trying to help *stop* obsessing about her body.

"I know some of your lists are very practical, Uncle Eddy," she proclaimed as she held up the paper to read aloud, "but this one is a bit odd." She cleared her throat and I held my breath.

" 'Things I Keep Meaning to Do,' " she began. Relief. " 'Become Fluent in a Foreign Language; Get Scuba Diving Certifi-

74

cation; Jump Out of a Plane; Use the Oven; Write a Novel; Take Figure Skating Lessons,' and my personal favorite, 'Join the Hare Krishnas.' " She pronounced it "hairy" and started to giggle while staring at me pseudointensely, awaiting an explanation.

"It's not odd," I answered in a thick British accent, ever fast on my feet, "it's simply overexpressive." I snatched the list from her grip. "That's a line from *Howards End*, a film about nonconformists that I highly recommend you watch."

"You rent it, I'll watch it," Tiffany responded. "Is it your OCD that makes you so neat too? Like, how when we watch a movie, you fold the blanket and fluff the pillow every time I get up to go to the bathroom or answer the phone?"

"Oh, I guess so, Tiffany," I answered with mock exasperation. "Look, I'm gay, so it's genetic. I have a special gene that makes me want to decorate and be neat and organized. You should be happy I don't have the opera gene as well. That would drive you *much* crazier."

Later that afternoon when I returned to the kitchen to begin cooking our Sunday dinner, I found a list written in Tiffany's handwriting. Each item was neatly crossed off with a line through its center:

~~Got up~~
~~Drank Orange Juice~~
~~Chatted on AOL~~
~~Listened to Eminem~~
~~Ate Breakfast~~
~~Talked to Uncle Eddy about OCD~~
~~Made a List and Crossed Everything Off~~

I howled with laughter and Tiffany came running down the hall from her room. Her devious grin made it clear that she was quite pleased with herself.

Our first Saturday together had not gone quite as planned. In fact, it would probably be remembered as my first big parenting mistake. I'd arranged to have a pizza party for the teenagers who lived in the immediately surrounding buildings, along with their parents, to celebrate Tiffany's arrival. I'd forgotten that, when sitting together with adults present, teenagers do not speak to each other. So there we were, a room full of about fifteen semistrangers eating pizza in silence. I made casual chitchat about the neighborhood and got an update on the new park being built along the Hudson River — the type of talk that probably made teenagers squirm all the more. I was sure they were *dying* to make fun of me. I would've been too, if I were they.

About a half hour in, there was a knock on the door followed by a muffled, "It's Aleksi." When I opened it, a striking young man stood looking directly into my eyes, his hand thrust forward to shake mine. "You must be Uncle Ed," Aleksi said as he stepped into the apartment, followed by his friend Liam, a tall, gangling but cute, young high-school-aged boy. Besides Aleksi's penetrating gaze, he was "striking" in that his tousled hair was partially dyed green, his fingernails were painted a dark brown, and his black eyes were rimmed heavily with eyeliner. As he walked, his hugely baggy, flared pants swept along the floor like the Bride of Frankenstein's wedding train.

Although Aleksi had lived in the bedroom directly below Tiffany's for at least two years, I had never laid eyes on him. I'd spoken to his stepdad, Marvin, a few hours earlier and he had promised that Aleksi would come by, though he himself couldn't make it. That was a relief, as things were still quite awkward between Marvin and me. Just after he'd moved in downstairs, he'd begun complaining constantly about the noise from my apartment. Although I believed I was quiet as a garden slug, he complained about every move I made. Our leases stipulated that all apartments must be 100 percent carpeted with wall-to-wall because of the shoddy workmanship of our building. Truth be told, I had zip: a few area rugs here and there, but no carpeting. After Marvin complained to management, I was forced to spend two thousand dollars to carpet the rear half of my apartment. I counted myself lucky that I was able to negotiate for the other half to remain gleaming hardwood, which was brand-new and gorgeous. What I never told Marvin or management, though, was that I was actually happy to put carpet between our bedrooms, as I couldn't stand the sounds of him yelling at Aleksi every night. Usually it was simply, "Shut off that computer!" over and over, but sometimes Marvin would launch into a full-scale tirade. Now, at least, it would all be a bit muffled.

I'd found out subsequently from other neighbors that Aleksi's mom was Russian-born and had come to the States when Aleksi was little. She'd hooked up with Marvin a bunch of years ago, making Marvin a sort of stepdad to Aleksi. Shortly after they moved into the building, Aleksi's mom had died of cancer, leaving Aleksi in Marvin's care.

Marvin and Aleksi were a huge improvement over my last downstairs neighbor, who used to smack around prostitutes all night long. I'd have called the police, but I could hear every word and had figured out that it was all part of the act. Burton was a horrific character who, when he wasn't at his luggage store on Eighth Street, was basically a shut-in. He'd blast his TV all night long and change the channel every two seconds, driving me and the neighbors below him insane. Burton suffered from diabetes and eventually had one of his feet removed; when he returned from the hospital after surgery, he actually left bloody stump prints all over the stairs. Within a year, Burton died. I'd had a Golden Globes party that night, and when my friends left at the end of the show, Eugene called me from the sidewalk to tell me that a dead body had been discovered in the apartment below mine. I ran down to the street to get the story. While huddled in a circle against the cold, we looked up to see Wendy, my neighbor who lived just beneath Burton and who'd been at war with him for years over the noise, standing in her window. She smiled demonically as she made the neck-chop gesture with one hand while pointing toward the ceiling with the other one. "Friendly neighbors you got here," Eugene commented sardonically. God forgive us, I remember thinking as we filled the night air with laughter.

Aleksi and Liam sauntered right into the center of the living room, grabbed some pizza, and sat on the floor. Aleksi spoke directly to Tiffany from across the room, seemingly without the typical self-consciousness teenagers display around adults. I knew he attended Stuyvesant, the best public high school in New York, and his level of intelligence was immediately clear. When he told Tiffany that he played the guitar and could often be found playing at various spots in the neighborhood, Tiffany's eyes went radioactive. I'd never seen her so animated around a boy before.

"Oh, that's so cool," she flirted.

"Yeah, when I play outside the Magnolia Bakery, all the yuppie dickheads give me money," Aleksi said casually.

"Language," I barked, as all the kids laughed. Aleksi apologized but I sensed that he knew I was impressed by him too.

"Hey, Uncle Ed," he said, "what do you

say Liam and I take Tiffany out for a walk and show her the neighborhood?"

"She knows the neighborhood, Aleksi," I replied. "She's stayed with me for chunks of the last two summers in a row."

"That's *your* version of the neighborhood, Uncle Ed," Aleksi said with a smile. "Ours is a little bit different."

"Well, I guess it's okay. That is, if Daniel's and Emily's parents consent to your taking them as well," I cleverly responded, avoiding eye contact with Tiffany. Daniel was a studious, shy boy from the first floor who was very close to his parents, and Emily was a sweet girl from the fourth floor who was at least eighteen months Tiffany's junior. Their parents said okay, as long as it was limited to an hour. Before they left, though, I ran through Tiffany's checklist, which embarrassed her to no end. It wasn't an *actual* list, like all my others; it was a verbal one, and I'd run through each item before Tiffany left the apartment and she'd answer yes if the item was in her pocket or bag — home address, phone number, ID, keys, map, money, that sort of thing. At six o'clock it was already getting dark outside, and I watched from the window as Tiffany wandered off down the Village streets with other kids for the first time. Unfortunately, the young Emily and the virtuous Daniel were back within fifteen minutes, with no sign of Tiffany and the boys.

The party — if you could call it that — wound down shortly and everyone began to leave. Even though an hour hadn't passed since Tiffany had left, the parents seemed downcast as they left, wishing me good luck and offering support, should I need it. I stood by the window and waited.

Tiffany showed up a mere fifteen minutes late, approaching the building alone, with no sign of Aleksi and Liam. She said they'd met up with some friends down the street and were staying out. So much for entrusting her to Aleksi, I thought. I didn't make a huge fuss, though, since it was her first time out with "friends" and her curfew had been a meager seven thirty.

I'd promised to dye Tiffany's hair for our Saturday evening pre-video activity, and I stood in the kitchen splattered with "roasted chestnut" and racing against the clock to get all the color in before it was time to start taking it out. I hated the mess but I loved the fumes, which reminded me of watching my mom color her hair thirty years earlier. The odor of the dye hadn't changed a bit over the decades, which struck me as odd but comforting. Dying Tiffany's long, thick hair was a much more challenging enterprise than bleaching the hair on her arms, toes, hands, knuckles, and the small of her back, which we'd done several nights before. The little spatula that came with the bleaching kit was adorable, and using it had been like icing skin cupcakes. Luckily, Tiffany had no facial hair, so I didn't have to apply the mixture to her face. "I'm sure the mustache is coming," she'd complained as she'd marched off to the bathroom to fly solo on her happy trail. "I hate being Italian."

"He's kind of hot, in a weird sort of way," Tiffany now replied when I asked what she thought of Aleksi. "But he has a big chin, kind of like Jay Leno, and he looks sort of gay too. No offense, Uncle Eddy," she quickly added. "But I really don't think he is. Liam is definitely not."

"None taken, sweetie," I replied, squeezing the bottle more firmly. "Yeah, so what is Liam's story?" I wondered if there was any chance she'd sparked to the more normal-looking of the boys. "Clip, please," I ordered, and Tiffany handed me one.

"He has a girlfriend and is a sophomore at Stuyvesant too," she answered, "and he seems nice. Just a lot less interesting than Aleksi."

"Yeah, I have to agree with you there. Aleksi does seem like quite a character. Definitely not someone you'd find in New Milford, huh?"

"Omigod, Uncle Eddy!" Tiffany yelled suddenly.

"What, what? Did the dye burn you, honey?" I ran around to look at her face.

"No, I'm just excited to finally have a friend in the neighborhood! And he's going to teach me the guitar too." She wiggled from side to side in the chair beneath me, her neck following her hips, all self-satisfied.

You've been here only a week, I thought, and he ain't just in the neighborhood, he's in the building. Right underneath you, in fact. How long will it be before you're sneaking up and down the fire escape into each other's bedrooms?

"That's great, Tiffany," I said. "I'm excited for you, I really am." Me and my stupid freaking pizza party, I thought as I clipped back another goopy section of hair and squeezed even harder.

"Hey, wait a minute. Stop the movie," Tiffany yelled out. We were watching *Rosemary's Baby*, which I'd selected from the list of "Videos to Be Rented" that I kept on the shelf next to the door. The list was at least twenty index cards long and I'd placed a straight line through the title and director of every movie I'd seen. Index cards stand up better to travel than regular paper, and I always tried to keep at least one with me in case I found myself in a video store scratching my head. (I'd recently started a card listing films to rent with Tiffany, which included *Desperately Seeking Susan*, *My Life as a Dog*, and *Ghost World*.) I stopped the DVD, as commanded.

"So, that lady, Anne Marie, she just got roofied by her husband and her neighbors and then got, like, raped by the devil?" Tiffany asked, her face the picture of skepticism.

"Yes, though that thought is so horrible that some in the audience might still think she's dreaming or deluded. I told you this was a real shocker." Tiffany loves horror movies and, since I was trying to educate her in cinema studies, I figured we could meet halfway with classics like this or the Coen brothers' *Blood Simple*. "And it's Rosemary, not Anne Marie," I added.

"A shocker?" she asked incredulously. "What's shocking is that she wakes up all covered with nasty scratches, having mysteriously passed out the night before. She looks at her husband and he apologizes, telling her that he's already trimmed his nails and that he couldn't resist having sex with her. And Maryrose is, like, 'Oh, okay.' *That's* the shocking part!"

"What do you mean?" I asked, thoroughly into riding Tiffany's high horse.

"First, if my husband or boyfriend, or *whoever,* had sex with me while I was passed out, I'd have them arrested for rape. Plus, if I woke up that scratched up, even if there was no sex involved, I'd run out of the apartment screaming. Well, maybe since you said their apartment used to belong to one of the Beatles, I'd have the police drag my psycho husband out for battering me."

We watched the rest of the film. When it was over, I turned to Tiffany and asked, "So, what do you think now? Are you scared?"

"Scared?" Tiffany feigned disbelief. "You can't be serious. That was so retarded. I can't believe that she didn't kill the little monster with that butcher knife. I'd have killed it *and* my Satan-worshipping husband too!"

"Very interesting, Tiffany," I said

thoughtfully. "I've never considered the film from a feminist perspective. The novel was written by a man and, actually, the director of the film fled the United States because he was brought up on charges of having sex with a girl younger than you. Even though he's never been back, he keeps making films in Europe; he has a new one coming out, called *The Pianist*, that's supposed to be great."

"It figures he's a pervert," Tiffany responded as she removed the DVD from the machine and tuned the TV to *SNL*. "This was a movie about a rape victim who never gets any revenge. Instead, Mary Ann becomes a servant to her rapists."

"You know, you're absolutely right," I agreed. "But you've got to remember the lead character's name. It's *Rosemary,* and it's iconic, which means symbolic, suggestive of a greater meaning."

"Yeah, whatever, Uncle Eddy."

A little while later, when Tiffany was on the phone with her friend Christina, I ran into my room and threw on a little blond wig from my collection in the closet, stuck a pillow under my shirt to look pregnant, and grabbed a big carving knife from the kitchen. I snuck up on Tiffany and started mimicking the singsong, creepy "la la la la" music from the movie.

"Oh my God, *'Christina, get the axe!'* " she screamed, and started giggling. I'd taught her that quote from *Mommie Dearest* and now she'd found the perfect time to use it. "It's Roseanne from the movie, complete with knife and unborn devil baby!"

Maybe Tiffany was unfazed, but goofing around helped me shake the serious heebie-jeebies that had set in from the movie.

# Expeditions

"Uncle Eddy," Tiffany began, her pitch nosediving from the *U* to the *Y*. I'd quickly learned that when a conversation began like this, Tiffany was invariably going to ask for something she knew was likely to be out of the question. Maybe she thought that by alerting me to what was coming, as well as to her awareness of its impossibility, I might just be charmed enough to cave.

"Yes?" I played along, swinging slowly up from the *Y* to the *S*. It was around noon on the Columbus Day holiday, and the brisk breeze was bracing against my freshly shaved face.

"Next month, for my birthday, can I have, like, ten friends down from Connecticut for the weekend?" We were passing by the recently renovated Jackson Square Park on our way up Eighth Avenue to catch the C train at Fourteenth Street. I loved the huge, cast-iron, nineteenth-century repro fountain now standing at the park's center. In the warm months it sort of gurgled water down into its tiered pools, making it a giant pigeon bath.

"How could we possibly put up ten kids in our apartment?" I humored her.

"The boys could sleep in the living room and the girls in my bedroom," she answered earnestly.

Uh oh, it sounds like she doesn't realize that I'm kidding here. "Will that be before or after you get your tongue pierced and your back tattooed?"

Tiffany giggled, understanding the game was over. Well, at least for this round. We both knew she was not nearly finished harassing me about her fourteenth birthday.

Columbus Day came just a few weeks after Tiffany moved in. An extra day off from work suddenly took on the dimensions of a two-week "rest" in a sanitarium. Let's face it: I'd been in a sort of thinly veiled panic since Tiffany had arrived. I'd been dashing out of work at exactly six o'clock, stressed about what I was going to make for dinner and how long it would take. What had Tiffany been doing since she got home from school? Would I have to reprimand her for being parked on the sofa in front of *Seinfeld* reruns, while a pile of dirty dishes sat crusting over in the sink? (I'd had the cable cut to the basic service and put a lock on HBO and Showtime, but that didn't stop her from staring at old sitcoms.) Would helping her with her math homework lead to yet another fight?

So far, a typical math session had gone something like this:

> ME: "Okay, what you need to do here is solve for $x$."
>
> TIFFANY: "What do you mean, 'solve for $x$'?"
>
> ME: "You have to find $x$."
>
> TIFFANY: "The $x$ is right there. What do you mean, 'find $x$'?"
>
> ME: "You have to figure out what $x$ is."
>
> TIFFANY: "I know what $x$ is. It's a letter. It comes after $w$ and before $y$."

I guess Tiffany's D in eighth grade math meant that her algebra skills were about equal to mine in astrophysics. I tried desperately to figure out ways to explain variables and equations without letting my voice grow louder or edgier, but I usually failed miserably. Tiffany would say, "You're getting that voice again." If I didn't take heed, it wouldn't be long before Tiffany would break into tears and her pencil would fly across the room. It didn't help that her daffy teacher was giving the class word problems that were virtually impossible to solve — I guess as a way of introducing them to how algebra could *ultimately* be used in everyday life (if you held a math PhD). It was a ridiculous approach, and one that led to extreme frustration. As an experiment, I'd given a particularly difficult word problem to half my office to solve, as well as to my dad, and everyone came up empty-handed. To make matters worse, Mr. Ling never went over the problems after he assigned them. Tiffany was up against enough of a challenge without being subjected to head games. I'd have to remember to have a little chat with Mr. Ling, who I would later learn was teaching for the very first time.

During the couple of weekends since Tiffany's arrival, I'd felt just as panicked as during the weekdays. I guess I'd imagined us picnicking in Central Park, sketchbooks in hand, or standing in front of a huge Pollock at MoMA discussing our visceral reactions to the genius's splatter paintings. Instead, I scrambled to keep on top of my bills, errands, the food shopping, and work reading. Trying to figure out the coming week's meals left me feeling anxious and inept. I'd decided that Sunday afternoons were for cooking ahead — which entailed making lasagnas, meat loaves, and huge batches of meatballs and sauce. (It wouldn't be long before the sight of ground beef would make me gag.) Tiffany slept late and, of course, spent the better part of her waking hours on my cell phone with friends from Connecticut. (I'd had the apartment phone's long-distance service shut off, so she could make outgoing calls to Connecticut only on my cell, and only after nine p.m. on weeknights — if she completed her homework — and on week-ends.) She also had a habit of keeping the television on at all times, something I perceived as a symptom of her "suburban malaise." Talking on the phone and watching TV were by no means mutually exclusive activities; Tiffany and her friends would watch whole programs together via telephone, giggling and commenting intermittently. I tried endlessly to get her to hold the cell phone on the side that would help stave off the brain tumors I was sure were already growing in her pretty head, but I could never keep straight which side that was supposed to be. In all fairness, Tiffany did her own laundry, which was a huge help, and she was willing to vacuum and dust for a small fee. (She'd not yet learned to clean a bathroom, so I added that lesson to my To Do list.) But there still didn't seem to be time for outside activities, so the weekends were not turning out as I'd imagined.

For our Columbus Day cultural outing, I figured we'd start simple — the new Rose Science Center at the Museum of Natural History. I didn't want to scare Tiffany off museums, so I decided I'd save places like the Tenement and Holocaust museums for later. Plus, the refurbished Hayden Planetarium at the Rose Center was featuring a cool-sounding show about alien life in the universe called *Are We Alone?* I hoped it might even be a little scary, and with Harrison Ford narrating, you couldn't go wrong. He's got to have one of *the* sexiest voices in our solar system.

The C train from the West Village up to Central Park West wasn't very crowded, so Tiffany and I were easily able to find seats. I decided to broach the subject of Courtney Holleran. The night before, Tiffany had been up late on AOL, IMing like crazy. She'd looked adorable in her oversized black sweatshirt with the hood up, her pale, heart-shaped face barely peeking out from under it. A regular street thug

94

homegirl, I'd laughed inside, just like Halle Berry in *Bullworth*. I'd gone to bed to read a manuscript for work when I heard her screech, "Omigod, omigod!" I ran out to the living room to see what was up.

"Courtney just keeps writing the same thing over and over." Tiffany typed furiously as she spoke, her eyes glued to the monitor.

"Well, what is she saying?" I asked impatiently.

" 'I'm going to kill someone. They're all going to die. I'm going to kill someone. They're all going to die. I'm going —' "

"I get it," I cut in. "I'm sure she's just messing with your head." I remembered that one time at a high school party I got really stoned and repeated everything I said twice for about two hours, just for the fun of driving my best friend, Mark, crazy. "Do you think she's high?" I asked.

"Probably. I'm going to try and get her to sign off and call me. Courtney wouldn't do this to be funny, believe me. I know Courtney. Omigod!" Tiffany was going full throttle now, pumped by the drama of it.

"Let me know if there's anything I can do," I offered weakly. "I'm going to bed, so if you get on the phone, try and keep it down." I plodded off to my room in my plaid drawstring pants, my arms wrapped around my bare torso to fight the October night chill. I heard only some faint whispering before drifting off into a sound sleep.

"So, did you find out what was up with Courtney last night?" I asked as the subway doors closed at Fourteenth Street. We had a fifteen-minute ride ahead, so Tiffany was my captive audience.

"I'm pretty sure she snorted some dust," Tiffany responded casually. "I thought at first it was heroin, but that usually makes people mellow. Dust can make a person crazy. And, like, totally paranoid."

I'd learned two summers ago that the most revealing information — stuff that you wouldn't expect a child to tell an adult — came out at the most unlikely times. It rarely, if ever, came out when you sat down together to have a chat; that was actually the best way to guarantee that *no* communication would take place and you'd learn zip. Tiffany was staying with me for six weeks that summer and we were on a trip up to Mystic, Connecticut. The weekend had been a special treat for Tiffany and me, as we'd been invited to travel up the coast on my friend's father's yacht. Our "captain" was quite wealthy and took the entire group to a fancy dinner in town the night we arrived. After we'd ordered our meals from the waiter, Tiffany turned to me and whispered, "I hope that when people see us together, they think you're my father." I could think of a dozen responses but not the right one, so I'd simply given her hand a squeeze and said, "You're sweet."

Later that night, after a stroll through town for some homemade ice cream, we went night swimming off the boat. When Tiffany and I jumped off the highest part of the upper deck into the black water of the harbor, a thousand tiny stars sparkled all around us, whole constellations shooting out from our fingertips and toes as we treaded water. Neither Tiffany nor our seventy-five-year-old host had ever seen phosphorescence. "Omigod, this is the coolest thing I've ever seen," she gasped, as our host stood on deck smiling ear to ear.

It was on the morning we were leaving, though, that Tiffany surprised me with a sudden offering of secret information. It was a perfect summer day and we were sitting on the bow relaxing while the yacht was being refueled, full from a big breakfast of bagels and lox. The mouth of the Mystic River was abuzz, and we marveled at the variety of boats that glided by as if choreographed, from fat-cat powertubs to elegant, teak-rimmed sailboats.

"This is so beautiful," Tiffany whispered in reverence. "It's like a different planet from my house in New Milford."

"Whaddaya mean?" I asked, keeping my gaze out over the river.

"Like, after we went swimming the other night, I slept so well with the gentle rocking of the boat. Then, yesterday, I felt so calm and the day went by kind of like a dream."

"Well, in New Milford you don't live on a boat, and weekends away are supposed to be relaxing, not like regular life."

"No, it's not just that. It's you, it's the people around you, it's everything. It's all just different." She was getting at something and I didn't want to lose it. Like fishing, when you know something is on the hook but if you yank too hard, whatever it is will be gone forever. I remained silent but turned my body toward hers.

"Like my last weekend at home, Mommy and Eric got really drunk and had this huge fight. Mommy went downstairs to her room but Eric stayed in the living room. Sammy had her friend Chrissy over and they were playing a game on the floor while I watched TV. Eric sat down next to them and said, 'You know Megan likes big black cock, don't you?' "

The blue Mystic morning sky fell onto my chest, but I said nothing.

"I screamed for Mommy to come get Eric, but he stormed out the door and started walking down the street yelling out nasty stuff about her."

"What did Sammy and Chrissy do?" I tried to sound matter-of-fact.

"They just kept playing Sorry! like nothing had happened. It was the weirdest thing. Then I hear police sirens down the street and Mommy goes running out the door. I tried to stop her, telling her to let them arrest that psycho freak, but I couldn't." She paused, then said: "So, you see, everything just feels really different."

"Yes, I see," I said softly, trying to find the air to make words. I wanted to grab Tiffany and hold her and cover her entire body with mine, like a shell. Then I wanted to reach into her brain, into her past, and yank out this poison, this ugliness. Instead I squeezed her hand tightly and pointed toward the east with my free hand. "Look" was all I could manage. The sun was caught behind a small white cloud, but its rays shot out magnificently from all sides, spotlighting the river.

Now, on the C train, I felt another window open and I knew I had to climb through quickly.

"You sound pretty knowledgeable about drugs," I said. "Have you tried dust or heroin?" I used a supercasual tone, but if she'd said yes, I probably would've pulled the train's emergency brake cord.

"No way, Uncle Eddy." She sounded slightly indignant. "I have no desire to do any of those drugs. I only do pot and alcohol." Just then a homeless woman came into our car and started her spiel a few feet away from us. She was obviously a heroin addict but claimed to need money because her apartment had burned down after she'd been diagnosed with cancer. No one looked directly at her except, of course, Tiffany, who I could tell wanted to give her some money. It was just like the '80s again, when you couldn't ride the train without being harassed for money.

"Then how do you know so much about this stuff?" I asked.

"Well, I've seen people high on all sorts of drugs, like crystal, GHB, E, coke, Special K, glue, and heroin. I'd never do any of that stuff, though, except maybe shrooms."

She shot me a mischievous grin to let me know she was enjoying telling me things she probably shouldn't. I hadn't heard a drug menu like that since my days out on Fire Island Pines. But I wasn't living under a rock either, and I knew that many of the drugs that had begun as expensive, designer drugs in the gay community fifteen-plus years ago had eventually found their way to the suburban teenage crowd. I guess I'd just hoped that they hadn't gotten so close to my thirteen-year-old niece. I'd have to remember to address her desire to do mushrooms another time.

"Why do you think Courtney would feel the need to do dust? Or heroin, for that matter?" I was fighting mightily not to sound pedantic but, judging from Tiffany's eye roll, I hadn't been successful.

"She doesn't *need* to do anything, but if you had parents like hers, you'd *want* to do heroin too. Her father is such a loser. I had the hugest fight with him before I moved down here." Tiffany's voice was never this loud in public; I must've really hit a nerve.

"What do you mean by 'a fight'?"

"Well, he told Kitt's mom that Mommy is a drunk and that she leaves me home alone so that I can do drugs and have sex with boys. He told her that Kitt shouldn't be allowed to hang out with me. She's my F-ing best friend!" Tiffany was working herself into a state now, her voice a vicious whisper. "No one disrespects me or my family like that. If they do, they're going to hear from me."

I wanted to tell her that saying "F-ing" is just as bad as saying the word itself, but decided now was not the time. "What did you say?" I was almost afraid to ask, but we'd come this far.

"I told him that if he had something to say, he should say it to my face next time. And that he should know what he's talking about before he talks shit about other people. I told him that, unlike him with his loser factory job, Mommy has a high-level executive job that requires her to use her brain."

"Oooh, that's harsh," I ventured. "Don't you agree that your mom *does* have a problem with alcohol, though?" I quickly added, "A problem she currently seems to have under control, thank God."

"That's not the point, Uncle Eddy!" Tiffany was getting exasperated with me. "Mr. Holleran *cannot* be F-ing calling people up and telling them to keep their kids away from us. Like they're any F-ing better or something? Plus, that stuff about me is all bullshit and lies."

*Whew!* That's what I was hoping to hear. When the train stopped at West Eighty-first Street, I realized I'd learned more in a fifteen-minute subway ride than during the last three days' worth of meals together. Tiffany had spoken to me like a friend, a peer, and in doing so let me glimpse a bit of her world from inside her skin. Later, between the IMAX *Stomp* movie and the Big Bang presentation, we ran into four girls Tiffany knew from school. When they all just stood there looking at each other, I attempted to start a conversation about the exhibits we'd seen. Tiffany cut me off, saying, "We gotta go!" When I asked her what that was all about, she scolded me, "Kids don't want to talk to other kids' parents! It's totally embarrassing. Please, if we ever run into anyone I know again, keep on walking and wait for me nearby." I knew then that no matter how many of these rules I learned or how many times Tiffany seemed to share certain secrets with me, to the world of teenage girls I would remain forever an outsider.

# An Inside Job

About a month into my new life I began feeling like I could breathe a little easier. Tiffany seemed to be adapting both to her new high school and to the quiet, structured weeknights in the apartment. With the exception of her possibly running away, my worst fear had been that she'd call me crying every day after school and spend evenings either shrieking about how much she hated it here or curled up in a ball, sobbing with homesickness. Though I knew Tiffany missed her friends terribly, she seemed to be taking the separation in stride so far, making me wonder if she didn't agree that coming to live with me was the best option for her at this point in her life. None of the kids from her new school lived in the neighborhood, so she hadn't started asking to go out on Friday and Saturday nights, and since she hadn't yet bonded closely with any girls from school, no friends had come back to the apartment. Though the kids had acted friendly when she'd first arrived, Tiffany said that the girls were pretty cliquey; the Asians hung mostly with Asians, the black girls stuck mostly with the black girls, and so on, leaving my niece with few choices for a best girlfriend. The boys were paying lots of attention to her, of course, but so far there wasn't anyone special. At least that I knew of.

So, while I breathed easier about Tiffany's adjustment, mine was a different story. Sure, the mania had begun to wear off, as expected, and I was sleeping better, but I was still trying to get used to the early morning schedule and to having such a big responsibility waiting for me when I got home every night. I always looked forward to seeing Tiffany at the end of my workday, but there were invariably several stops I had to make on the way home for dinner items and the latest list of sundries Tiffany had dictated to me over the phone. There were looseleaf reinforcements to be found and lip gloss to be bought . . . and a protractor, a memo pad, tampons, thong shields, a black-light bulb — the list went on and on. Who knew kids needed so many *things* to make it through their days? Daily shopping added to my already constant stressing about money. Although

Megan was sending two hundred dollars a month, setting Tiffany up with the proper wardrobe and new school supplies had left me scraping. I'd lost five hundred dollars in monthly income from Dr. Harland and was always worried that my meager savings weren't going to last. So my walk home from work through beautiful Greenwich Village usually involved an internal battle between *Screw it, I'm going to pick up takeout like I've always done* and *Don't be foolish; you need to cook every night, so pick up microwavable Hot Pockets and cans of soup.* Then, after flip-flopping back and forth, if I was good and chose the latter, I'd start beating myself up about what I was planning to make. *Pick up some precut vegetables, you moron, and make a stir-fry. Tiffany loves fresh veggies!* It would have been so much simpler to decide we could eat takeout *x* nights per week and cook on the others. But, no, I had to be the captain of the debating team every single weeknight, further tightening an already tight inner coil.

By the time I arrived home, I was more than ready for a time-out. I'd kiss Tiffany hello and then go into my room for twenty minutes of structured relaxation. My niece, of course, thought it was bizarre that I'd play "weirdo" music in a room lit only by candles, with cold compresses or cucumber slices over my eyes. For me, though, Paul Horns recordings from the Taj Mahal or the Grand Canyon calmed me down and helped me catch my breath before I shifted into a whole different gear. For the five years that I'd been at my current company, I'd gone to the gym almost every night directly from the office. Between the physical release of exercising and the visual stimulation provided by the eye candy that crammed the place, I'd easily stop thinking about thorny negotiations, needy clients, and a creeping sense of frustration with my work. Now, with the incredible life force known as Tiffany waiting at the apartment for me each night, a buffer between the office and home was no longer a luxury: it was a necessity.

On a Tuesday night in late October, I kissed Tiffany hi, grabbed the mail off the dining table, and headed to my room to do my timeout. Before I lay down, I rifled through the regular junk and found a letter from my father. After I'd whined to my parents about my financial straits, they'd pledged to send three hundred dollars a month to help us out; the first check was in the envelope, along with a note from my dad. In his chicken-scratch cursive, my father had written:

Dear Eddy,
I am so proud of you for taking on this incredible responsibility. You're doing a great job.

Love, Dad.

Now, that might not seem like a demonstrative note to most people, but when you consider that my dad had predicted to my mom that this whole thing wouldn't work out, it was a watershed. Without realizing it, my father had admitted that he'd underestimated both me and Tiffany — a small victory, to be sure, but these victories were rare, so I'd happily savor it. More important, he'd said he was proud of me. I knew he bragged about my accomplishments to other people, but he'd told me I made him proud only once that I could remember — when I'd graduated law school near the top of my class, which was almost ten years earlier. I cranked up the volume on the CD player, lit a candle, and killed the lights. Holding my father's note against my chest, I lay there stoically for my allotted twenty minutes, unable to cry because of the thickly sliced, ice-cold vegetables I'd laid against my weary eyes.

My father was the only son of poor Irish immigrants. He grew up in a tiny apartment in the South Bronx with his parents and only sibling, my aunt Geraldine. The South Bronx would later become crime-ridden and eventually be leveled with a bulldozer. The immigrants would flee to other parts of the Bronx, upstate, and out east to Long Island, which is where my folks went after they married in their early twenties. My dad claimed to be an adventurous kid who swung from the nets over the East River and dove in naked, but I knew that he was more likely to be found at the ballet with his lonely albino friend, Whitey, who my dad would later admit was probably gay. As Carrie Bradshaw so eloquently put it on *Sex and the City*, my dad is a "gay straight man." He's always been just as girl-crazy as I am boy-crazy, but his interests run toward the effete. In addition to inculcating me with an intense appreciation of art, books, film and, above all, nature, my dad has every Barbra Streisand record made and at least three different versions of *Les Misérables*.

Though he never attended college, my

father eventually replaced an executive at his company who'd graduated from the Wharton School of Business. He'd worked his way up in companies like Woolworth and Squibb and eventually became a vice president of distribution for a national cement company based in Greenwich, Connecticut. He had three children, his second house, and a shiny new red Mustang by the time he was thirty-two. Such a trajectory, though, was not without its price. He worked long hours, commuted four hours a day between Greenwich and Long Island, and returned home well after we'd all eaten dinner, wildly stressed out. In addition to that load, which would send most young men of today straight to psych wards, my dad also suffers from a lifelong case of road rage. Years later for a brief period he and Megan would commute together, and she would often come home shaking and crying, ranting about all the drivers Dad had chased after allegedly being cut off.

During the weekends of my boyhood my dad was very busy. There was the yard to tend to, the precious cars to be washed, and *Wide World of Sports* to be watched on Saturday afternoons. (The latter held no interest for me unless, of course, figure skating was on.) Five o'clock was cocktail hour, when he and my mom would retire to their formal living room to listen to Frank Sinatra on the hi-fi and sip Manhattans. Though we children were of course welcome to stop by, this was not family time.

The times I felt closest to my dad as a boy were when we'd watch *Star Trek* on Sunday evenings after my bath, and at Christmastime when he'd sit me on his lap and guide me through the Sears catalogue to create my wish list for Santa. I'd learned quickly that I'd be lucky to get even one or two items from the list, but I looked forward to this ritual all year long. (One year I retrieved my completed list from the cookie jar, where all the lists were kept for safekeeping until they were mailed to the North Pole, and added to it all the Barbies and accessories I ached for. Obviously, when I found out there was no Santa a few years later, I was *mortified*. Neither my dad nor my mom ever mentioned this, for which I remain grateful to this day.) My dad and I never really became friends while I was growing up, though; he remained a mystery to me, and I suspect I was simply incomprehensible to him.

As two adults, my father and I finally got

to know each other, warts and all. Though our relationship would always feel booby-trapped, the tender moments we somehow managed over the years were its sustenance. Once, when I was visiting home during my early twenties, Dad called me outside after dinner to look at the stars. It was cold and he stood on the wooden deck off the kitchen, a glass of red wine in his hand. He put his right arm around my shoulder and with his wineglass pointed toward the night sky.

"You see that trapezoid shape up there, with the three stars making a straight line that shoots down from its center?" he asked, warm clouds of breath billowing from his mouth.

"Yes," I answered, and I actually did.

"That's Orion's belt, part of Orion, a winter constellation," he said, sipping his wine while holding his gaze. "It was the first constellation I taught your mother when we were dating. Now I stand here twenty-odd years later showing my youngest child, my grown son, the same formation." He paused and breathed in deeply. On the exhale he continued, "It's something, I tell ya. It's something."

My father had never said anything like this to me before, so I'd believed that everything in his life had proved a disappointment to him, including me. I snaked my left arm behind the small of his back and briefly touched my head to his shoulder. We stayed standing there in the frigid winter air, staring up at the stars, for several perfect, silent seconds.

Now, as I lay in bed listening to my New Age music, I thought about how vulnerable I'd been feeling since Tiffany moved in. I wasn't quite sure why exactly, but it was as if I'd been pried wide open and my insides turned out. It was a lot like I'd felt when I was younger, especially in my twenties when I was acting and my emotions were always close to the surface, accessible at a moment's notice. When I left acting and started law school at twenty-eight, I'd had to toughen up and hide the sensitive guy behind the aggressive, ambitious attorney. Maybe that's why, despite doing better than I could have dreamed my first year, I ran smack into a wall of depression the following summer and then again after I graduated. As a result, I've spent the intervening years on antidepressant medication, which has leveled out my emotions for the most part, making me what I guess you'd call a regular grown-up guy — one who no longer cries at corny television commercials and can spend his days sparring with perfidious Hollywood producers. I know several depressed and anxious people who refuse to go on medication because they're afraid they'll go "flat" and lose their personalities. But in my case, a little level land was a welcome break from the emotional mechanical bull I'd ridden throughout my teens and my twenties. Besides, it wasn't as if I couldn't feel the experience when exceptionally good and terribly bad things happened. When I fell in love it was like I'd tumbled off a cliff, and when my niece Heather died I felt the pain of a wound so deep it could never completely heal. But overall, I'd become hardened to life's battles and multitude of disappointments, and maybe even a little inured to its wealth of tiny beauties.

Tiffany's arrival, though, seemed to break straight through my Zoloft-Wellbutrin shield and stir up the old inner currents. Since the moment a month and a half earlier when I'd made the decision to become her guardian, everything had taken on a different sheen, a more vibrant tone, like it all meant more somehow. It felt as if I were firing on all cylinders for the first time in years and aware of every moment as it passed. Of course I was completely exhausted from the whole experience, which can make a person feel on the verge, but much deeper things were at work here, I was sure. I spent many late nights on the phone with my best girlfriend, Orly, or my therapist friend, Steven (the one safeguarding my porn), trying to map out some of the feelings I was experiencing. Where was this river of sadness coming from? Was I remembering the loneliness and terror I felt at thirteen, a skinny little kid trying to make the switch from a small Catholic grade school to a scary public high — one filled with older boys and cool, tough girls like Tiffany? Or were the joy and comfort I felt making me mourn the fact that I'd never had children of my own? Probably both were accurate, we figured, plus a dozen others. One thing was for sure, though: Tiffany was showing me not only how meaningful it is to care for a child but also just how good a father I might have been.

# Guns

"Republicans Regain Control of the Senate and Increase Margin in the House," screamed the headline in the *New York Times*. I'd known this since morning, when the election results were announced on the radio, but seeing it in black and white made my stomach turn. I could already hear Justices Rehnquist and O'Connor arguing over retirement dates. So I switched to the Dining In/Dining Out section to read a piece on truffle season in Tuscany. I love the *Times*.

Tiffany was in her usual spot at the dining table, IMing madly on the laptop, with the cell phone to one side and the cordless on the other. How she could hear anything through her homegirl hood always puzzled me. An Instant Message chime would be followed with a giggle or a gasp and then furious typing. Contentment washed over me. We've fallen into an after-dinner, after-homework routine. We're going to be okay.

"Uncle Eddy, what's an AK-47 and a thirty-eight?" Tiffany's typing paused momentarily.

"They're types of firearms." Did I sound casual, or could she tell that the Republicans had just become very small potatoes?

"Thanks," she mumbled, and resumed her banging.

"Tiffany, you can't just ask me that and go back to typing. What's going on?"

"Uncle Eddy, I have to deal with this right now. It's important. I promise we'll talk in a little while."

"Okay, but I want you to sign off in a half hour." I went back to reading but the words refused to form sentences. Was this the same girl who just this morning was using maple syrup to draw flowers on her pancakes?

Later, after tucking her in, I lay on Tiffany's crescent-moon-and-star-covered bed.

"So, what's up? Why were you asking about guns?"

"You promise you won't freak out?"

Oh good, I thought, she doesn't know I already did. "I promise."

"You're sure?"

I nodded.

"Well, a few weeks ago, Luke and Toby broke into Toby's next-door neighbor's house and stole a whole bunch of stuff. They took stereos, TVs, VCRs, a DVD player, computers, jewelry, and cash. And the guns. Now the police are questioning them, and Luke is blaming it all on Toby. He is such a jerk for doing that."

I was stunned and speechless, but I knew I had to say something. If I reacted badly now, I would cut off the flow of information. And knowing what was *really* happening in her world was crucial. Tiffany sensed my hesitation.

"You're not going to tell Mommy, are you?" She sat up straighter.

"No." I had no idea if I could keep that promise, but I had to make it. "Have you known about the burglary since it happened?"

"Yes."

"Did the boys know there were guns in that house? Is that why they broke in there to begin with?" Tiffany could cut me off at any time, so I needed to get the most important information first. Maybe there was a plan to shoot up the school or something.

"Of course not, Uncle Eddy." She sank down into the bed, disgusted that I would even suggest such a thing.

"You're sure, right?" The window was

definitely closing now, but I had to push this point.

"Yes, I'm *sure*. My friends are not into guns and there is no big, evil *Zero Day* plan." She'd read my mind: *Zero Day* was a client's Columbine-inspired film in which two "normal" boys break into someone's house, steal guns, and slaughter half their high school. At first I was thrilled that Tiffany had liked the film so much, but when she'd watched it for the fourth time, I started to get a little nervous. She continued, "They're good people. They're just stupid and they got caught." She rolled onto her side, away from me.

"Was Tommy Dash involved?" I'd suspected for some time now that Tiffany and Tommy were romantically involved, but she would never let me get near the subject.

"No, he had nothing to do with it. Good night." I'd been dismissed. To Tiffany I was now just another annoying adult, asking all the wrong questions and jumping to irrational conclusions.

"I'm so glad you're here" was all I could think to say. I walked around the bed, kissed her on the forehead, and shut off her light.

Back in my bedroom I lay awake,

thinking about how dark and frightening her world seemed — not the world of childhood at all. Removing her from New Milford had seemed like the first step toward changing all that, but how could I be sure that it wouldn't simply start all over again here in New York, with a different cast of characters? And there had to be so much more that I couldn't possibly know.

# Rappin'

Shackin' with my niece,
She's a freshgirl.
But she ain't too happy
'Cause her hair don't got the curl.
See, she was born white,
And she wishes she was black.
'Cause when it comes to the rappin',
She just don't got the knack.

Tiffany usually doesn't like it when I break into song on the street, which, admittedly, is a pretty annoying habit. But tonight was an exception. Tonight I was rappin'. See, we'd just seen *8 Mile* with Eminem — on opening night no less — and we left the theater pretty spiked. She tried to hide her smile by bringing her sweatshirted hand to her mouth. I'd spotted it first, though, plus her slitty eyes betrayed her anyway. When Tiffany smiles, her whole face smiles, making her eyeballs virtually disappear. It's the kind of smile a person wants to work for and, when it comes, makes your heart crack open like a coconut. Kind of like Renée Zellweger, only better. The tension I'd carried in my neck through the entire film drained off. We were on the same side again.

We had arrived twenty minutes early for the movie, even though I'd bought the tickets during my lunch break. Seeing a movie on opening night in Manhattan requires major planning, especially when it's the acting debut of a rap superstar.

"I spoke to your mom today," I said when we sat down, looking straight out toward the screen. "She knows."

"About the guys in Connecticut?"

I nodded.

"How?" she asked.

"She ran into Jackie's mom, and apparently, it's all over town. She said they found guns at both Luke's and Toby's. And drugs at Toby's house too. Enough to charge him as a dealer." Jackie was a girlfriend of Tiffany's who'd recently lit the girls' room on fire at Tiffany's old high school, causing the building to be evacuated for two hours. She'd been expelled. For good.

"That's bull crap." I could tell she wanted to say "shit." Then, through clenched teeth, "I'd like to punch that bitch in the face."

"Tiffany!" I tried not to raise my voice. "Why are you angry with *her?* What does she have to do with anything?"

"It's not her business. She has no right going around saying that. Plus she doesn't know what she's talking about. I hate her. Everyone does. She's so stupid."

I was silent. There was some moronic movie jumble on the screen. A third grader would know in a second that the answer was "Tom Hanks." I was relieved of making the next move when Tiffany spoke first.

"Why are you mad at me now?"

"I'm not mad. I'm concerned. You just . . . seem so hardened to me, so angry. And angry about the wrong things and at the wrong people. Of course Jackie's mother is going to talk about it, especially with your mom. Their daughters are friends with boys who've committed a major felony. And it involved burglary and guns, and now maybe drugs too. It's a very scary thing. And you're so casual about it all. Plus, I thought your boxing days were over." The one time she'd punched another girl in the face, she'd thrown up at the sight of the blood spurting from the girl's nose.

Tiffany sort of humphed at my joke, but she was gone already. Eyes glazed, she'd pulled to the far side of her seat and slumped down. But I was glad I'd said what I said. Who knows if it was the right thing to say, or if it was even remotely helpful to the situation; it was all I could come up with. We were in public, and the movie was going to start. I'm sure neither of us had any doubt that there would be more conversations about guns.

Now, as we walked west on Thirteenth Street, Tiffany was laughing and we were a team again. The early October night air was exhilarating — slightly crisp, with summer still lingering at its edges.

"So, I take it you liked the movie?" I asked in normal speech, having exhausted the little rhythm I could muster from my nonmusical brain. "I thought it was cool, if a bit contrived, the way Eminem apologized to the gay community for his past sins by sticking up for that guy in the movie."

"Oh, Uncle Eddy, you've given me the Eminem homophobia lecture a million times, and I still say he has no reason to apologize. He wasn't speaking for himself in all those old songs; he was playing a character." I think I'd told Tiffany that this was Eminem's defense, and now she was throwing it back at me. Do kids forget anything?

"Okay, gotcha," I conceded.

"What does 'contrived' mean?"

"Oh, good, it's probably an SAT word." I was glad that Tiffany never let a word she didn't understand go by unquestioned. "I think it means 'artificially created' or something. I mean, everything in a movie is artificial and a product of artistic collaboration. But when it feels 'contrived,' I guess it seems even more obviously fake, usually to make a point, I think."

"Then I guess you could say it was contrived that there were no drugs in the entire movie. That's ridiculous and unrealistic — a whole movie about rappers without a single drug in sight. But I really liked it. Eminem is so hot."

"Wow, you're right. That never even occurred to me." This kid is really on the ball. "I guess the filmmakers contrived it that way so that people would not equate rappers with drugs. But, my God, the violence. Isn't it awful that kids have to grow up around that?" We'd stopped at the corner of Seventh Avenue and Twelfth Street, and a group of young pseudo-homeys came running toward us, trying to beat the light. Hoping to spot a sexy, New York version of Eminem, I quickly scanned their faces. When I walked the streets with Tiffany, I tried to curb my awful habit of rubbernecking after every hot guy that walked by. With homeys, though, it wasn't a problem; their long, baggy shirts and low-crotched, oversized jeans were designed to hide any trace of ass whatsoever.

"There's pretty much violence everywhere," Tiffany said, confirming that none of the passing boys were worth our attention. "I met a guy in Danbury who murdered eleven people."

"Okay," I said, going up three octaves on the second syllable. "And your encounter with a psychotic serial killer would have been when, where, and how, pray tell?"

"I went with friends to his house. It was no big deal. I guess I thought it would be cool to meet someone who'd killed people." This was delivered completely deadpan, with no trace of irony or humor. She's got to be putting me on, I thought. Or maybe it's a suburban legend. Kids love to freak each other out with this kind of stuff. I decided not to blow a gasket, reassuring myself that the story was on its face implausible; anyone who was known by hordes of local kids to be a murderer would have been caught long before getting to number eleven. Instead, I played along to see where this would go.

"So, what was he like?" I asked nonchalantly.

"He was nice, I guess, kind of funny even."

"Nice, huh?" This was getting interesting. "But if you knew beforehand that he was a killer, why would you want to meet him?"

"Because I don't prejudge people, Uncle Eddy. That's prejudice. If someone's nice to me, then I'm nice back to them. If they mess with me or disrespect me, then they're history." Tiffany was taking a stand, which I admired, but she clearly had it all wrong.

"That's not the way it works, Tiff." I tried to not go into lecture mode but failed miserably. "Prejudice is when you judge someone based on a characteristic they can't change, like someone's race, skin color, gender, or sexual orientation. Behavior is exactly what a person *should* be judged on. Choosing to not associate with murderers is not being bigoted, it's just using good judgment and being selective."

"You're still talking about Toby and

Luke, aren't you?" Tiffany stopped and turned toward me accusingly. "This isn't about the murderer, and I still think you're too judgmental. My friends can make mistakes and I'm not going to desert them for it. They stood by me when I had no one, and I'm not going to condemn them for one stupid action."

Luckily, we were now standing on the corner of Bank and Bleecker Streets, only one block from Magnolia Bakery.

"Look, the fabu-line isn't too long," I said, pointing toward the five or so trendy Villagers spilling out the door. "How about a cupcake?"

I'd learned in just six short weeks that when I could no longer get through, it was best to disengage and move on. Maybe she heard something, maybe something had sunk in. Either way, though, we could both use a major dose of chocolate icing.

# Soldiers

"Have you heard anything else about the burglary?" I asked Megan from my desk. "Was there anything about it in the papers?" We'd taken to speaking from work one or two mornings a week, where we could talk without danger of Tiffany's overhearing.

"No, nothing in the papers, but I confirmed that it definitely happened through someone I know at the sheriff's office." Megan was kind of like Erin Brockovich that way: she always knew who to call and how to wheedle information out of them. "And the boys aren't in custody, which I expected."

"Well, I hope their court dates happen before Thanksgiving, and that they're sent somewhere away from New Milford," I said, knowing it was wishful thinking. "Tiffany's still e-mailing Toby, but I think she's had a falling out with Luke, thank God."

"How is she this week?" Megan asked.

"Not too bad. I actually heard her practicing songs in her room when I came home from work last night. Her voice is just unbelievable. I sat on the carpet outside her door and practically wept when she did 'In My Own Little Corner' from *Cinderella*." Tiffany had been taking a musical theater class on Tuesday afternoons at her "old" conservatory on the river. "So over dinner I negotiated a deal with her and she's going to sing on Thanksgiving."

"What do you mean, 'negotiated'? Are you going to pay her?" Megan sounded surprised.

"Of course. There's no way she'd do it otherwise. She's getting thirty dollars for three songs. I offered her twenty for four, she countered with forty for two, and we wound up at three for thirty." I laughed.

"Sounds like she's taking after her uncle, the agent," Megan teased. "She probably wants to buy pot with the money while she's up here, especially for her birthday."

"Well, let's hold her accountable for how she spends it. I have her on a strict receipt system, so we need to be consistent." I swiveled my chair toward the window, away from my office door, and lowered my voice. "You know, Megan, despite everything that's happened, you did an amazing job with Tiffany. She is one awesome young woman; she's smart, kind, funny, and boy, is she tough."

Megan started to cry.

"What's wrong?" I asked. "She's doing okay now, studying more and singing. Her attitude seems a bit better." I didn't tell her that Tiffany had spent the last two Saturday afternoons in Washington Square Park with Aleksi from downstairs and that she'd come home with eyes the size of saucers. She'd looked just like one of those 1960s Keane paintings of children with huge heads and giant, sad eyes. Both evenings she'd eaten dinner ravenously and fallen asleep in front of the television. If Tiffany wanted to buy pot, she probably didn't even have to leave our building.

"I know, it's not that." Megan wrestled her voice back from her tears. "I miss her, Eddy. I miss hearing her singing in her bedroom. I miss the funny things she says. She's going to graduate high school and go off to college, so really, she's already gone for good. My little girl is gone." She broke down into sobs.

"Megan, that's not true," I whispered, trying to protect Rob from overhearing something so personal. "This arrangement may only be temporary — maybe just till you're solidly back on track and Tiffany's got her act together," I said, secretly hoping it wouldn't be the case. "And you and Tiffany have long lives ahead of you as mother and daughter. There are decades for you to be best friends again." This part I meant with all my heart.

"I hope you're right, Eddy."

When I clicked off my headset, I felt bad that Megan was upset, as well as a little bit guilty, like I'd taken Tiffany away from her or something. But I was also glad to hear her express such tender thoughts about her daughter. It was a major turnaround from a conversation we'd had shortly after Tiffany moved in with me. "She's got the life of Reilly, that one," Megan had said bitterly. "Everyone should be so lucky. I wish I could've gone to school in New York City." Megan often seemed jealous of Tiffany — of her talent, her looks, her youth, even her relationship with me. She seemed to have little empathy for the difficulties in Tiffany's life, so it was moving to hear that she at least missed her.

I was glad too that I didn't tell Megan about Tiffany's dream of the night before. Sharing dreams was a ritual that never seemed to grow old for mother and daughter; I knew they'd continued it even when they were fighting, and Megan must surely miss that as well. I, on the other hand, found other people's dreams excruciatingly boring, but I never told Tiffany that.

During this particular night, Tiffany had dreamt about guns. She'd come into my room in the morning before my alarm went off, all puffy-eyed and innocent, and sat on the edge of my bed.

"I was putting together a gun, but I couldn't figure out how to do it." She launched right in, having dispensed with the standard "I had this dream last night" intro weeks ago. "It was one of those long guns, practically half the size of me."

"Like a rifle or something," I coached.

"Yeah, and I was standing in a big toy store, like Toys Я Us. There was no one around and I was about to give up when this huge group of men came walking down the aisle, in straight lines. They had on pointy hats, like this." She pulled the sides of her head out into imaginary points.

"Did they have on uniforms too? They sound like Revolutionary War soldiers."

"Exactly." Her eyes grew wide, then just as quickly her brow furrowed. "Except I got a little scared because I couldn't figure out if they were fighting or just in a parade."

"Ah," I surmised, ever the sage, "giant toy soldiers, like in that old Laurel and Hardy movie, *March of the Wooden Soldiers*."

"No. They were real," she corrected, rolling her eyes. "So this one guy comes out of the line and somehow I know that he's going to help me put my gun together, and I'm not afraid anymore. But all of a sudden I'm in this beautiful meadow on a hill and the sky is really, really blue. The soldier is standing right behind me, helping me balance the rifle against my shoulder so that I can shoot it. I can feel his breath on the back of my neck."

"And did you fire it?" Alarm bells sounded in the back of my brain.

"Yeah, which woke me up." She sounded disappointed. "But first I turned my head and saw that the soldier was Tommy Dash. I'm going back to bed for a while." She walked out as suddenly as she'd walked in.

I was glad Tiffany didn't ask me what I thought her dream meant, as she usually did. Though it didn't surprise me that my niece's subconscious had wrapped her romantic longings in guns and violence, it made me sad all the same. Tiffany is caught in two worlds at one time, I thought. And there is no middle.

# I Hate You

In the middle of November, on the evening before my forty-first birthday, Tiffany told me that she hated me. It felt monumental, like a rite of passage, being told I was hated. It was inevitable, I suppose, but I guess I just hoped it would be longer in the coming.

We'd had a relatively smooth week or two, once the gun incident had receded into the wings. I'd begun to relax into the situation a bit more, feeling a little less like a writhing ball of exposed nerve endings. Tiffany seemed to have made a few friends at school, and I was happy to observe that nearly half the phone calls that came in were *not* from Connecticut. Believe me, I was keeping tabs. Most of the calls were from boys, though, many with deep voices and heavy street accents. There was Niko and Kevin and Jesus and Jonathan. There was also a sweet-sounding kid named Ari, whom Tiffany described as "a nice little Jewish computer-geek-next-door." And of course, Aleksi from downstairs.

And two girls seemed to have finally made their way into Tiffany's sphere, though there was still little opportunity for getting together outside of school. One was Sade (pronounced sha-DAY, like the singer), who had transferred in the same day as Tiffany, but she lived all the way up in Harlem. I wasn't sure if Tiffany felt at all close to Sade or if they'd become friends by default. The other was April, whom I'd actually met one day when she and Tiffany stopped by my office after school. April was a sophomore who seemed extremely intelligent, street savvy, and reasonably polite. She was a mix of retro and current punk, with her blue hair, pierced tongue and eyebrows, and outrageously colorful thrift store ensembles. Tiffany told me April was the only punk in the whole school, which, in my opinion, took balls. Her fierce individualism would be a good example for Tiffany, who tended to over-value fitting in. Plus, I'd recently learned that she had moved from Long Island to live with her single aunt because her mother had a drug problem, so she and Tiffany had a lot in common. Unfortunately, though, April lived on the Upper East Side, which takes three trains to reach from our apartment, and worked many afternoons and weekends at Baskin-Robbins.

That left lots of time for Tiffany to spend with Aleksi. He too was a real individualist, and I'd initially been extremely impressed that he attended Stuyvesant. But I'd since found out that he was likely to be asked to leave because of a lack of motivation, which, judging from the condition in which Tiffany returned from their last two Saturday afternoons together, was probably due to excessive pot smoking. I also worried that with him living directly beneath us, they had ample opportunity to be alone in one of the apartments together. Tiffany made fun of Aleksi's eyeliner and makeup, and joked about his unwillingness to "label" his sexual orientation, but I feared she might be fooling around with him just because he was there. I knew from reading Oprah's magazine, as well as from other sources, that it wasn't like it was when I was a teenager back in the '70s. Nowadays kids didn't have to be "going out" or even really like each other to have sex: they would just "hook up" on a whim. Blow jobs were given out by girls like party favors, I'd heard, and they weren't even considered sex. And I knew from experience that when pot was involved, people did things they might not otherwise do. But then again, wasn't I thinking just like a typical, old-fashioned parent? Isn't it always worse today than the "innocent" way it was back then? I mean, I started fooling around with boys every chance I could get when I was about twelve years old. But I was gay, so I *couldn't* properly date and fall in love prior to getting my rocks off, right? And the girls I knew, including my sisters of course, were always crazy about the guys they fooled around with, weren't they? I was sure they didn't do it just for entertainment, like the kids seemed to today. Or, did I deep down think it was okay for me to be promiscuous because I was a boy, making me guilty of the sexist double standard I loathed? In any event, I couldn't escape the sneaking suspicion that maybe back then *everyone* was behaving the way I did and that I was just being a big fat hypocrite with Tiffany.

Still, I figured it was my job to at least not make it too easy for her to have sex, as well as to repeatedly mention the dangers involved and explain how she could protect herself against them. The conversations never went as planned, though. Just as Tiffany had proudly told me she does *only* pot and alcohol that day on the subway, whenever I brought up sex she'd either clam up or cut me off by saying, "Don't worry, Uncle Eddy, I'm still a virgin." Still, I persevered and one night at dinner brought up both sex *and* drugs in the context of talking about Aleksi.

"Look, Tiffany, I know you're spending a lot of time with Aleksi lately, and I know you're getting high together." I tried to make it sound like I thought that was okay.

"Whatever, Uncle Eddy. Can't we just eat, please?"

"But Tiffany, when a person gets stoned and gets into a potentially sexual situation, they might find themselves doing things they might not normally do. Their judgment gets impaired."

"Are you afraid I might get donkey-punched, Uncle Eddy?" Tiffany asked me casually. "Or that Aleksi might pull a Polish dump truck?"

"What do those things mean?" I asked, slightly afraid to find out.

"Well, 'donkey-punched' is when a guy and girl are having sex and the moment after he has an orgasm, he pulls out his you-know-what and punches the girl in the face." Tiffany giggled and took a bite of her Green Giant broccoli in cheese sauce. "And a 'Polish dump truck' is when —"

"Okay, okay, Tiffany." I saw where this was going. "I get it; you don't want to have this conversation." She continued laughing, but I ate in silence for a moment.

"Do you know what 'misogyny' means, Tiffany? It's an SAT word that I think you should look up and memorize."

"No problemo, Uncle Eddy. I will."

"So you were kidding the other morning when you told me you had sex with Aleksi at the pizza place, right?" I had to get at least that much out of her.

"Duh," she answered, raising her eyebrows and widening her eyes. "I think he's actually kind of gross with that pancake makeup line going along his huge jaw. Give me some credit, Uncle Eddy; I'm going to be a lot more selective than that when I decide to give it up." Tiffany laughed as she scooped up a big forkful of Hamburger Helper Beef Stroganoff.

I decided to quit while I was ahead, and we ate in silence. Though I now believed that she wouldn't lose her virginity to Aleksi, I still wasn't convinced there wasn't some serious diddling going on.

Regarding drugs, I wasn't going to tell Tiffany she absolutely could not indulge. My parents had done that with Megan and me when we were teenagers and it hadn't worked; I had no reason to think that approach would be any more successful today. No, my strategy with Tiffany would be to *discuss* her drug use — to *explore* the reasons she felt the *need* to put substances into her system. And I planned to do this without telling her that I myself had tried virtually every drug under the sun before I'd graduated high school. Well, that strategy was abruptly aborted one evening when Tiffany confronted me with my yearbook, which I'd foolishly left on the bookshelf in the living room.

"Uncle Eddy," she'd begun, smiling mischievously, "why do all the people who signed your yearbook end with things like 'stay burnt' or 'never stop partying'?"

Totally busted, I thought. Think quick!

"And what's a 'bone zone'?"

"Never mind about the bone zone," I snipped. "Yes, I smoked pot in high school, Tiffany. But my friends are grossly exaggerating, as teenagers tend to do. I was obviously not a burnout; I got good grades and went to a great college. Of course they're not going to write about our good times in English class."

"Okay, chill," she'd replied, putting the book back on the shelf.

If it was so acceptable for *me* to smoke

pot in high school, why was I getting so defensive? And why would I be horrified if my niece behaved the same way I had? Was I being a hypocrite yet again? Tiffany knew that I'd gone to Binghamton University, arguably the best state school in New York, but she didn't know that I'd needed to use my art portfolio to apply as a "talented student." And though I had decent SAT scores and won a Regents scholarship, my average had been a below-par 87, and I'd failed to make the National Honor Society because my Spanish teacher told the committee I fell asleep too often in class. But I'd wound up at a top Wall Street law firm, surrounded by attorneys from the country's top law schools, so it didn't matter that I'd been a pothead in high school, right? A legal career had turned out to be the wrong choice for me, though; maybe if I hadn't spent so much time partying, I'd have known myself better and been more confident creatively. Didn't I fail at acting and not pursue writing because I had no confidence? Hadn't I become a lawyer to prove to myself and the world that I was just as smart and capable as all those happy, shiny, athletic kids I never really knew in high school and college? Had I become an insecure outsider because I did drugs, or did I do drugs because I was already one? It all seemed so confusing, but no matter how I looked at it, the bottom line was that I hoped Tiffany wouldn't waste as much time killing her brain cells as I had.

Progress in honestly and openly discussing sex and drugs was going to be slow and difficult for both of us. I reminded myself, though, that no matter how ill-prepared I felt for so many aspects of this job, I was providing Tiffany with a fairly stable, quiet environment and that she seemed to be getting most of her schoolwork done. Regarding Aleksi, between Tiffany's singing classes and tutoring, there weren't that many weekday afternoons where she could see him. I'd told her that he wasn't allowed in our apartment when I wasn't home and I'd asked Marvin, who worked irregular hours, to help police the situation. I could only hope that, with time and my influence, Tiffany might be able to begin making good decisions for herself.

On the evening that Tiffany said she hated me, I'd sat her down and told her what Megan and I had planned for the Thanksgiving/birthday weekend. It would be her first trip back to Connecticut, and her mom and I were pretty nervous about it. The boys who'd committed the burglary were free until their court dates, and Tiffany's remaining girlfriends were far from model citizens. I say "remaining" because one by one her girlfriends were hitting the road. Jackie, who'd torched the school, had been sent away; Kimberly's parents had resorted to having her kidnapped by that outward-bound, military-rehab outfit in Idaho; and Serena's family had up and moved out of the area to get their daughter away from her friends. Of Tiffany's remaining three girlfriends, two had shoplifting convictions on their records and the third had been caught stealing from her mother. Megan and I were determined to wean her off these kids and, for better or worse, help turn her focus toward the friends she was making in the city.

Remembering a technique I'd learned in couples counseling years ago, I decided to not simply talk *at* Tiffany but instead told her we would have a "structured discussion." I would speak for ten minutes, she would speak for ten minutes, and then we'd have five more minutes each to respond. This method of communicating had led directly to the breakup of my relationship, but I figured what the heck, it was better than diving right into an argument. I also told Tiffany that what I was going to tell her was not up for negotiation; I was structuring it this way so that I could listen to her thoughts and feelings because they mattered to me but that nothing would change. This sounded like total bullshit to me, so it probably sounded even worse to her.

We sat at opposite ends of my huge hunter green sofa and faced each other. I opened with a recap of the reasons Tiffany was living with me in the first place, followed by a list of all her talents and how bright her future could look if she'd only focus on it. Then I outlined her trip to Connecticut. She would spend Thanksgiving with the family and have the entire next day — her birthday — to do whatever she wanted. That evening, though, she had to come home for dinner, after which she could then go back out until eleven o'clock. If she would like, her friends could come over for pizza and cake, and several of her girlfriends could sleep over. But they'd all have to be in by eleven, and each of their parents would be called in advance to discuss the plan. The following day, Saturday, we would return to Manhattan in the late afternoon, after she'd had a good number of hours to spend as she liked.

When Tiffany heard that she would not have Saturday night and Sunday with her friends, tears the size of marbles popped out of her eyes. With all the unsupervised time I had just offered her, Tiffany could focus only on the loss of that one day.

"I have waited two months to go back and see my friends. It's the one thing that's kept me going through all this crap." She was buying time; I could see in her eyes that she was quickly strategizing how to make her argument.

"Uncle Eddy, I have not been happy here." She paused for emphasis, as though this revelation would send me into an emotional tailspin.

Of course you're not happy, I thought. You're a teenager; it's your job to be miserable.

"I know why you're doing this and it's not fair. You're judging my friends based on the mistakes they've made. Everyone makes mistakes."

Exactly. We're thought well of when we do good things and we're thought ill of when we do bad. Forgiving people for their mistakes shouldn't result in having only criminals for friends.

"They've all given up on themselves, but

146

I'm not going to give up on them. They were there for me when no one else was, not even the family. One night I was freaking out and Luke came over and calmed me down. I didn't even ask him to. He helped me with my homework and covered my book."

Covered your book? Was that before or after he burglarized the neighbor's house? Even my inner sarcasm couldn't fight the fact that, with those words, Tiffany had transformed into a little girl again. Her world was brown-paper-bag book covers and *Puff the Magic Dragon.* But was this simply what she wanted me to think? Had Luke actually brought her a hit of E and a shot of Southern Comfort? It was becoming increasingly hard to know what was real. I longed for a crystal ball.

"If anyone, including you, Uncle Eddy — and I don't mean to be disrespectful — has a problem with my friends, then it's their problem. And they have to work it out themselves. It's not my problem, it's their problem." Tiffany folded her arms and her now-dry face went stony. I was surprised she didn't snap her fingers and jut her jaw from side to side.

To be honest, I admired her loyalty to her friends, and I told her so. A forgiving friend who never forgot an act of kindness is hard to come by and will always be greatly valued by others. I also told her that my job, above all others, is to keep her safe. I had twenty-five years more life experience than she did, which entitled me to make judgments regarding how to avoid danger. Tiffany, of course, had a rebuttal.

"Safety? You're concerned with my safety?" Her incredulity seemed real. "Can you honestly sit there and say that I'm safer down here in this crazy city than I am up in Connecticut? I can't walk down the street without creeps harassing me: 'Short and sweet. Just the way I like it!' Or, 'Hey honey, can I carry your books?' Then, when I actually get to school, it's even worse. You should see the size of these girls. Their wrists are the size of my thighs! It's like I'm this little white girl lost in this sea of huge boobs and asses. I have to watch my back all day long. I've never felt so unsafe!"

God, she's good, I thought, but time's up. Saved by the bell.

"Thank you," I said, "I really appreciate your honesty. Now let's get ready for bed." Tiffany stared, mouth agape, as I got up from the sofa.

"What? That's it?" She couldn't believe

that she'd made no headway — that I hadn't compromised with her in some way.

"Yes. We've heard each other out and it's finished. I meant it when I told you that this was not up for negotiation."

Tiffany combusted into tears. "I can't take this anymore," she sobbed as she ran toward her room. "I don't deserve this," she screamed, slamming her door shut for the first time.

Sitting on the edge of my bed listening to her sobs, I had a realization, however obvious it seems to me now: This is simply about her being told no. She's always gotten her way, so every cell in her body is revolting against this.

Tiffany's sobs were interrupted by muffled screams. "I can't fucking stand this" and "I'm going to lose it." Then the pounding started. I wasn't sure what she was hitting, but it was loud and I got scared. I guess this is it, I thought, the inevitable meltdown has arrived. I knocked on her door.

"Don't you dare fucking come in here," she yelled, not missing a beat in her pounding. "I fucking hate you." I walked in and found Tiffany kneeling on top of the bed, hunched over and pounding her fist against the mattress. She had a wild look in her eye — one I hadn't seen before — and there was blood on her sheets. She kept pounding, so I grabbed her arm by the wrist. The side of her hand was bloodied and looked bruised.

"Don't you lay a fucking hand on me," she screamed in my face as she jerked her arm away. It would have been so easy to smack her right then, or to pin her down and scream at her until she gave in. But somehow, despite the adrenaline pumping through me, I knew it was the wrong decision. I left and sat on the sofa and tried to catch my breath. A strange calm came over me, and I knew what to do.

The middle-income housing complex where we live has a staff of security guards who patrol during the evenings. Often there were a couple of them standing in front of a building on the next block — between Eleventh and Perry Streets. Despite the fact that I was in my drawstring pants, a T-shirt, and slippers, I sneaked out of the apartment and ran down the three flights of stairs to the street.

Sure enough, there they were — two African-American men standing against the wrought-iron fence in their navy uniforms, complete with hats and bright orange vests with the word *Security* written boldly across them. One of them was extremely tall and brawny.

How am I going to explain this? I thought as I approached them.

"I have an hysterical thirteen-year-old girl on my hands," I began.

"No problem," the bigger of the two interrupted. "Do you want us to come up and speak with her?" I nodded and nothing more was said.

We slipped back into the apartment, where the smaller guard knocked loudly on Tiffany's door and said, "Security." The pounding inside stopped and, to my surprise, the door swung open.

"Everything okay in here?" the big guy asked Tiffany, who'd pulled down her sleeve to cover her hand. "One of your neighbors called us because of the noise," he said.

How did he know to say that?

Tiffany immediately burst into tears and sat on the edge of the bed.

"Yes, yes," she stammered, swatting at her tears with her other hand. "I'm fine, and I promise I'll be quiet." She continued to weep softly. I closed her door and saw the men out.

"Thank you," was all I could think to say.

"You're welcome," the smaller one answered with a sympathetic smile. "Good luck."

I didn't see Tiffany again that night. Later, after I'd taken a tranquilizer and gotten into bed, I heard her stereo playing softly.

I find it kind of funny,
I find it kind of sad,
That the dreams in which I'm dying
Are the best I've ever had.
I find it hard to tell you,
I find it hard to take,
When people run in circles,
It's a very, very
Mad world.

Over and over she played the same song from *Donnie Darko*, and I drifted off to its strange, sad lyrics.

# Passages

I awoke abruptly at four thirty in the morning, my mouth parched and my mind racing. Damn it, I thought, I wish I'd taken half a Klonopin, but I'd taken only a quarter. As I'd need to wake Tiffany in just two hours, it was far too late to take the remaining pebble of tablet now. I knew that sleep — a most precious commodity these days — would elude me for the rest of the morning. The memory of the evening before quickly flooded my mind and I was struck by a sudden urge to smoke a cigarette. This was pretty rare for me these days, and usually happened only after a few drinks, but since it was the morning of my forty-first birthday, I decided to indulge myself. I found the stale old pack of emergency Marlboro Lights hidden in my underwear drawer and was leaving my room to put on some coffee when I saw that Tiffany had stuck a note halfway under my bedroom door.

I hate you.
You did this to me.
I can't breathe, I am so angry.
I want to scream out my emotions,
all at once.
I want to kill you with them.

How would you feel
if I stole your life
and made it what I wanted it to be?

Just remember,
one day can make your life,
one day can break it,
and one day can bring
a lifetime worth of happiness.

When I lock you up,
and take you away,
then tell me how intense the need is
for that one day.

What a lovely birthday card, I thought.
Now I *really* feel like having a cigarette. As
soon as the coffee was ready, I headed
downstairs to the backyard.

The housing complex in which Tiffany
and I live is an expanse of forty-two five-
story, reddish brick buildings bordered by
Bank Street on the north and Morton

Street to the south. A couple of buildings face the Hudson River, the complex's western border, but most face side streets or our street, Washington Street, which is the eastern border. What thirty years ago was a thinly populated area, forgotten as old shipping piers on the river were abandoned, is now a swanky residential district with new luxury high-rise apartments sprouting up monthly. We even have a new name — the Far West Village — and Nicole Kidman, Calvin Klein, and Martha Stewart live around the corner in über-architect Richard Meier's new "blue glass waterfall" twin towers.

Our yard is a manicured little court that we share with our fellow West Village Houses middle-income neighbors on three sides. We're mostly teachers, artists, actors, and writers — a bunch of leftover hippies, really — who never made it big, with a few cops and firemen thrown in. There are two squares of grass (one artificial to withstand children's play) surrounded by common walkways and little private gardens that serve as consolation prizes for the "G"-floor apartments that are, in actuality, partially underground and constantly flooding. The yard was now a place where I sought refuge when the apartment seemed simply too small to contain the pyrotechnics of Tiffany's and my outsized personalities, and I often paced its concrete paths.

I realized as I smoked that I had been only eight years older than Tiffany when I first moved into the complex. After graduating from college, I'd found a share through the Gay Roommate Service and gotten a sweet deal on an apartment that looked out on this very yard — for four hundred dollars a month, to be exact, including utilities. The only thing that wasn't so sweet was my three-hundred-pound depressed roommate, who was wasting an MFA from UCLA by lying around the apartment moaning about how fat and old he was. Jonah Goldfarb had just hit thirty. He was a brilliant talent, as evidenced by the way he brought the house down every Saturday night at a wonderful subterranean piano bar called the Five Oaks on Grove Street. Jonah would belt out "Down in the Depths on the Ninety-Eighth Floor," employing every ounce of his girth and charisma, and the denizens of the smoke-filled room would go nuts. Then Jonah would pass the elderly pianist's tip jar around as he swept through the crowd before making a grand exit. Occasionally he would stay and sip a pink cocktail

156

through a tiny red straw.

Jonah did word processing at big law firms for weeks on end until he had a pile of money and his eyes were so red he needed to close them or he'd bleed to death. Then he'd buy a half pound of pot, smoke himself silly, and order out for food five times a day. He'd descend into some strange dreamworld where he'd yell at his Aunt Candice as though she were in the room when, in reality, she was out in Los Angeles running the family's pornography empire. When he wasn't having imaginary arguments, he was watching selections from the cartons of gay porno tapes Aunt Candy so kindly shipped to him. Neighbors complained of Jonah's screaming, but even more of his habit of throwing empty takeout containers, pizza boxes, and dozens of plastic Diet Coke bottles out the apartment's fifth-floor window and into the very courtyard where I now sipped, smoked, and paced.

I think Jonah wanted me to move in so that I might save him by pulling him out of his funk. Instead, my twenty-two-year-old relentless optimism, combined with my blind ambition to become a successful actor, probably drove him even more crazy. I was always running from dance class to dialogue coach, from audition to my agent's office, and I was constantly checking in with my answering service, Bells Are Ringing, for the latest updates on my busy schedule. (Answering machines were just about to proliferate, rendering the kitschy Bells extinct.) When Jonah chased me around the apartment with a rather large kitchen knife one evening, I decided it was time to hit the road. The next day, as I was packing my stuff, I got a peek into Jonah's bedroom, which he usually kept locked. There was no furniture other than a sheetless bed, and the floor was hidden by old newspapers, magazines, and porno. But worst of all, the walls around his bed were brightly speckled with spots of color which, upon closer inspection, turned out to be wads of chewing gum Jonah had stuck there every time he threw himself into his dirty bed to pass out.

The courtyard wasn't so manicured back in 1984, and neither was New York City in general. The subways were covered in graffiti and rarely air-conditioned, Times Square was the quintessential red-light district, and there were no men and women in red suits sweeping the streets to fulfill their Giuliani-inspired community service sentences. In fact, the whole city was a lot grimier, sleazier, and more unpredictable. I remember frolicking on a hot summer afternoon in the unmown weeds of this yard with a group of waiters and waitresses from the huge restaurant in the South Street Seaport where we worked lunches. I'd invited them back for a party of beer, pot, and rolling around under the sprinkler. The boys all may or may not have been gay and the girls all may or may not have been in love with the boys. No one really knew what they were, and nobody really cared. It was a New York that seemed impossibly dirty and decadent and inviting and scary. And, in its own strange way, perfectly innocent.

Those days were long gone for me now, but their ghosts lingered on here in this grassy little square. There were Tom and Jack, a glamorous older couple (probably all of thirty) who lived in the ground-level apartment with the biggest private garden. I'd carried on secret affairs with both of them simultaneously, canceling out (I'd figured back then) any moral turpitude on my part. Tom had long since relocated to South Beach after Jack withered away to a skeleton from AIDS and died a gruesome death. And there was Carly, the twenty-four-hour party girl whom I'd spotted wandering down Bank Street crying hysterically over a doomed affair. She was six feet tall and blond, and when I'd offered my assistance, she'd grabbed me to her, hugged me, and pulled me into her apartment for an all-night, drug-induced rap session and game of Monopoly (her alternative to sex after she'd discovered I was gay). Carly gave up her wily ways in the late '80s and moved home to Main Line Philadelphia to marry the rich boy next door.

When I moved out of Jonah's, I signed up on the complex's waiting list for apartments. Just when I was starting law school five years later, I got the call that I could move back into Manhattan's coziest neighborhood. Now, as I stood here on the morning of my forty-first birthday, the differences between 1984 and 2002 seemed unfathomable. The trees in the courtyard had grown taller, fancy fences had been installed, and flowers had been planted. Hudson Street, the closest busy boulevard, had been gentrified and was now a thriving district of outdoor cafés filled with beautiful people. The rich had moved into gorgeous new apartments on the river's edge, which was once reserved for anonymous sex trysts and where "Stop the Movie *Cruising!*" had been stenciled everywhere in blood red paint by gay rights activists.

Sure, all of that had changed, and many would say for the better. But in the intervening years I would know fifty people — forty-eight men and two women — who'd be taken in their primes by a hideous and terrifying illness. (Yes, I've kept a list — one that I'm afraid is still not complete.) And on a crystalline September morning I would make my way south along the Hudson River, walking against a torrent of people, some covered in white ash, as I went to help a friend who sat paralyzed with fear in her apartment. Clutching each other for support, we would watch in disbelief as two skyscrapers imploded, killing thousands. Later I would be told to duct-tape my windows and hoard extra water, batteries, and canned food because I might, at any time, have to seal myself in my apartment for days on end. The zany innocence of my city that I'd cherished so dearly had died over those eighteen years, taking my youth and a part of my heart along with it.

Tonight a young girl was sleeping peacefully upstairs, exhausted from her rage and her tears. Did she dream about the city that pulsed around her? To her, was it as new and wondrous and mysterious and exciting as I'd found it all those years ago?

One thing was for certain: if I was now to play Jonah Goldfarb to Tiffany's Eddy Wintle, I could not reveal any newfound cynicism. Instead I would encourage my niece to partake of the city's magnificent bounty, all the while standing alert, at the ready, to second-guess its many, many perils.

# Moo Shu Birthday

"Come on, Tiffany, get up. It's seven o'clock already." It was the third time I'd gone in to try to rouse her from bed. "I don't want to have to come back in here again." I shuffled off to the kitchen to put on more coffee and pour us some orange juice. I also took the Banana Nut Crunch cereal from the cabinet and placed it on the counter, next to a bowl and a carton of milk. The scrambled eggs and toast had fallen by the proverbial wayside a couple of weeks back, when Tiffany declared she couldn't stomach another cheesy egg and that it would be quite some time before she could even *look* at one. Breakfast was now juice and cereal, which she usually ate alone at the dining table. So much for the Norman Rockwell mornings. I grabbed my *New York Times* from the vestibule outside the apartment door, poured myself some coffee, and headed back toward our bedrooms.

"Uncle Eddy, can I stay home today? I

feel really exhausted." Tiffany was sitting on the edge of her bed, with her hands tucked under her thighs. I passed her the juice, which she accepted with her good hand.

"Welcome to New York, Tiffany, where we're *all* exhausted *all* the time. Now come on, let's get a move on." I went to my room and jumped back under my warm covers. Since it was my birthday, I'd decided to skip the gym and take an extra glorious hour to read the paper in bed, which meant that Tiffany would have to walk to the subway on her own. In a moment, though, she appeared in my room and curled herself into a ball at my feet. Tiffany knew I loved it when she did this; the fact that it was the morning after our first huge fight made it all the more manipulative.

"Uncle Eddy," she began, with that telltale slide down from the *U* to the *Y*.

Doesn't she realize that's a dead giveaway?

"I have barely missed a day of school for a bunch of weeks now, so I think I've earned the right to take a day off." Then, quickly: "Mommy always let me do it in Connecticut."

"Well, Dorothy, you're not in Connecticut anymore," I said, refusing to pet her hair as I usually did. "Your eighth grade transcript showed eighteen absences and thirty-seven tardies, and that ain't gonna happen here. We'll save missing school for when you're sick. And by sick I mean you're either puking or running a fever."

"Who says 'tardy' anyway?" She immediately tried to cover her sarcasm with a giggle.

"Listen, Tiffany, we're both still recovering from last night, which, by the way, we need to talk about at length. You're really in no position to be starting an argument. Now, please get ready for school." I cracked open the Arts section and buried my face behind it. Tiffany dragged herself off the bed and shuffled into the bathroom. We didn't speak again until she was ready to leave.

"Here's your lunch money," I said, handing her three dollars.

"You're not walking with me?" she asked, seemingly disappointed.

"No, I'm going to relax for an hour. I'm a bit worn out." I waited to see if she'd remember it was my birthday. "Your thong is totally showing." I pointed to it as Tiffany turned around to grab her jacket. "If you've got to wear a thong, please make sure it's tucked in, especially when you sit down." Though the school required collared shirts and prohibited jeans, with the superlow hip-huggers girls were currently wearing, Tiffany's tops rarely met up with her bottoms. Luckily (for me, anyway), her belly button had been infected since she'd had it pierced over the summer, so she made darned sure her shirts never rode up more than an inch in front. I was sure that wouldn't last, though, and that great midriff wars lay ahead.

"Let me see your hand," I said, taking hers in mine. She'd placed a Band-Aid over the spot where the skin had rubbed off, but the side of her palm that surrounded it was black-and-blue. "We've got to talk about this," I said as I kissed her on the cheek.

A "Good-bye" was all I got as she slung her huge backpack over her shoulder, grabbed her keys, and left.

"Happy fucking birthday, Uncle Eddy," I said aloud to myself as I locked the door behind her.

"Oh, my, it sounds like she needs much more than in-school counseling. You should think about enrolling Tiffany in a drug and alcohol program as quickly as possible. And she should be attending Alateen meetings at least three times a week too." I was speaking for the first time to Judith Martin, the District 2 counselor assigned to Tiffany's high school one day a week, and I already wanted to reach through my headset and wring her neck.

"Look, Ms. Martin, I can only take this one step at a time, and right now I need to know if *you* can do anything for Tiffany. She's already been through your office's intake process with Ms. Wong."

"Okay, sure, I'll see her on Wednesdays. I'll check her schedule and see which period works best. In the meantime, I'll fax you a consent form and a list of referrals I think you should look into."

"Thank you, Ms. Martin. If there's any way possible, please, *please* don't pull her from math class. She really can't afford to *ever* miss that one." Tiffany's algebra skills were actually coming along, but losing a class a week would certainly set her back.

"Gotcha, Mr. Wintle. I'll call you and let you know how it's going in a few weeks."

Why do counselors and therapists always do that? I wondered as I hung my headset on its hook by the phone. Here I am, just coming off a night of crisis, and I'm already trying to take an action, to do something about the situation. And she goes and makes me feel like I'm not doing enough, like I have to plan a fucking mental health *schedule* for Tiffany.

Ms. Martin sounded like my own therapist, whom I'd started seeing ten months earlier when I was thinking about breaking up with my then boyfriend. I realized in the first session that I absolutely had to end the relationship, which I did, but I'd stayed on in therapy anyway. Now that Tiffany had moved in, I was glad I had. But then one day, right in the middle of my moaning and whining about the stress of my new responsibility, my therapist tells me that I really need to join his group. *Haven't you heard a word I've said?* I wanted to shout in frustration. Another hour-and-a-half appointment to fit into my insane schedule was exactly what I *didn't* need. Group, my ass. I about canned him right then and there.

"Ed, Francis Ford Coppola is on the phone," Rob called out from his desk, grinning. "And happy birthday." Yikes, I'd better take this one, I thought as I reached once again for my headset. And this had better not be a birthday prank.

"Therapy is retarded," Tiffany announced, "and I'm not going."

I'd come home to find a Hallmark card and a single red rose on the dining room table. Tiffany had remembered my birthday after all. Though in the past she'd always made the cards she gave me, at least she'd taken the trouble to buy a card and fill it out. Sublime was blasting from her bedroom, but I'd pulled her out to talk.

"I'm sorry, Tiffany, but you need to be in some sort of counseling right now. What happened last night is not okay, and I want you to talk to someone."

"That's what I have friends for," she responded, flinging herself on the cream love seat. I sat diagonally across from her on the hunter sofa (with matching cream piping). She continued, "I don't *need* to speak to any strangers about my personal life."

"Think of it as a luxury. That's how I look at it." I wasn't sure if this was the right approach but, then again, I never was. "I get to lie on a sofa for forty-five minutes once a week and talk to an objective ear about me, me, *me!*" I raised my arms higher with each "me," à la Charles Busch doing Joan Crawford. The attempted humor fell flat.

"Well, that's you," Tiffany responded

curtly. "We're not the same person, Uncle Eddy."

"That's for sure," I replied. "Look, Tiff, it's not a matter of choice here. Overall you've been doing well with this whole transition. When you didn't want to continue after speaking with Ms. Wong, I agreed. But you've got to work through your anger with some professional guidance. I know your friends are a great support, but this is out of their league." I sat up and leaned toward her. "Tiffany, you've got a lot to be angry about, I know. But it's going to get in the way of your becoming the incredible adult I know you're going to be."

"I couldn't understand Ms. Wong because of her accent," Tiffany said. "And I don't know why you make such a big deal about everything. Teenagers are supposed to get angry and punch things."

"I won't let you make light of what happened, Tiffany." Scenes like last night's were probably commonplace in Connecticut and felt familiar to her. "You'll be seeing Ms. Martin on Wednesdays, and the only accent she has comes from a faraway land called Brooklyn. Now, in honor of the much-maligned Ms. Wong, let's go meet my friends for some Chinese food." I stood up and stretched. "I could use a hot and sour fix."

"And I have a little something for Miss Tiffany too!" Eugene announced to our table of nine. Leave it to Eugene to bring something for Tiffany on *my* birthday, I thought. He and his new boyfriend, Tom, had just given me a fabulous double DVD collectors' edition of *Polyester* and *Desperate Living*. I adored the former and couldn't wait to show it to Tiffany; the latter, however, I'd have to keep well hidden until I had a chance to preview it. Early John Waters — I'm sure even *I* can't imagine.

"Oh, how beautiful," my niece cooed when she opened the little box containing a colorful Tiffany glass–style votive candle holder. "It's perfect," she added as she turned and gave Eugene a peck on the cheek. He'd known that anything that burned, smelled, or lit up would work in Tiffany's bedroom and might even be used for her alleged practice of Wicca. Eugene *loves* witches.

"Eugene gives *the* best gifts," I whispered loudly to Tiffany, so that he could hear. His pursed lips, arched eyebrows, and batted eyelashes thanked me. I secretly gave him the okay sign and nodded toward Tom. It was my first time meeting him, and I got a good feeling. He was handsome, serene, and seemed to possess a quiet, confident intelligence. I was pleased for Eugene, as he hadn't been this serious about anyone in years, and it was clearly mutual. Eugene, it could be said, is larger than life, which makes him a lot to handle at times. We'd spent many a late evening drinking coffee in diners, discussing how, if we ever married, it would have to be to the strong, silent type. It appeared that Eugene might have found exactly this in Tom. Only time would tell, though, as in my experience Strong and Silent often turned out to be Brooding and Fucked-up.

I'd decided to keep my forty-first birthday low-key; several of my best friends and their spouses joined Tiffany and me in one of my favorite neighborhood restaurants. There are probably ten Chinese restaurants within a three-block radius of our apartment, but Sung Chun Mei had existed when I'd first lived in this area eighteen years ago and so had stood the test of time (which says a lot in New York). Plus, it had the best hot and sour soup around; I'd done extensive research, which had led to a serious, active addiction. In addition to Eugene and Tom, there were Steven and his husband, Julio, a graphic designer who hailed from Puerto Rico. My closest girlfriend, Orly, whom I'd met in law school, had come alone since her partner, Marisol, was visiting her homeland of Peru. And Georgia, a dear friend of almost twenty years, was flying solo as well; her husband, Connor, was an artist/interior designer who painted every spare moment he could. Understandably, nonlandmark birthdays of his wife's friends were definitely "spare moments" in Connor's book. Rounding out the group was Stewart Fischer, my favorite colleague and confidant from work. A major food maven, Stewart ordered for the entire table, giving the crestfallen waiter special instructions for preparing each and every dish.

Tiffany was sandwiched between Eugene and Georgia, which I'd carefully arranged. She'd met Eugene once before, albeit briefly, and had immediately taken to him. Eugene has a gift for making people feel special in his presence, and he is particularly good at working his magic on females. When he'd met Tiffany, Eugene had focused on her with great interest, commenting on her "lustrous" hair and "model-like" posture. He used words like "glamorous" and "mature" and made reference to his wild teenage years. Eugene was nobody's fool. Georgia was currently getting a PhD in literature, but she was also a kick-ass musician who'd spent years gigging at New York's hottest rock clubs while writing songs for Chrysalis records. Between her persistent stage fright and never getting that coveted recording contract of her own, Georgia had chosen this new path of words and ideas. She seemed endlessly stimulated by her studies, but kept up her guitar playing and poetry at the same time. Georgia is also a radical leftist who'd been a rebel since she could walk; time hadn't mellowed her at all and Dubya kept her in a perpetual lather. I knew she and Tiffany would be thick as thieves in no time, and I was proven right when Tiffany had agreed to sing for Georgia, without recompense, the first time Georgia had visited our apartment. The evening had ended with the three of us singing and dancing to a CD of Georgia's old tunes.

By contrast, Steven and Orly didn't seem to have a clue as to how to relate to Tiffany, although ironically, both of them have teenage nephews. Orly's nephew, Zeevi, is a bit older, and though he and Tiffany had spent some time together, they didn't seem to connect. Steven's nephew, Noah, is almost exactly Tiffany's age. While they don't really remember each other from the weekends we'd gone skiing together when they were little, now that they'd hit puberty and liked to party, they were partners in crime when given the opportunity. Despite this, I encouraged Tiffany to see Noah because he was a nice kid who did okay in school, played the guitar, and had a loving and caring family. Plus, I figured the devil you know is better than the devil you don't, an adage that I adhered to often these days. Doubly ironic was that Steven is a social worker/psychotherapist who was then earning a nice living evaluating preschoolers for placement with mental health professionals. He has the mind of a Venus flytrap; he insatiably devours every bit of information that comes within his orbit and never forgets even the tiniest morsel. Steven can quote an article about the movement of the earth's tectonic plates that appeared in the Science Times nine years ago, and he loves to do so.

Though Orly is much closer to Zeevi than Steven is to Noah, Orly didn't seem comfortable around a girly-girl like Tiffany. Being foreign, a bit butch, and not

Barbie Doll pretty, Orly, I suspected, had been ostracized by popular girls who looked like Tiffany when she arrived in Great Neck, Long Island, from Israel in the middle of high school. Orly is also a brilliant prosecutor who loves the art of the discussion. Never one for small talk or cocktail party chitchat, she could literally go silent when faced with a child. I hoped that, with time, my two favorite gals would somehow get to know and love each other. For now, though, I tried not to force them to spend time together, especially one on one.

For a small gathering, the dinner was lively. Over the years, my good friends had all come to know and care for one another and, in some cases, developed friendships of their own. It had taken a long time and great effort on my part — many weekends in Montauk and Vermont, innumerable Oscar parties and game nights at my apartment — to bring people from the various strands of my life together. But this little group, which represented just a few of those strands, was proof of my success, and I toasted them in gratitude. I was glad for Tiffany's presence and I knew that she was impressed with the quality of my friends. Several times throughout the dinner we locked eyes and once I thought she may have smiled slightly at me. Had she forgiven me, at least temporarily, for trying to ruin her life by not agreeing to let her stay in Connecticut for her entire birthday weekend? I couldn't know. I doubt that she wondered whether I'd forgiven her, as she knew I could never stay angry with her for very long. Plus, in her mind, I'm sure there was nothing to be forgiven for.

# Seventh Ab Inventist

Tiffany never mentioned our argument again, and I never acknowledged receiving her poem. The next couple of weeks flew by, hurtling us toward the much-anticipated Thanksgiving weekend and Tiffany's first trip home. Unfortunately, the weekend got off to a very bad start when, the night before the holiday, I lost my temper with Tiffany for the first time and, in my rage, intentionally hurt my niece's feelings.

I had been looking forward to that Wednesday night — Thanksgiving eve — as a chance for us to relax together. We wouldn't have to practice algebra for a change, which would reduce our chances of fighting, and Tiffany would likely be all excited about seeing her friends and about her birthday on Friday. We could just enjoy each other's company and maybe even start the holiday season off by watching *It's a Wonderful Life*, which I of course own on videotape and watch dutifully every year.

It had been a very difficult (albeit short) week for me. On Monday I'd found out that I would need surgery for a hernia in my abdomen. Back in July, when I'd gone to the family camp up in the Adirondacks, I'd caught my sister Kathleen staring at my stomach. "Pretty cut, huh?" I'd asked, proud as an annoying peacock. "You sure are, Ed, except you see this here?" she'd asked, pointing to a little lump of flesh between two of the abs in my six-pack (okay, more of a four-pack plus a seventy-two ounce). "Yeah, I noticed that, but I thought it was just a detail of an ab, or maybe an ab that doesn't always show on people less defined." I am often self-deluded when it comes to my body, for better or worse. "Wishful thinking, Ed. That's a hernia and you'd better have it looked at fairly quickly." Kathleen had been a nurse for twenty-five years, so I'd certainly heeded her advice . . . eventually. When I told Eugene this story, he'd called me a "Seventh Ab Inventist" and said I should form a church of Latter Day Weight Lifters.

I should have been relieved about the surgery because when I'd initially consulted my primary care physician, he'd said I had a condition where my right and left ab "plates" had split apart — that the fiber connecting them had deteriorated and torn — and that my entire midsection would have to be sewn back together. I'd made an appointment with the surgeon immediately, picturing myself a monster with bulging abs on its sides and a huge sack of guts hanging freely out front. But Dr. Garbowsky, the surgeon, had laughed at all that. He'd said I had a simple hernia, one that could go untreated but might eventually become larger if not repaired. Vain as I am, I hadn't worked so hard at the gym only to have a protuberance that didn't belong; I scheduled the surgery for the second week in January, giving myself a week to recover from the holidays first. Dr. Garbowsky was hardly anyone's idea of a dish, with his long, Ichabod Crane neck and sun-starved complexion, but I found him sexy all the same. (Okay, I admit it: when it comes to men in positions of power — doctors, lawyers, policemen, professors — I find an inordinate number to be attractive.) Though I dreaded my first surgery ever, I looked forward to seeing him again.

Tuesday of that short week wasn't much better. I'd spent all day trying to sort out a touchy political situation at work involving one of the agency's major clients. Then, in the evening, Tiffany had gone apoplectic when Megan said no to her including a boy in her birthday slumber party. "What century is she living in?" Tiffany had yelled when she'd hung up the phone. Then, "I'm not allowed to do anything!" No boys at a sleepover? I thought sarcastically. How old-fashioned can you get? But I didn't say a word to Tiffany, refusing to let her engage me when she tried to bring it up. Even if Tiffany's progress seemed nonexistent at times, at least *I* was changing the way I handled things. Or so I thought.

I took advantage of Wednesday's half day at work to go down to Tiffany's school, as I'd missed parent-teacher night because of a business function. Tiffany's report card had arrived a week or so earlier, and though not terrible, the results were not what I'd expected. She'd gotten a 65 in math (despite all of *our* hard work), in the 70s in science, Spanish, and gym, and an even 80 in English, history, art, and her elective course, Council for Unity. We'd both been disappointed — me because of her low average and Tiffany because she'd only made $12.50. (Since she had no regular allowance, I'd decided to incentivize her by offering her $20 for an A, $10 for a B, minus $5 for a C, and minus $10 for a

D. Courses that carried fewer credits cut the figure in half, and if she failed anything, all bets were off.)

As I emerged from the subway entrance at East Broadway, a skinny little man hung over the railing hawking cigarettes for four dollars a pack — some generic brand he probably bought wholesale out in New Jersey for two bucks each. So much for Bloomberg's seven-dollar cigarettes preventing kids from smoking, I thought ruefully. Indeed, there were throngs of kids crowding the sidewalk just beyond the stairs, smoking in huddles to fight the cold and drizzle. It was the kind of late autumn day that makes you want to curl up in front of a fireplace with a cup of tea and a good book — or, for these kids, maybe in front of a good video game with a pack of Kools. In any event, I was relieved to see that Tiffany was not among them.

The school was overheated and had that familiar cafeteria-food smell of canned corn, ketchup, and mystery meat grease. Does one go to his grave with this odor seared into his brain? I wondered as I presented my driver's license to the security guard on duty and signed the thick register.

I was told to report first to Tiffany's

guidance counselor, Mr. Rodriguez, whose office was on the third floor. The stairwells were narrow but painted in cheery primary colors and, because of the high-ceilinged stories, the stairs seemed to go on forever. (The building made up for its tiny lot by reaching up six floors.) Running up and down all these stairs must be how Tiffany's managing not to show the fattening crap she eats every day after school, I thought as I climbed. The hallways were polished to a high gloss and lined with bulletin boards dedicated to particular themes. Because the school was in partnership with a university, it had been exempted from the strict curriculum requirements being enforced by the Bloomberg administration, which had done away with the epically unpopular Board of Education. Here, if students were reading Christopher Marlowe in English, then they were studying the Renaissance in history and creating art projects using that period as their subject. Apparently some class was reading *Othello*, as the wall to my right was covered with about twenty depictions of the Moor smothering his beloved Desdemona. How sweet, I thought as I entered the guidance counselor's office.

Mr. Rodriguez was an adorably odd-looking little man. Beneath his balding pate his huge brown eyes peered out over bifocals that had slid down the tiniest ski-jump nose I'd ever seen. Its drastic, last-second upturn made me want to push his glasses back to the top to see if they'd sail right off — and maybe perform a daffy along the way. (I managed to restrain myself.) Mr. Rodriguez was cute in the way of a pug or French bulldog, where you coo and coo but don't exactly want to pick it up and nuzzle it. I suddenly remembered my much-loathed guidance counselor in high school — a lesbian who wore culottes and had framed portraits of her poodles on the walls of her office.

"You must be Tiffany's father," he said as he stood and offered me his hand. I saw now that he had an intense underbite, which added to the canine appeal.

"Ed Wintle," I replied, giving him a hearty shake, "and I'm her uncle. It's very nice to meet you."

Mr. Rodriguez's office was the size of a classroom and we sat at a large makeshift conference table at its center. (It was actually a bunch of desks pushed together.) He spoke quickly, with a Spanish accent, and tended toward speeches when discussing his philosophy of education and discipline.

His approach must be a real hit with the students, I was thinking just as the conversation turned toward Tiffany. He produced a large manila folder and inquired as to why I'd become her guardian. After I explained the situation by blaming almost everything on the kids Tiffany had been running around with in Connecticut, he proceeded to tell me that both of his young children had been killed in a car accident. Caught severely off guard, I had no idea what to say.

"I'm so sorry," I offered, though I failed completely to see how his children's deaths connected to my guardianship of Tiffany. But this endeared Mr. Rodriguez to me, as I tended to like people who told way too much too quickly, catching the listener by surprise and redefining the word "inappropriate."

"We've got some problems on our hands with Tiffany," Mr. Rodriguez informed me over his specs. "She's got a real temper on her, that one, and she does not like to be told what to do."

"Have there been incidents?" I asked, trying not to sound defensive. He was, after all, describing a side of Tiffany I knew all too well.

"Oh, yes, several," he replied, scanning

through the file. "She received three demerits just last week after being removed from her science class for insubordination."

"What happened, and where was she removed to?" My heart was sinking, as I had thought the school thing, at least, had been going fairly smoothly.

"She had to sit right here for the rest of the period," he said, pointing toward a lonely desk in the corner. He began to read from the file: " 'Tiffany had been asked repeatedly to stop talking during the lesson, and when she kept talking, Ms. Wilkinson asked her to move to an empty desk across the room.' "

"And then what happened?" I felt like an attorney leading his witness through rehearsed testimony.

" 'Tiffany spoke inappropriately to her instructor and I was called in to intervene,' " he read. "So, you see, there's an adjustment in attitude that needs to be made here. If she receives ten demerits, she will be suspended and further infractions will lead to expulsion."

"I understand, Mr. Rodriguez, and I assure you that is not going to happen. In fact, as I'm sure you know, Tiffany began seeing Ms. Martin last Wednesday. She has a lot of anger over things that have happened in the past, not to mention the usual teenage hormonal rage. I'm sure with some time and counseling, things will improve."

After some discussion of academics, the community service requirements, and Regents exams, I said good-bye and left Mr. Rodriguez's office with a mild anxiety buzzing at the back of my brain: If Tiffany gets thrown out of here, she'll wind up at Humanities, of all places. A woman I knew told me it was awful . . . and she taught there! As I walked around the school to meet with several of Tiffany's teachers, I looked closely at the student body. It began to dawn on me that Tiffany may have deliberately chosen to define herself as someone not to be messed with. Though the kids I saw didn't look particularly menacing to me, when you're a five-foot-two skinny white girl, things probably looked pretty fucking different. This was a response to her new environment that I hadn't predicted; I'd need to figure out something to counteract it, and fast.

Except for my meeting with Mr. Ling, Tiffany's math teacher, the other conferences all yielded the same results: Tiffany seemed bright with lots of potential, but she needed to behave in class and spend more time on homework. For Mr. Ling, though, I'd planned a sort of ambush. After learning from Mr. Rodriguez that it was Mr. Ling's first semester teaching, I asked that his supervisor be present at the meeting. Besides assigning ridiculously hard problems and refusing to go over them in class, Mr. Ling had failed to return the last exam he'd given until the morning of the midterm. Because of that, Tiffany and I weren't able to focus on her weak areas before the bigger test. I left with assurances from all parties that that would not occur again, as well as with the distinct feeling that I was Mr. Ling's worst nightmare.

Interestingly, two of Tiffany's teachers — one a man, one a woman — had separately mentioned an additional issue. Tiffany was apparently extremely popular with the boys and seemed to revel in their attention; both teachers feared, though, that adolescent boys could misinterpret her friendliness, possibly putting her into unpleasant or even dangerous situations. They weren't calling her a tramp so much as suggesting that she might be somewhat naive and that I might speak to her about establishing firmer physical boundaries.

Regrettably, I didn't get to see Tiffany's

art teacher, as she'd dashed out after her last class to get a jump on the preholiday traffic. I was very interested in meeting Ms. Robichon, who my niece referred to simply as "the psycho bee-otch."

By chance I bumped into Tiffany and April, the punky one, as we all left the building. It was still drizzling and, as we walked past the projects and the little parks that separated them, the air was filled with that fecund fall aroma of rotting leaves.

"I love that smell," I said to the girls, taking in a deep breath.

"Ewww," Tiffany replied, making April giggle. "You love the weirdest smells, Uncle Eddy." She turned to April and added, "He even likes the smell of skunk."

"Skunk is a refreshing, protonatural aroma," I said, deciding not to reproach her for using a pronoun when referring to me. My mother always did that, and though I guess I could see how it was somewhat disrespectful not to refer to an adult who was present by name, it drove me crazy.

"What the frig does 'protonatural' mean?" Tiffany looked dubiously at April.

"Yes, I may have made it up, but you need to learn how to glean meaning by breaking words down." I hugged my shoulders against the damp chill.

" 'Proto' means 'primitive' or 'original,' I think," April chimed in.

"Exactly," I said, smiling. "Someone's going to do well on her SATs."

We entered the subway at Rutgers and Madison Streets (yes, that's its name — and Madison Avenue it ain't) and rode the train together, changing from the F to the 6 at Broadway-Lafayette. The girls were heading to the East Village so April could return a CD and I was heading back to work on Astor Place. Their plans to see *Harry Potter 2* had been thwarted by April's aunt, who'd insisted she come home to help lug Thanksgiving potatoes from the store. That's pretty lame, I thought; I'll have to do better than that when making up reasons for *my* niece to come home. Tiffany was anxious to know what her teachers and Mr. Rodriguez had said, but I wanted to wait till we were back at the apartment to go through it class by class. For some stupid reason, though, I decided to broach the subject of boys. It didn't go well.

"That's ridiculous. Who said that?" Tiffany barked up at me. The girls had found seats and I stood above them, hanging from the overhead hand rail.

"It doesn't matter who said it; what matters is that two teachers observed the same thing." April was listening but was laying low. "It wasn't meant as a criticism, Tiffany, but just as something to think about."

"It's still ridiculous. I have 'boundaries.' " She sarcastically repeated the word I'd relayed. "And I can take care of myself. If a boy does something that makes me uncomfortable, believe me, I will tell him to stop."

"But how can you be sure he will?" I asked.

"Are you talking about, like, getting raped?" Tiffany rolled her eyes and turned to April. "He thinks I'm going to get raped in school."

Again with the pronoun thing, I thought, but now's definitely not the time.

"Well, girls have gotten raped in New York City public schools before," April answered. "Not in our school, but it's only been around for four years." I knew I liked this kid.

"Most rapes are committed by people known to the victim," I added. "I'm sure you've heard of date rape — hey, remember *Rosemary's Baby*?" I tried for some levity, to no avail. "I don't think anyone who's raped on a date ever, in a million years, could've imagined that their date would turn out to be a rapist."

"April, could you picture Ari, the sweetest guy in the school, turning into a rapist?" Tiffany laughed, making April smile. I could see this wasn't getting anywhere and I was now supremely annoyed.

"All right, just forget it, Tiffany," I snipped. "You know everything and don't need advice from anyone." I swung my body away from the girls and read the ad on the opposite side of the car touting how cheaply and efficiently Dr. Zizinor could cure even the worst case of acne.

Later, when I met Tiffany back at the apartment, my annoyance had dissipated but the pesky headache I'd been nursing all day still throbbed behind my temples. I'd taken a nice long time out when I'd gotten home from work, which calmed me but hadn't relieved the pain. Over a dinner of stir-fried vegetables and salad, Tiffany pushed for more information about my teacher conferences. After each report she said things like "I hate that woman more than anyone" or "I'd like to set him up to take a fall." (I didn't know B-noir lingo was back, I remember thinking.) There was no contrition, only pure defiance.

While I was doing the dinner dishes, Tiffany excitedly showed me the Nirvana CD she'd bought at the store with April.

"Great," I said. "But that reminds me: fork over the ten bucks I gave you for *Harry Potter.*"

"I don't have it," she said sheepishly.

"Ha ha. Now hand it over."

"Seriously, I don't have it. I spent it."

I was silent, incredulous.

"Why does it matter? You gave me that money, so it was gone, right? You'd already spent it."

I felt my pulse quicken and the blood rush to my face. Tiffany knew this was not how we handled the "money thing" together. If I gave her money for something, it was to be spent on only that *and* she was to bring me a receipt to prove it. She cannot be standing here flouting that rule in my face, I fumed.

"Give me back my money." My voice grew louder.

"I don't have it!" Tiffany's volume now matched mine. "Why are you making such a big deal out of ten dollars? Can't we just say that you bought me the CD for my birthday?" She'd switched to negotiation mode.

"Don't you dare presume to buy yourself

a birthday present from me with my money." I was furious now. The stories my sister had told me of Tiffany's sense of entitlement stormed my brain. There was the $250 phone bill that was Megan's responsibility "because you're my mother," and the time Tiffany had been given $200 to shop for school clothes and had come home with two pairs of jeans and a couple of pairs of panties. (She'd admitted to me later that she'd given some money to Toby for his birthday.)

"What happened to the other ten dollars you had?" I asked. "You left here with twenty this morning and the CD was only ten."

"We ordered out Chinese for lunch."

"I gave you money for Chinese food last Friday when your Council for Unity class was ordering. We can't afford for you to order out for lunch all the time." (School lunch cost only a dollar, but Tiffany refused to eat the cafeteria food. "It's repulsive," she'd said. So I gave her three dollars a day, which she usually saved for spring rolls, pizza, or bacon, egg, and cheese sandwiches after school.)

"What do *you* eat every day for lunch, Uncle Eddy?" she challenged.

I saw red. "None of your business. That

does it!" My voice was louder than it had ever been with Tiffany. "You're punished. No cell phone, no cordless, no TV, and no AOL. Get into your room!" I poked her in the back with my index finger as I followed her down the hall. It was the first time I'd ever touched Tiffany in anger.

"All right, all right. Stop freaking out and making such a big deal out of it," she said as she closed the door to her room, which made me even angrier. I stood outside and kept on yelling.

"Can't you just admit you're wrong? Just once, can't you say, 'I'm sorry, Uncle Eddy. You're right and I shouldn't have done it'? Instead you just argue and argue." I continued ranting as I walked toward the living room. "Don't you have a conscience, for God's sake?" At that moment something inside me snapped. I did an about-face and stormed down the hall to her room and threw open the door.

"Your behavior is beyond selfish," I shouted. Then I moved in for the kill. "That you could even suggest that the CD be for your birthday is incredible. On *my* birthday, you gave me a Hallmark card, for Christ's sake! You could've scribbled something on a piece of looseleaf paper and I'd have been happier. But no! You didn't even wish me a happy birthday before you left for school that morning. All you think about is yourself!" I slammed her bedroom door as hard as I could and marched back to my corner.

Boy, I told her, didn't I? I consoled myself. And how wonderful that there are so many things to take away when punishing a child these days!

Immediately I felt utterly miserable. I tried to watch a movie but needed to call Steven to confess that I'd turned into a nasty, abusive parent. My worst fear had been realized. I'd recreated Tiffany's home in Connecticut, complete with accusations, yelling, tears, and slamming doors. I begged Steven to tell me that I should run down the hall and apologize to her for getting so angry.

"Absolutely not," he said. "You both need to sit with this for a while. You had a right to be angry, and though you may have gotten carried away, if you apologize to her now, you'll be sending the wrong message."

"What do you mean?" I asked Steven through my sniffles.

"She's the one who is recreating her home life in Connecticut, not you. This is what she's used to — yelling, screaming, and fighting. It's what she knows. And I'd venture to guess that every episode at home ended with Megan feeling terrible and seeking forgiveness from Tiffany. Provoking an adult to lose his temper is the easiest way for a kid in trouble to turn the tables. You can apologize for hurting her feelings later, but it's okay to be angry with her for now. Your desire for immediate resolution is understandable, but sometimes you have to allow time for process."

I was floored. How the hell did he come up with all of that so quickly? *And* it seemed to make perfect sense. It's incredibly helpful to have a therapist for a friend, I thought, and they don't get any better than Steven.

I returned to my movie, though it was still difficult to concentrate. My anger had frightened me and left me shaken. I wasn't sure where it had come from, but it reminded me of my father. Once, when I was around nine, I spied a bunch of boys from a nearby street in the little patch of woods near our house — a small stand of trees that I considered mine. I went there often to be alone: I'd climb to the very top of the tallest pine and point my face into the wind as the tree swayed. On Sunday mornings after church I'd go there to visit "my" rabbits, whom I'd always find waiting for me in the same spot. When I ventured closer to the interloping boys that day, I saw that they were shooting rocks at squirrels with slingshots. I yelled for them to stop, but they laughed and called me a sissy. Their fancy ten-speeds were all lined up, one next to the other, so I knocked the end one over and ran. They fell like dominoes. Later my father got a phone call from one of the boys' fathers, who claimed that I'd done $120 worth of damage to the bicycles. My dad yelled out my name as he made his way down the hall to my bedroom, and when he entered, I barely recognized him. His rage was so great that after he'd slapped me across the face, he picked me up over his head and hurled me across the room, where I hit the wall and fell limp onto my bed. Only after it was all over did I discover that I'd been so terrified I'd wet myself.

I knew now that, somewhere inside, I might be capable of treating Tiffany the same way. After all, I'd just chased her down the hallway poking my finger in her back over a mere ten dollars. If it was her ingratitude that I was so angry about, was I expecting too much in return for what I was doing? Had I been resenting helping my niece this whole time? Certainly, a teenager who'd been through so much shit in her life couldn't be expected to walk around her uncle's apartment feeling grateful every minute. I'd once told an older, wealthy friend how wonderful I thought it was that he was supporting his grown nieces and nephews. "Wonderful?" he'd replied incredulously. "They hate me for it." Was Tiffany acting out and breaking the rules because she was mad or ashamed about needing my help? In either case, it wouldn't do any good for me to mirror the anger right back at her.

That night, for the first time in quite a while, I got down on my knees to say my prayers. I asked God to help me control my temper and for Tiffany to know some peace. I also prayed that I would emulate my father's good qualities, which were legion, rather than his rage.

# Uncle Rose

Thanksgiving morning started abruptly at nine a.m. with banging on the front door of the apartment. "Who's there?" I shouted. I'd taken a quarter of a tranquilizer and slept for nine hours; in my fog, I'd completely forgotten that my old friend Beth and her family were coming in from New Jersey. They were heading to the Macy's parade and wanted to drop off a change of clothes they'd need later for a holiday dinner on Staten Island. As the snowsuit-clad kids bounced in noisily and Beth dashed for the bathroom, Tiffany emerged from her bedroom wrapped in a small blanket, with her tousled hair pulled into a loose, floppy bun behind her head. She had that milky innocence of a freshly awakened child, and she beamed a bright holiday smile for the family.

Tiffany glanced my way and her smile softened. "Happy Thanksgiving," she said. I could tell she was as relieved as I to have this boisterous, happy little family to help us usher in this awkward holiday morning. The scene of the night before would be our secret, and we could now move easily into the Ed & Tiffany Act we loved to do for visitors, especially first-timers like these. We'd never spoken of this; we didn't have to. I believe we both had the same view of how we were perceived together, whether accurate or not. Our easy, comfortable affection for one another, our shared giggles and stolen grins, all hinted at an exclusive world of hidden meaning and inside jokes. And the performance gene is something we certainly share.

Maybe, for my niece, the feeling was more like having one's first off-campus apartment during college. I remember how grown-up I'd felt when friends would come by unannounced on weekend mornings; I'd "throw on" a pot of coffee and regale them with my escapades of the night before. It was obvious that, for all her studied nonchalance, Tiffany was proud to be living in New York City, away from her parents. We were, after all, two single people living coed in a Greenwich Village apartment. And Tiffany knew that, in front of guests, I could be counted on to treat her at least somewhat like a cool and admired roommate. Not your typical life situation for a thirteen-year-old girl, and

Tiffany enjoyed working it a little, as did I.

After Beth and her family left, we prepared for our trip upstate mostly in silence. The Macy's Thanksgiving Day Parade was on television, and we'd occasionally run into the living room at the same time to catch a musical number from *Nine* or *Into the Woods*, but we didn't say much. Though the parade is basically one big tacky promotion for Broadway shows, watching it with my parents was a ritual when I was growing up, and it wouldn't feel like Thanksgiving without it.

Later, when we were cozily squeezed into a two-seater on the Metro North train to Brewster, I broached the subject of the previous night with Tiffany. "I'm sorry I said that about my birthday last night."

"I forgive you," Tiffany answered with a slight grin. "And I'm sorry I spent your money without your permission. I won't do it again." She cracked open Ellen Wittlinger's novel, *The Long Night of Leo and Bree*, about a troubled teenage boy who abducts a rich, preppy girl who'd ventured alone to the bad part of town. Over the course of a night, they come to understand each other and even forge a friendship.

"I need to ask you something," I said. "And you're not going to love it."

"Uh-oh. Is it something we *have* to talk about now?" she asked warily.

"Yes," I answered. "I need you to promise me you're not going to see Luke or Toby while you're home." Tiffany tended to go berserk when Megan, Tony, or I tried to limit whom she associated with, which is probably why I'd waited until we were on a crowded train to bring it up.

"I haven't been speaking to Luke since he tried to blame everything on Toby," she said. "He's a total loser and I hate his F-ing guts. But I miss Toby so bad, Uncle Eddy. He's really a good kid who just got sucked into this by Luke." She looked at me pleadingly.

"Okay, I guess. But please try to steer clear of trouble. If things don't go well, you won't be able to spend Christmas break in Connecticut."

"Yeah, I realize that," she said, biting some purple polish off the nail of her index finger.

"What about Tommy?" I asked. "Do you plan on spending time with him?"

"I hope so," she answered sadly. "He hasn't been calling me much anymore, and I think he has a new girlfriend."

"You have feelings for him, don't you?" I asked softly.

"No, Uncle Eddy, I don't 'have feelings for him,' " she mocked. "He's a friend who just happens to be incredibly hot. Now, can we talk about something else?" She looked at me with one eyebrow raised.

"Don't be nervous about singing today," I told her. "You're going to be sensational."

"Well, I don't know about that." She sighed deeply. "But I do know you haven't forked over the thirty bucks you promised me."

"Payment will be made when services are rendered," I said as I gently squeezed her knee.

"Yeah, I figured that's what you'd say, Uncle Eddy. Two months, and you've already become so predictable." Tiffany giggled, closed her book, and rested her head against my shoulder.

I'd like to swim in a clear blue stream
Where the water is icy cold;
Then go to town in a golden gown
And have my fortune told.
Just once! Just once!
Just once before I'm old!
I'd like to be not evil;
But a little worldly wise;
To be the kind of girl designed
To be kissed upon the eyes.

Tiffany's soprano rang out true and crisp and clear. She stood at the end of my parents' long, paneled family room facing a small crowd of surprised relatives that included Megan, Sammy, Kathleen, Tyler, my mom's two brothers, Tommy and Barry, and their second wives, Patricia and Crystal. When my niece hit and held the high note on the titular "much more" at the end of this song from *The Fantastiks*, the audience cheered and Tiffany curtsied; she *actually* curtsied, something I had no idea she could do. And then she agreed to do a fourth song — gratis. As an agent, I couldn't help but momentarily gloat that Tiffany was now bringing down the price I'd paid per song. She decided to finish with "Somewhere Over the Rainbow," a good choice in my book because it wouldn't leave a dry eye in the house. I knew the song reminded everyone of my grandfather — my mom's dad — and all three of his children were present.

As I queued up the music and ran back to my spot against the wall (where I nervously mouthed the lyrics as Tiffany sang them), I wondered if I was acting more like Mama Rose in *Gypsy* or Lee Grant in *Valley of the Dolls*. Either way, it was not a pretty picture. Though Tiffany actually seemed to be enjoying herself once she got through the first song, there might be some who would think I'd forced her to do it and, perhaps, that I was pushing the "performing thing" a little too hard in general. I certainly questioned my own motives. Am I trying to live vicariously through her? If Tiffany becomes the star that I never was, will I too have succeeded in a way? Will it feel like delicious revenge on a world that had treated me so cruelly? Classic stage-mother stuff, I'm sure, but ever since the first time Tiffany had performed an entire song for me, I'd known that she was a natural, and that she had gifts that far exceeded my own.

It was autumn, and Orly and I had taken the train to upstate New York to check out the foliage and have dinner with my parents. We'd borrowed one of my folks' cars for the afternoon and, since Sammy was still a tiny baby, we figured we'd take Tiffany off Megan's hands for a few hours. We were driving down a particularly scenic road in western Connecticut, supposedly looking at the explosion of colors all around us but instead discussing law school, when a tiny voice came floating up from the backseat. I'd almost forgotten

Tiffany was there, she'd been so quiet, all strapped in and staring out the window. Now I heard something about a "blue corn moon" and a giant sycamore — words evocative of the fall and the world she watched pass by outside the car.

"What's that you're singing, Tiffany?" I asked, looking at her in the rearview mirror. I'd intentionally sat her behind Orly so I could see her while driving.

"It's from *Pocahontas*," she answered, "and I know all the words."

"Could you please sing it for us?" I asked in my sweetest tone. "From the little I heard, it sounded so pretty."

"How much will you give me?" she asked, her Minnie Mouse voice turning steely. Tiffany was five.

"What?" Orly screamed. "You people pay your children to sing?" She was incredulous, probably because she is from Israel, where even prayers are sung.

"Well, I've never paid Tiffany to sing before," I replied. "But she does have a beautiful voice and she's smart to know that it's of value to others. She's talented *and* has a head for business."

Orly laughed and shook her head. "So, how much will it cost to hear that whole song you were singing, from beginning to end?" she asked. I could see Tiffany counting something on her fingers in the mirror.

"Well, it's a long song with a lot of verses." She paused, possibly as a negotiation strategy. "Five dollars."

"Done," said Orly, as she dug into her pocket and pulled out some bills. "And it's my treat," she added, peeling off a fiver.

"I'll need to take my seat belt off, though, so I can sit in the middle," Tiffany informed us. "Or else only Orly will be able to hear me."

"Okay, but just this once," I said as Orly and I smiled at each other.

Tiffany began her song slowly and softly, but with a steady sureness that was astounding, especially considering she was singing *a cappella*. I'd never heard "Colors of the Wind" before and was taken aback by its strong political bent. It was a plea for the white man to stop raping the earth — to try to understand the sanctity of nature and appreciate the diversity of beliefs among the different races on earth.

Tiffany's father, Tony, had been adopted, so one-half of her heritage is unknown. Tony is round-faced and stocky, with black hair and a rather prominent nose, all of which were easy to reconcile with his Italian last name of Adeletta. My niece, on the other hand, was harder to figure out. As a small child she looked somewhat Asian, Inuit even, with her angled, narrow eyes, raven hair, and fair skin. But as she'd grown and begun to shed her baby fat, Tiffany became even more exotic. Her gold-green eyes had opened more fully but still slanted up and out from her nose, giving her a slightly feline quality. Her skin had darkened to a light olive and her arrow-straight hair got even shinier and thicker as it grew longer; Tiffany could easily be Native American. Hearing her sing Pocahontas's plaintive song with the clarity and innocence of a child made it all the more powerful.

As predicted, several sniffles could be heard when Tiffany finished her ballad from *The Wizard of Oz*. My mom reached for the tissues, and Megan, tears streaming down her face, jumped off the love seat to hug her daughter. They'd been having a lovefest all day, which had pleasantly surprised everyone. During several rough moments over the last two months, Tiffany had angrily accused her mother of getting rid of her to make her own life easier. Though it would have been easy to suspect that Tiffany's solicitous behavior was manipulative, I knew that deep down she missed her mom terribly. When she wasn't mad about something, she often spoke about funny things her mom did or special routines they shared together. At one point earlier in the afternoon, I'd been simultaneously shocked and moved to see Tiffany sprawled across Megan's lap on one of the overstuffed chairs in the living room. Even her attitude toward Sammy seemed to have improved; Sammy was more desperate than ever for her big sister's attention — a need that often manifested itself in negative behaviors like pulling or even hitting — but Tiffany was treating her with more patience and affection than I'd ever seen.

"Eddy, I can't believe her voice," Uncle Tommy said as he cornered me in the family room. Everyone else had gone into the dining room to sit for dinner. "She sings beautifully; what a talent. And she's behaving like such a lovely young lady. Were things really that bad between her and Megan?"

"Yeah, trust me, they were. She's a complicated kid, this one, with several very different sides to her." I decided to put it to him directly: "So, do you think she has a future as a singer?"

To me, Tiffany has a voice that could

rival Barbra, Celine, and Mariah combined, but I'm not musical and Uncle Tommy is. The most magical nights of my early childhood were summer parties where everyone sat around the yard listening to him play his guitar and sing. Eyes closed, his high cheekbones and strong jaw lit golden by kerosene lantern, he would sing "The Sound of Silence" or "The First Time Ever I Saw Your Face" with such feeling that I thought I should turn away. They were songs about adult emotions that I couldn't yet understand, but I knew they were powerful and sad, and that my Uncle Tommy was the most handsome man I'd ever seen. And I knew too that I wasn't supposed to think that, and I believed that if I kept looking, everyone would know what was in my head. But I never could turn away.

"Maybe," he answered, "but would you really want to steer her toward that kind of a life? Especially after how difficult it was for you as an actor." He's definitely cut from the same cloth as Mom, I thought. Don't take too many risks; slow and steady wins the race. Uncle Tommy has worked for the phone company his entire adult life. In fairness, he's a smart man who's pursued a hundred interests, especially sailing. He'd earned his captain's license and has owned his own small sailboat for many years. His wasn't the life of your average Irish boy from the Bronx who never attended college. But he never seemed engaged by his work; his job was just a job, not a calling.

"Yeah, but Tiffany's been writing and singing since she was so little. She has more talent in her pinky than I have in my entire body. And Uncle Tommy, I don't regret for a *minute* the four years I spent pursuing an acting career. If I hadn't tried, I'd still be wondering, 'what if?' "

"That makes sense," he said. "And you have to do those things when you're young, I guess." He sounded wistful, and I wondered if he wished he'd pursued his singing professionally. "Plus, it was a lot of fun to come into the city to see you in those plays. I still can't believe we got your grandmother to go see *Vampire Lesbians of Sodom.*" We both laughed.

"Yeah, I wonder what she made of *that?* At least I wasn't playing any of the 'women's' parts."

"That's true," he said, "but she was more with it than you might have thought. The world changed so fast last century, but she did her best to keep up, at least somewhat." He paused, then: "God bless her sweet heart."

"I miss her too," I replied.

"She would be very proud of what you're doing for Tiffany," he said as we walked toward the aroma-filled, candlelit dining room, lively with the presence of those we loved, both living and gone.

Though my acting "career" had been brief, those four years felt like an eternity at the time. The world turns more slowly when you're young, and it seemed that I was always waiting, waiting, waiting for something big to happen. The highlight had indeed been the year I'd spent in Charles Busch's *Vampire Lesbians*, which went on to become the longest-running comedy in off-Broadway history. I was a huge fan of Busch's troupe, Theatre-in-Limbo, and, as one of the first replacements for the original cast, was thrilled to share a dressing room with the diva himself at the historic Provincetown Playhouse on MacDougal Street. Bette Davis had trod the boards in early productions of Eugene O'Neill plays at this very theater.

Charles was generous and kind, but I suffered from crippling self-doubt and his acerbic wit could occasionally crush me. His work is based in vaudeville, a type of comedy with which I'd had no experience.

I remember one night when I'd failed to get my laughs on one of my key bits and turned to Charles for advice. "What would you do if you were me?" I'd asked. "Quit the business," he'd answered in his best hard-boiled dame voice. The other cast members within earshot laughed. I played a modern-day version of Prince Charming — a nutrition guru — and on another occasion, Charles had told me that I was the best Craig Prince he'd seen yet. Of course it was only the negative comments, even if made in jest, that remained with me.

There was also the esteem-draining difficulty of being a gay man in an extremely homophobic business. Even though many of the agents, casting directors, and directors were themselves gay, the talent could absolutely not be. I'd been signed "across the board" by a major talent agency within a month of arriving in New York at twenty-two. This meant they represented me for theater, film, television, commercials, and print work — all the areas in which a young actor might hope to find employment and exposure. Well, that relationship never amounted to much, except for my getting harassed by Fern Sapperstein. I supposedly had a team of agents working for me, but Fern was the junior agent directly responsible for mentoring me. She'd call my apartment at nine o'clock in the morning and whine loudly into the phone, "You sound like shit! Get out of bed and do your vocalizations. When your voice is tired, you sound *gay.*" Horror of horrors, I'd thought. There's nothing worse than being perceived as a homo. Thanks to Fern, and the business in general, I became paranoid about my every intonation, my every gesture. If I crossed my legs or smiled too much, would they label me "light in the loafers"?

About two years in, I'd become friendly with a crowd of young, up-and-coming actors in which all the men were gay but had girlfriends. I had a big crush on one guy in particular; he had thick, messy hair and dimples you could plant tomatoes in, and he'd driven me home one night on the handlebars of his bicycle, just like Redford did for Katharine Ross in *Butch Cassidy.* During a party to celebrate his landing the lead in the national tour of a hit Broadway play, he flirted simultaneously with me and a young television actress. She and I both picked up on this, so we decided to "show him" by leaving the party together. Though inside we were both longing for him, we smoked a joint and laughed at his expense

215

as I walked her to her tenement building on the east side of Tompkins Square Park. She would go on to win an Academy Award, the object of our desire would have a lucrative television career, and I would quit the business within a couple of years. My ego just wasn't strong enough to take it.

Tiffany would have no such problems, I was sure. She was a gorgeous, multi-talented straight girl, and just being herself would make her eminently castable. My niece wouldn't need to fake anyone out, pretend she's something she's not, or worry about letting her true self shine through. In fact, the more herself she could be, the farther she would go. She'd been training in New York City since middle school, and we hoped to get her on the audition circuit during high school, as soon as she could pull off consistently good grades. And Tiffany had something I never had: me — a cheerleader, someone to show her the ropes, someone to say, "You can do this, I know you can!" I often wondered how my acting career would have turned out if I had had someone — a teacher, another actor, a parent, anyone — to play Mama to my Gypsy Rose Lee.

# The Immaculate Conception

Tiffany's first weekend back in Connecticut had gone relatively smoothly. There was no sign of the boys who'd been arrested. On her birthday Tiffany and her friends had come home on time, so Megan let them hang out in the yard for an extra hour. Tommy, who lived just down the street, was the only boy among them. From the living room window Megan could see them all lying in a big circle on the driveway with their heads touching at its center, like a giant flower. Cigarettes glowed in the dark and laughter pierced the night air. Tiffany lay next to Tommy. Listening to Megan describe the scene, it was obvious that she longed for those teenage nights of her youth; I knew she considered them the best times of her life. Megan figured the kids must have been drinking or they never would have been able to stand the cold. Plus, Courtney had puked during the night and there was an empty bottle of Southern Comfort lying on the grass the next day.

Since Tiffany seemed sober, Megan decided not to make a big issue of it at the time.

"Well," Megan had joked to me on the phone, "at least now that she's fourteen, there are only seven more years till she's legal."

"Yeah, it's too bad the drinking age isn't eighteen, like it was when we were kids," I replied. "That would probably get her into a rehab all the sooner." For some reason, Megan didn't think this was very funny.

A driving, cold rain fell as Tiffany and I wound our way toward Sixth Avenue. It was now early December, and though there was still a trace of decaying gingko leaves in the air on Perry Street, winter's chill had set in with a vengeance. We huddled under a single umbrella and clung to each other for warmth.

"This sucks," Tiffany complained. And indeed it did. "The streets seem so crowded with parked cars today," she said. "What's up with that?"

"You just don't miss a thing, do you? In order for the streets to get cleaned by those huge machines, cars can only park on one side or the other on certain days, as dictated by the signs. It's called 'alternate side parking,' but today the rules are suspended, so people can park on both sides of the street."

"Why are they suspended?"

"I heard on the radio that today is the Feast of the Immaculate Conception."

"Oh, yeah, we learned about that in catechism class when I was little," she said as we sloshed through curbside puddles to cross Seventh Avenue. "That's where the Virgin Mary has sex with God and gets pregnant with Jesus, right?"

"Something like that," I replied. "Only I don't think any sex was involved — just your regular, PG-rated miracle." I paused. "Now that I think of it, why *would* they suspend the parking rules over something so obscurely religious? The public street cleaning crew can't possibly have the day off from work because of the Feast of the Immaculate Conception." My sarcasm grew. "And it's not like people can't move their cars because they're running off to church to worship the Virgin Mother." Catholic basher, party of one, I thought, but I couldn't stop; I'd attended Catholic school for five years and just the word "immaculate" begged a tirade. "And why is it called a *feast?* I'd say getting pregnant without having the sex to go along with it is more of a famine than a feast." Oops, I probably shouldn't have said that.

"You're crazy, Uncle Eddy," Tiffany laughed. Then, after a moment: "Hey, wait a minute! Since Christmas is less than three weeks away, that would mean that Jesus was born eight months early — a total preemie. Do you think they had an incubator in the manger?" I stood laughing in the rain as she folded up the umbrella to take it with her.

"I couldn't care less how long you worked at Miramax," I shouted into my headset, completely exasperated. I was selling a client's book to a novice producer who'd turned around and hired this clown to negotiate his option agreement. Apparently, Wendel Gooch III thought that because he'd spent several years in Miramax's business affairs department, his young client should get every protection and benefit ever won in any negotiation by a big studio. As a result, this deal was heading down the toilet . . . on power flush. Another fucking colossal waste of time.

Just then Rob came into my office waving a pink message slip with the words "Mr. Rodriguez on 582" scrawled on it in his chicken scratch. Despite his handwriting, Rob was by far the best assistant I'd ever had. He could have simply broken into my conversation with Gooch to tell me about Rodriguez, but he knew that. In my current state, I was likely to botch the "whisper back" feature and say something ugly *to* Gooch when I thought I was "whispering" to Rob *about* Gooch.

Rob was the quintessential Gen Y'er. An ardent vegan who spent his nights DJing at exclusive dance clubs in the Meatpacking District or on the Lower East Side, he was a bit pasty-looking and prone to illness. But he was also tall and adorable, with a '60s mop of mod-London hair and an utterly secure sense of his own masculinity. The son of ex-hippies, Rob read *The Nation* and the *New York Observer* and could convincingly spout any hot political conspiracy theory. He was the least angry person I'd ever met, though, and seemed to have nothing to prove to anyone. At twenty-four, he appeared neither lazy nor wildly ambitious, but rather had perfected a "go with the flow" attitude born, I was sure, of an underlying certainty that the universe (and his family) would provide. (What was his parents' magic formula? I'd asked myself again and again since Tiffany moved in. Besides money, of course.) In short, he was unflappable, which provided the perfect counterpoint to my high-strung volatility.

I nodded to Rob that I would take Mr. Rodriguez and told Wendel I'd be recommending that my client forget this deal. "Your author would be foolish to pass up this opportunity," he retorted.

"Right, Wendel. Good-bye." *Whatever.* I switched lines.

"Mr. Wintle, we have a big problem," Mr. Rodriguez said, somehow conveying that he was still peering at me over the top of his spectacles.

"And what would that be, Mr. Rodriguez?" I tried not to sound snippy but I was in no mood.

"Well, it seems that Tiffany has managed to place herself at the center of what could turn into an out-and-out gang fight," he said matter-of-factly, I suspected to add to the impact.

"What? You've got to be kidding me. What happened?" I could literally see Rob's ears perk up at his desk outside my office. Like me, he was fascinated with all things Tiffany, and he knew something juicy was up.

"Apparently Tiffany was seen kissing a

boy in the hallway and word got back to his girlfriend. Written messages were going back and forth between the two girls; Destiny was in the cafeteria and Tiffany was on the fifth floor. By the time one of my informants told me what was going on and I intercepted their courier, the messages had gotten threatening."

Informants? Couriers? It was all sounding very cloak-and-dagger. "Where does the gang aspect come in?" I interrupted, trying to keep it rooted in the third millennium.

"Well, the couple is Puerto Rican and Destiny apparently told all her friends what's going on. Tiffany then sent a note saying Destiny had better, quote-unquote, watch her back. As you know, most of Tiffany's friends are black." A certain tone in Mr. Rodriguez's voice made me wonder if this all wasn't terribly exciting for him.

"Sounds like you're pitching a remake of *West Side Story*," I joked.

"Pardon me? Mr. Wintle, this is a very serious matter. Destiny apparently called her mother, who has now threatened to call the police. She's afraid Tiffany's going to have her daughter jumped after school. If this were to escalate to a fight, both girls would be expelled."

*"Jumped?"*

"Yes, so you'll need to come down here at three fifteen to meet Tiffany. We've decided that both girls need to be escorted from school by their guardians today. Tomorrow the matter will go before student arbitrators." I pictured Tiffany having her kissing lips sliced off before a bloodthirsty, multiracial tribunal.

"Okay, I'll be there. Thank you, Mr. Rodriguez."

I pulled off my headset and buried my face in my hands. A part of me wanted to laugh at the absurdity of it all. The idea of Tiffany mobilizing a gang of kids to attack somebody seemed preposterous. But is it? I wondered. She'd had fistfights in Connecticut, the police had been called to intervene more than once when Megan and Eric fought, and her friends stole guns. How far could things go? I knew then that I would spend the entire next four years asking myself this very question. And the answer would always be the same: farther than I'd like to imagine.

"That is so fucking ridiculous," Tiffany practically yelled when I told her about my conversation with Mr. Rodriguez.

"Language, Tiffany." I ground my teeth and scrunched my eyebrows together, showing her that I was serious.

"They're hysterical at that school. It's like they have nothing better to do because that place is so damned boring. So they totally overreact to everything."

We were sitting in a pizza place on Madison Street, near the subway entrance at Rutgers. I wanted to have a discussion immediately, rather than talking in hushed tones on the train or waiting until tonight's dinner. We sat in wobbly yellow plastic chairs and leaned on a chipped orange Formica table. The place was brutally lit with fluorescents, but at least there wasn't a chance in hell I'd run into someone I knew in this part of town.

"Why were you making out with him in the first place?" I asked, sipping my Diet Dr Pepper.

"We weren't making out. It was a joke is all. He was flirting with me and he dared me to kiss him, so I did." She wasn't maintaining eye contact with me. Don't they say that means a person is lying? Or is it the other way around?

I actually knew Tiffany was lying because a couple of weeks earlier, before her birthday weekend, I'd let her go down to a boy's apartment for a few hours on a Saturday afternoon. I didn't know the boy, nor did I know Latoya, the girlfriend with whom she said she was going. Tiffany had admitted to me that there would be no parents home but said that she and Latoya were "just friends" with the two boys and that they were merely going to watch a movie. Since she'd been up front with me about there being no supervision — and because she literally had no social life outside Aleksi, so I was starting to feel sorry for her — I'd let her go.

Late that evening, after Tiffany had gone to bed, I noticed the computer was on and that she was still logged on to AOL. When I went to shut it off, a window containing her last e-mail popped up on the screen. I couldn't help but read it before clicking on the *x*. A friend had written, "sorry, no shrooms 4 yr b-day." (So, she's actively *trying* to do mushrooms now, I'd thought, horrified, and made a mental note to add this to my list of Conversations I Keep Putting Off.) Tiffany had typed, "s'cool. guess what? i got with the hottest porto rican boy 2day — sooooo fly!!!" She'd gone on to describe some of what was called "petting" in the middle of the last century and then wrote, "never done that b4!!!" I was relieved to read that last bit and decided not to mention it to Tiffany, especially since I'd been wrong to read her e-mail in the first place. Now I could only assume that Mr. Fly was Destiny's child.

"Were you threatening to fight with her?"

"No, she was threatening me, so I was just trying to scare her off. I wouldn't even know how to have somebody *jumped.* That sounds like it's out of some bad Julia Stiles hip-hop movie. Nothing like that ever happens at my school. We have a friggin' dress code, for chrissakes!" Tiffany was making far more sense to me than Mr. Rodriguez had. Does she simply know what I want to hear, or are we truly on the same wavelength?

"I *will* duff her, though, Uncle Eddy, if she comes near me," she said with finality as she leaned over her Sprite and sipped from the straw without picking it up.

"I assume that means 'hit' and you will not *duff* anyone, Tiffany. You've got to start thinking about how to make situations like this go away, rather than escalating them to the point of the whole school getting involved." I was trying not to raise my voice, as the place was filling with kids, some of whom probably knew Tiffany from school. "I know it's hard when you're angry, but I need you to try and make better decisions. Honestly, it will ultimately be to your own benefit."

This was advice that I was still very much trying to follow in my own life, especially at work, so I felt like a hypocrite preaching it to Tiffany. My two biggest shortcomings in business are my desire to resolve things immediately and my habit of telling people off when they act like assholes. I could name at least a few situations where it would've been smarter to bite my tongue and wait to use someone's bad behavior against them down the road.

"Can we not talk about this here, Uncle Eddy? I should probably get going before Destiny comes walking in with her posse." I couldn't tell if Tiffany was kidding, but the last thing I wanted was to referee some teenaged melee.

"Please, Tiffany. Just promise me you'll try. You're a smart girl and I know you understand how this game is played. You just have to want to play it." I stood up and put on my coat.

"What game?" she asked, simultaneously chewing her straw and sucking air through the ice.

"The game of life, Tiffany, where you try to get ahead by working things to your advantage. People who play badly are called 'losers' — a term you use all the time.

Losers make consistently bad decisions because they refuse to learn from their mistakes. They keep getting in their own way and wind up screwing only themselves."

"I get it," she said, putting on the cream-colored, hip-length down jacket I'd bought her. It had vertical quilting and fit snugly, so it was her first winter coat in which she looked like a young woman rather than a little girl.

"So do you promise you'll at least try to win at it? I don't want to be called down here again, Tiffany, unless it's to watch you perform or win an award or something." She'd lost the umbrella I'd given her in the morning, so we made a dash for the subway entrance.

"No, Uncle Eddy, my goal in life is to be a total loser. I want to live in a trailer, have no teeth by the time I'm thirty, and spend all my spare time drinking Budweiser at the VFW." She giggled as she slid her school MetroCard through the turnstile. Rather than being annoyed by her sarcasm, I was thrilled that she could so readily articulate the exact opposite of what we both hoped her life would be.

Tiffany and I lay beneath a magnificent night sky. There were mysterious constellations, plunging comets, multiringed planets, and tiny stars that sparkled off into the distant blackness.

"I still can't believe you did this, Uncle Eddy," she said in a whisper, as though reverent of the glow-in-the-dark night sky I'd affixed to her ceiling while she was away. I'd gotten the idea from *The Dangerous Lives of Altar Boys*, which Tiffany and I both loved.

"I remembered that you told me the stars are what you miss most about Connecticut," I said softly, "except for your friends, of course." The rain had started again and the cold December wind whipped it against her bedroom window.

"I want to talk a little more about what happened today at school," I said.

"This is such a perfect moment, Uncle Eddy. Do we have to ruin it?"

"It's also a perfect moment to talk, Tiffany." I rolled on my side and faced her. Though the room was dark, I could sense that she continued to look at the stars. Natalie Merchant's *Tigerlily* played softly in the background. "If you're too friendly with the boys too easily, they won't respect you and treat you right."

"Oh, no. Not the boys talk again, please," she whined.

"Look, Tiffany, I have a lot to offer in that department. First of all, I *am* a boy, so I can tell you firsthand what we're after twenty-four-seven. Secondly, I grew up with two sisters and most of my best friends are girls, so I know a thing or two about men's behavior toward women. And, finally, I *date* boys. In fact, I've dated *hundreds and hundreds* of them. So, I'm more than qualified to advise you on this topic."

"You've already explained that double thingy to me, and you don't have to brag about what a big whore you've been." She giggled.

"Double *standard,* and don't forget it," I admonished. "And think of it as *me* having been a whore so *you* don't have to. I did it *for* you and lived to tell the tale, luckily." I was keeping it light in an effort to keep the conversation going.

"You're so weird. I don't understand half the things you say." Tiffany now turned on her side and faced me. I reached up and flipped on the black light over her bed. Her teeth and the whites of her eyes leapt out at me.

"Omigod!" I feigned fear. "You look exactly like the Cheshire Cat in that scene from *Alice in Wonderland,* where he disappears except for his eyes and grin." She smiled demonically. "But seriously, Tiffany, boys are praised and admired if they make it with lots of girls. Girls, on the other hand, are called 'sluts' and 'whores' and treated like shit by the guys and by each other. I know things have changed a bit, but not that much. It makes no sense whatsoever and it's an unfair —"

"Double standard," she interrupted. "I understand, Uncle Eddy."

"Right. So, if you're going to give it up for somebody, why not make it special? Why not wait until you're with someone you really care about and who knows you and appreciates you for the person you are inside?" Jesus, I sound like a public service announcement, I thought.

"Well, I'm not planning on giving it up any time soon, so you don't have to worry," she said, turning again toward the stars, which were now a pale chartreuse from the black light. "I was just *kissing* Ricardo today, that's all."

"I know, Tiffany. But people, boys especially, will figure that if you do that, you'll do more. At least try to stay away from boys who have girlfriends, okay?" Now it was me who was whining.

"Okay," she replied, "but it's not going

to be because I respect that bee-otch Destiny."

"Well, then, it'll be because you respect yourself."

I stared off at the little planet with two sets of rings and imagined it was a world ruled by women and that I could magically beam Tiffany there. Like that wonderfully awful Zsa Zsa Gabor movie *Queen of Outer Space*, where the men were enslaved by glamorous women in glittering outfits. Of course, since it was made in 1958, the movie was hardly a feminist manifesto; it was a cheesy men's fantasy with skimpy costumes and lots of catfighting. Not unlike the world in which Tiffany lives, it occurred to me, where the clothes are certainly revealing and the glitter is that of belly button jewels and face tackle.

# Be My Bitch . . . Now Cook!

"Pardon my skin cells," Tiffany said as she curled up on the foot of my bed at six forty-five in the morning.

"That's okay. A few hundred thousand more shouldn't make a difference."

I'd told her weeks ago that my allergist said my ongoing itchy eye problem might be due to dust mite feces. When I explained that there were bazillions of the little critters living in my bed with me, feeding off microscopic skin cells and leaving piles of their toxic poo behind, she'd freaked. This was probably the first time she'd lain on my bed since, even though I'd pointed out that hers was probably worse because she refused to change her sheets every week. ("Teenagers are supposed to be sloppy and live in filth," she'd say glibly whenever I'd get on her case about her room. This argument made me nuts and she knew it, which is precisely why she used it all the time. "Teenagers are supposed to watch endless hours of mindless television." "Teenagers are supposed to eat tons of crap and be full when it's time for dinner." "Teenagers are supposed to poke holes in their bodies and cover their skin with art." Art, my ass.)

I'd forgotten what a strange relationship young people have to the world of germs and microorganisms. Tiffany had no problem with leaving her hairbrush on the kitchen counter or with using a towel she'd left in a wet heap on the floor the day before. Or with eating five-day-old Chinese food. But getting her to use a public lavatory or to share a Jacuzzi with strangers was another story. Maybe her paranoia of other people's bodily gunk would serve her well when it came to STDs. It hadn't worked that way for me when I was a kid, though. For the first couple of years of high school, my mom still packed my lunch in a brown paper bag. (It was invariably a baloney and cheese sandwich, with a Ring Ding or Devil Dog for dessert.) I'd peel back the plastic baggie from the sandwich so that it covered my hands and no part of my skin touched the food as I ate. I was a freak and I didn't care who noticed. But that hadn't stopped me from fooling around with any boy or girl I could get my hands on.

"My throat is killing me, Uncle Eddy, and I'm not making it up."

"All right. Let's take your temperature and I'll look for a flashlight." I found the digital thermometer in the top drawer of my bureau and placed it gently under Tiffany's tongue. The flashlight was another matter altogether. The big Eveready in the back of the utility closet was practically dripping with battery acid. Boy, I'm really prepared for the next terrorist attack, I thought as I pitched the damned thing into the trash. The best I could come up with was the tiny toy flashlight that came in my goody bag at *The Rocky Horror Show* on Broadway. I'd gone with ten friends for my thirty-ninth birthday and we'd gleefully waved the little torches as Brad and Janet sang, "There's a light over at the Frankenstein place."

When I went back into my bedroom, Tiffany still lay there, all curled into a ball, dutifully waiting for me to remove the thermometer. Her almond-shaped eyes looked up at me expectantly, and I felt a funny sensation in my chest. It was so easy to forget that, for all her bluster and bravado, Tiffany was still a child. Just then, the thermometer beeped softly.

"No fever, so that's good. Now open

wide." I peered into her mouth and, with the help of the little light, I saw that the sides of her throat were a deep red and that the texture was incredibly bumpy, like scarlet cauliflower.

"Hold on a second," I said and ran into the bathroom to check out my own throat. Since I didn't know what to look for, I figured a comparison was the best place to start. The sides of my throat — my tonsils, I guessed — sloped gracefully outward from my epiglottis, which hung uncrowded at its center. I knew that Tiffany had a history of recurring strep, but she wasn't running a temperature and I hadn't detected any white spots. Still, the shape of her throat alarmed me. I would have to find her a doctor.

"Let's get you back into bed," I said, gently pushing the hair from her face. "Your throat looks very red, but you don't have strep. I want you to gargle with warm, salty water and aspirin every four hours. Let the aspirin dissolve first and, after you gargle, swallow it. It will soothe and numb your throat, I promise." I led her back to her room after draping the afghan my grandmother had crocheted for me over her shoulders.

"That sounds disgusting, Uncle Eddy," she

muttered as she climbed under her covers.

"Please, Tiffany, just do it. I'll leave everything out for you in the bathroom. Gargle first thing when you get up, okay?"

"Okay," she whispered as her eyelids fluttered to a close.

I climbed back into my own bed to luxuriate with the *Times* and some freshly brewed mocha java. I'd opened the drapes in my bedroom to confirm the radio's report that it was snowing heavily outside, and I now watched as the trees in the yard were quickly blanketed in fluffy whiteness. Even though Tiffany wasn't feeling well, an enormous sense of peace washed over me. Could this be what it feels like to be happy? I wondered as I cracked open the paper. New York was still under a code orange alert, thanks to the holiday season being such a perfect time for terrorists to try to kill us in mass numbers. So much for inner peace, I thought as I closed the paper and anxiously trudged off to the shower. And you'd better be damned sure to pick up a new flashlight!

Before I left for work I sat on the edge of Tiffany's bed and felt her forehead. It was a bit clammy but not perceptibly warm.

"What time is it?" she asked without opening her eyes.

"Nine fifteen."

"I can't wait till I get a job where I can show up at, like, a million o'clock," she said, eyes still closed. I had to laugh.

"Sick, half asleep, and still spunky. Nothing can keep you down, my dear. Call me when you get up." I kissed her on the forehead and headed out, looking forward to the magic of a walk through Greenwich Village in the snow.

"You've miscalculated your leverage throughout this entire negotiation," I told Wendel Gooch III through my headset. Nastassja Kinski gave me her usual come-hither look from the huge *Paris, Texas* movie poster that adorned the far wall of my office. The Wim Wenders film had been my first true American Independent Cinema experience and I'd bought the poster to remind myself why I was in the movie business, especially during negotiations like this one.

"What's that supposed to mean?" Wendel asked with obvious irritation.

"It means that my author couldn't care less about this deal. This whole thing has been more or less a favor to your client, and you've pushed too hard and too far. Plus, you've been incredibly condescending throughout this entire process."

"Wait a minute, Ed, I —"

"Here's what we're going to do," I interrupted. "I'll messenger over our agency's boilerplate contract with the financial terms we've agreed upon, and your client can sign it or not. Not a single change will be made to it. End of story."

"What about all of these hours I've spent negotiating and marking up contract drafts? You're being completely unprofessional, Ed." I imagined he saw his client's hefty bill just go up in smoke.

"I'm sorry you feel that way, Wendel. In my opinion, you blew this deal and we're being generous in still offering your client a chance to option this property, albeit on our terms. Good-bye now." I hit the button on my phone that terminated the call. I wasn't proud of myself, but it felt damned good to punish a smug, know-it-all lawyer for being a total asshole. Plus I would never have to speak to this man again. (With my luck, though, he'd probably end up being the head of Universal Studios.)

I decided to do something I'd done only twice before: I created an e-mail rule that would block any messages from Wendel from entering my box *and* automatically send him a note saying, "At recipient's request, your e-mail has been blocked from entering his mailbox." God, I can be a real prick sometimes, I was thinking when Rob announced that my father was on the phone.

"How's it going, Eddy?" Dad sounded upbeat, which was nice to hear.

"Oh, you know, same old, same old," I said on the back of a world-weary sigh. "I just told some jerkwad lawyer to basically go blankety-blank himself."

"Burned another bridge, did you? In my experience, that's not such a good thing." Who asked you? I thought, but of course he was right.

"Yeah, well, the wreckage in my professional wake is looking more and more like Dresden at the end of the war."

He laughed.

"Luckily, there seems to be no limit to the number of intact bridges beyond this one."

"If you say so," he said, obviously disagreeing.

"So, what's up?" I asked, looking out at Cooper Union. Covered in fresh snow, it looked like a Dickensian orphanage.

"I just wanted to let you know that we've invited Eric over for Christmas dinner." He knew I wouldn't like this, or he wouldn't have called to tell me.

"How did that happen?" I was incredulous. "I thought Megan was ending that ridiculous relationship." I could literally feel the blood rush to my head and my temples begin to throb. I dug through my desk drawer for some aspirin as we talked.

"Well, I guess she hasn't ended it completely. I think she feels more sorry for him than anything. And really, Eddy, he's not such a bad guy. Not the brightest but —"

"Dad, we all know he's as dumb as a box of hair," I interrupted, "but that's not what worries me. He's got a crazy look in his eye, and from things I've been told, he can turn mean." Megan, Kathleen, and I had shielded our parents from most of the goings-on in New Milford. It would kill them to know that Megan had had to call the police because Eric had pushed her, and that the Department of Children and Families had gotten involved because Sammy had seen it. The department had considered it potentially dangerous to my little niece, so they now had their eye on Megan.

"Jesus, no, don't tell me. I don't want to know anything. But he's coming, so we'll just have to make the best of it." On the one hand, my father didn't want to hear all the bad stuff, so he could keep himself in at least a little denial. But despite this, he usually managed to have the most negative assessment of any given situation. If the clothes dryer broke, he'd run around the house cursing God and asking him why he'd been chosen for such punishment. (Once when some appliance conked out, he actually threw a framed portrait of Jesus Christ down the stairs.) I guess if he knew all of the awful things that had been happening at Megan's, he'd have to run himself through with a sword or something. Sometimes it surprised me that my father wasn't at least part Greek. But I guess the Irish are dramatic enough.

The fresh snowfall helped to calm me on my way home from work that evening. Tiffany was sick, so I desperately wanted to pull myself out of the black hole I'd fallen into before I arrived. I felt strangely horny and, as I hadn't had sex since Tiffany moved in — probably a record period of abstinence since my teenage years — I toyed with the idea of stopping off at some trashy bookstore to have an anonymous wank. The more I thought about it, the more compulsively I ached to do it. This made me realize that it wasn't horniness at all that was driving me; it was simply that I felt like shit and having some sex would black out these feelings, even if only for a little while. I spent my days at work fighting with lawyers and producers or, worse, hand-holding terminally disappointed clients; some psycho alkie who said horrible things to my nieces was joining us for Christmas; our country seemed to be heading toward war; and I was afraid I wouldn't know how to make Tiffany better. I wanted *out,* I wanted to find an escape hatch, but I knew a tumble with some stranger wasn't the answer. Wearily, I pointed myself toward home, stopping only once along the way — for four containers of piping hot chicken soup.

Tiffany had taken to watching the cooking shows instead of *Seinfeld* or *That '70s Show* reruns. She could sit there for hours and hours on end, occasionally breaking from her trance to jot down a recipe. When her father was working, Tony made his living as a chef, so I think my niece found a certain comfort in watching people cook, especially men. Since it was educational and I stood to benefit directly from any skills Tiffany learned, I was much more tolerant of her watching this than sitcoms.

Tonight I came in during an episode of *Emeril*, who, I have to admit, does possess a certain cooking charisma.

"How do you feel, sweetheart?" I asked as I bent over the love seat to kiss her forehead.

"Better, though it still hurts a bit when I swallow."

"Have you been gargling religiously every four hours?" I asked.

"Yes, I even wrote it down. The list of times is in the kitchen." A girl after my own heart, I thought. "Oh, and Uncle Eddy, I wrote down the best meat loaf recipe. Martha Stewart had an old woman on her show who made it with her. It has carrots and cheese and looked really good." I guessed my mom's meat loaf recipe hadn't passed muster.

"Did you know Martha Stewart is currently under criminal investigation for insider trading? Look, there's a picture of her in today's *Times*."

"What's insider trading?" she asked.

"Oh, it's a white collar-crime that basically involves cheating when trading stocks. She might do time in the slammer. Can you imagine? She's got to be one of the richest women in the country."

"Well, maybe she can improve the prison

food and teach the other inmates how to cook," she said without taking her eyes off Emeril's handiwork.

"Yeah, they could even make a show out of it," I said. *"Cooking in the Clink with Martha Stewart."*

"Or maybe *Be My Bitch . . . Now Cook!"* Tiffany responded.

We both started giggling and couldn't stop. When we regained our composure, we broke out the soup and slurped and stared happily, soothed by Emeril's thick fingers and bad jokes. The worries of the day melted away — the Wendel Gooches of the world fading, fading — and I counted myself lucky to have this bewitching young woman under my care. Sure, my life as I'd known it was over and most of the time she drove me insane to the point of distraction. But there was something so inherently right — something that fit to a T — about the new life that was growing up all around me.

# Part Two

# Winter

# Silver Bells

On weekend mornings, especially on Saturdays, I still tried to sit down to a hot, home-cooked breakfast with Tiffany. As I could no longer be sure that I'd have the pleasure of her company for dinner on Saturday nights, I wanted to know that she'd had at least one nutritious meal before she hit the streets of New York. Tiffany slept until at least eleven o'clock most weekends and she always woke up ravenous. Since I don't like to eat when I first get up, the timing worked out perfectly. I'd putter around or catch up on work reading until Tiffany would emerge from her darkened lair and patter across the carpet to the bathroom. On this particular Saturday the menu featured a giant frittata with scallions, chopped tomato, sharp Vermont cheddar, and fresh basil.

Tiffany's lack of a weekend schedule was a constant source of tension between us. She didn't socialize on weeknights and had to call me at work for permission if she wanted to hang out with friends for an hour or two after school. If she went straight home, she was to phone me when she reached the apartment. Tiffany's daily phone call had become as certain — and as welcome — a marker of my day's passing as lunch hour and my four thirty Starbucks run. She honored our weekday arrangement, which pleased me to no end. We were establishing a somewhat calm, fairly consistent rhythm to our life together that I think she secretly valued. It certainly had improved both her attendance and performance at school.

The flip side of this progress, however, was that Tiffany viewed weekends as time for total relaxation. "I've earned it," she'd tell me every Saturday when I insisted she turn off the TV and make a list of things she needed to accomplish during her two days off. She liked nothing more than to wake up late. Immediately flip on the television to whatever, and lie on the sofa for a couple of hours (breaking for breakfast, of course). While I didn't want to be a slave driver, I simply couldn't abide this routine. *Evenings* were for watching television — preferably a *film* — as a reward for completing the day's activities, and only if nothing else was planned. I'd grown up in a home where the television was turned on only to view specific programs, after which it was turned off; it was not constant background noise, and no one ever simply sat and flipped from channel to channel. (Okay, so we didn't have remotes back then. But still.) I sensed that things had been quite different in Tiffany's home. Since she'd moved in, she'd asked again and again to bring her TV and VCR down from Connecticut and was supremely irritated each time I said, "Absolutely not." Sometimes I'd add, "You should never have gotten your own TV and VCR in the first place," which invariably earned me a homicidal glare. Somehow, though, a treaty organically emerged whereby she'd ask me if she could turn on the TV and I would oblige, conditioned on there being a preagreed shutoff time.

My unrealistic vision of weekends spent running from museum to art gallery had been replaced by my equally unrealistic vision of Tiffany running from dance class to kickboxing. I'd bought her a membership to the spanking new, deluxe YMCA on Fourteenth Street, and she'd gone only a handful of times, never attending a teen yoga class or swimming in the Olympic-sized pool. Her Thursday afternoon musical theater class had ended, and I'd tried to get her to enroll in a Friday night teen acting class at the same conservatory, but Tiffany didn't want to have a commitment on Friday nights. "I want to keep myself open," she'd said.

One weekend I managed to coax her into going up to the venerable Steps dance studio on Broadway and Seventy-third Street, where I'd taken jazz and modern classes almost two decades earlier. Tiffany wanted to study hip-hop, which, it turns out, one can actually do. In fact, there was a *selection* of hip-hop classes to choose from on weekends; she opted for Saturday's beginner session. We rode the elevator up several floors but then had to walk up a well-worn wooden staircase to the dance studios. I could hear piano accompaniment and the voice of a ballet instructor firmly calling out steps. It was impossible not to think of "At the Ballet" from *A Chorus Line*; "Up a very steep and narrow stairway, to a voice like a metronome" echoed in my brain.

The lobby was crammed with dancers — most quite young — stretching, chatting, and cooling down. I stood still for a moment and a flood of memories rushed in —

images of a long-ago me that I hardly recognized — and it was bittersweet, as nostalgia always is. I was an interloper now — a lawyer, a sellout — and when Tiffany went into the changing room to prepare for class, I feared the dancers would think I was some old pervert come to gawk. If they only knew how I once soared, I thought, however briefly.

Tiffany had asked me not to hang out with her while she waited for class to begin, so I retreated to the little café that had been created at the far end of the lobby, for exactly this purpose, I imagined. I ordered a coffee and sat facing the dancers. My niece had pulled her hair up into a high bun and, as she sat with her legs extended outward and apart, gently arcing her long neck and arms toward her right shin, she seemed the quintessential ballerina. But Tiffany hadn't had any formal dance training, and I watched surreptitiously as she tried in vain to keep up with the class's wildly paced combination of footwork and spins. Tiffany has natural rhythm and a body made for dancing, but the class was simply moving too quickly for her. Halfway through, she came running out in tears, cursing the substitute instructors and swearing never to return. I hadn't known Tiffany to give up on things so easily, but I think trying something new in a room full of adults — all strangers — made her too self-conscious. Inside, I was disappointed, but I recognized her frustration from my own experience and knew this wasn't something that could be forced. On the way home, I described some of my own more embarrassing dance class moments, prompting Tiffany to say she'd give it another try when the regular teacher was back from vacation. But she never did.

"How's the frittata?" I asked, even though Tiffany appeared to be devouring it.

"Great."

"It's a perfect day to go pick out a Christmas tree. Crisp and sunny. Oh, listen!" Light FM had begun mixing Christmas carols into their play list; Johnny Mathis was crooning "Silver Bells." "It's Christmastime in the city," I sang along.

"What a weird voice," Tiffany commented with her mouth full.

"Maybe this year we'll buy our tree from that family that comes down from Vermont and lives in their camper over on Jane and Hudson. You remember, the family that wrote that little book I bought for

Grandma last year, *Christmas on Jane Street?*"

"Oh, yeah," she said, smearing gobs of preserves on her English muffin. "Listen, Uncle Eddy, I kind of have plans today. Maybe I could meet you back here later and help you decorate it?"

"What sorts of plans?" I asked, trying to hide the irritation in my voice. What could be more fun than picking out a Christmas tree on the streets of New York City? "We've been over this before, Tiffany. You're supposed to *ask* me about your plans *before* you make them."

"Oh, no, they're not *plans* plans. I was just going to meet Aleksi, Liam, and Peter over in Union Square and check out the craft fair there. Maybe do some Christmas shopping. Speaking of which, can I have twenty dollars of my birthday money?" I'd deposited her birthday checks in my account and was meting the cash out slowly for specific expenditures.

"Sure," I said, "but I'm going to want to see the merchandise."

"No problem." She paused to sip her calcium-fortified orange juice. (I'd learned that older women with osteoporosis had failed to get enough calcium during their *teens,* so I was always nagging Tiffany to

255

drink her morning juice and evening milk, and to eat all her broccoli.) "Unless of course the merchandise is for you," she added.

"Oh, don't buy me anything, Tiffany. Really. Just make me a card that I can keep forever." I sat back and folded my arms, having scarfed my breakfast far too quickly. I always finished eating before her and had to force myself not to jump up and start cleaning.

"We'll see about that," she replied with an impish grin.

"Just last year Kurt and I chopped down our own Christmas tree. It was a spectacular day, like today. I'd never done that before; it was pretty special." It feels like a lifetime ago, I thought.

"Why did you guys break up again? I know you've told me, but I can't remember."

"Actually, I don't think I have told you. But in a nutshell, it was because Kurt couldn't communicate well. He couldn't talk about his feelings. If he was angry with me or upset about something, he'd retreat into his shell and not speak to me for days on end. Then, when he was finally ready to discuss it, we'd talk for five whole minutes and then go on like nothing had happened.

We never really processed anything together, so we never really grew as a couple. Plus, it hurt me when he wouldn't speak to me. It was kind of abusive, in a passive-aggressive way. Does any of this make any sense to you?"

"Sort of. Passive-aggressive is when someone hurts you by *not* doing something, right?"

"Exactly." I leaned in and put my elbows on the table. "I don't know what's worse, fighting a lot or never fighting."

"You don't put up with shit from boys and I think that's good. Not like Mommy."

"Language, please." I looked at her sternly for a second and then smiled sadly. "I don't know. Sometimes I wonder if I don't put up with enough. Seems like I spend every relationship weighing the good against the bad the entire time, and I always decide the bad is too much."

"Oh, oh, oh, I love this song!" Tiffany bounced in her chair, hands aflutter. We always listened to music while we ate, and Sheryl Crow and Kid Rock's duet seemed to come on at every meal lately.

"What about Peter?" I asked. "Do you like him?" I'd met him once before, when Aleksi and Liam had come by for Tiffany and had brought him along. He was blond and blue-eyed, and he wore glasses, which, I was sure, made him seem a lot more innocent than he actually was. But at least his looks enabled me to kid myself that he was the boy next door.

"Peter? He's sweet and sort of cute, but no, Uncle Eddy, he's not my type." She sang along with Sheryl and Kid as she cleared our plates: "I put your picture away. I wonder where you been."

Yeah, well, Kurt was exactly my type and that was part of the problem, I thought. Otherwise, I'd have put his picture away a lot sooner.

Kurt had hands the size of squash racquets. They could sail boats and build decks and plant gardens. He was a few years older than me and the skin on the backs was beginning to get shiny — crepey even — but his palms were meaty and his fingernails square. They were the hands of a grown, capable man.

I met Kurt at a tired gay club on eastern Long Island, where I was attending the Hamptons Film Festival. It was a chilly October night, and he'd come into the fairly empty disco wearing a thick sweater, which he removed by pulling it over his head. While most gay men would make a beeline to the men's room for mirror access, Kurt did this right next to the dance floor, his huge hands barely leaving his sides as he quickly patted down the dark, bushy hair that was just beginning to gray. Errant strands flew back up from static electricity, making me wonder if he wasn't a married man out on a sexcursion. Naturally, I was intrigued and determined to find out. I quickly introduced myself, and we went outside into the garden, where we could talk.

Kurt's deep-set, royal blue eyes twinkled mischievously beneath wiry brows as he rattled on about the upcoming presidential election or some scandalous local story he was working on for the eastern Connecticut newspaper where he was an editor. He was smart and had the gift of gab, which I enjoyed, but it was his eyes, hands, and a jaw as square as Jan Michael Vincent's (or Seann William Scott's, depending on your decade) that held me rapt. I have a long face and round brown eyes, with no jaw to speak of; Kurt was my opposite and I needed him to find me attractive. He was the aging Bruce Weber model and the missing Kennedy cousin for whom I'd been searching.

Kurt and I went home together that

night and I learned the next morning that he had indeed been married — for ten years — but that he had no children and had had a long-term relationship with a man after his marriage ended. Kurt began visiting me in New York and I soon started spending every other weekend with him in Old Saybrook, Connecticut, where he lived in a charming little house perched on a hill overlooking Long Island Sound. In the panoramic view from the master bedroom, you could practically see where he moored his sailboat. After only two months, I fell deeply in love with him — the kind of falling where you wake up at six in the morning riddled with both anxiety and joy, where you wonder how you'd ever slogged through your days before this miraculous person entered your life. The relationship would last less than a year and a half.

Kurt had everything I'd ever imagined in a partner. He was engaged by his work, and it was work that I admired and thought important. He was kind and considerate and seemed to not have a bitter, cynical, or jaded bone in his body. He was an avid reader and loved films; the television was turned on only for morning news, while he dressed for work. Being a former reporter, he was innately curious about everything and knew how to converse with anyone (with the exception of children, to whom he didn't seem to relate). He loved food and dining out, as I do, and every Saturday night that we were in Connecticut, we drove to different towns to try the best restaurants. Kurt taught me how to sail and we took weeklong vacations on his boat, sailing from harbor to harbor. He was a traveler too; we spent a long weekend in Paris and flew to St. John for my fortieth birthday. A die-hard snowboarder, I got Kurt back on skis after ten years, and for our second Christmas together he gave me a deluxe trip to Vail. Kurt never showed up at my apartment without flowers and a bottle of wine, and every time I got off the train in Old Saybrook, he was standing on the platform with a smile, no matter the weather. And the sex only got better as the months progressed.

In many ways, it was the kind of life and relationship that I'd almost given up hope of ever having. Early on, there were winter mornings when, as we lay in bed reading with our legs entwined, I felt a sense of peace and perfection that made me think, "This is it." But, as I told Tiffany, there was one big problem — a problem that arose only a couple of months in, but one that I mistakenly thought we could work through or that I could live with.

Kurt had been a "change of life" baby for his parents, born many years after his brothers and sisters. His folks were prominent Philadelphians, and I quickly got the feeling that he may have been subjected to the "speak only when spoken to" philosophy of child rearing and reprimanded harshly and often by his parents and much-older siblings. The first time I ever expressed any sort of criticism or complaint, Kurt curled up into a ball and cried off and on for nearly six hours. He refused to speak to me until he realized I'd called a taxi to take me to the train station. I'm aware that I can be controlling and sometimes hypercritical, but I'd never gotten this response before. It was the strangest behavior I'd ever seen — all the more surprising coming from a man like Kurt — and it eventually became our undoing. His crying bouts later turned to anger, and I often wouldn't hear from him for days and days after some little spat. Our discussions of these events lasted a matter of minutes, and I began to walk on eggshells around him, frightened that something I might say would elicit some wildly disproportionate reaction. The seemingly beautiful life we had together was corroding from the inside out, and I decided to say good-bye.

Though I haven't often questioned that decision, in retrospect it was more fortunate than I could have realized. The first summer that Tiffany had visited me, I'd managed to "subject" Kurt to her for only two weekends, and he'd seemed very uncomfortable the entire time. If we'd stayed together, taking my niece in would have been out of the question.

Thinking of Kurt always reminded me of one of the great revelations regarding my relationship with Tiffany; with her there was no weighing of pros and cons, no calculating how much I could or couldn't put up with. She was family, blood, and my love for her had to be unconditional. Breaking up was not an option. After Kurt and I split, he sent me a letter copping to his problematic behavior. He had no plans of getting help or of changing; he simply hoped he could find someone who would accept him "as is." I'd chosen not to, but with Tiffany, there was no choice involved. And somehow there was great comfort in that.

I was just finishing putting the lights on the Christmas tree when Tiffany came home from her afternoon with Aleksi, Liam, and Peter. Her cheeks were rosy from the cold but her eyes seemed glazed, almost blank, and she complained of being exhausted. I knew she'd gotten stoned but that she'd simply deny it if I said anything. She'd bought no gifts but showed me that she had fifteen dollars left, having spent five on pizza and hot chocolate.

"What's new with your friends?" I asked as I neurotically continued tucking the lights' green electrical wire behind branches, despite the fact that it blended fairly well with the tree and we'd be hiding it with decorations anyway.

"Well, since you asked, Liam's girlfriend is pregnant *and* she's a heroin addict." Tiffany curled up on the love seat, facing the tree.

"Oh, my God, how old is she, Tiffany?" She had my undivided attention now.

"My age — fourteen," she answered casually, pulling a little plaid blanket over herself.

"Please tell me you think that's retarded," I pleaded.

"Superretarded, Uncle Eddy," she said, as her head fell against the billowing cushions and her eyes gently closed. "Don't worry," she whispered.

That's all I do is worry, I thought. If only there were an off switch. For all I knew, Tiffany could have snorted some heroin that very afternoon. I had no way of knowing for sure but rather had to trust that she was telling me the truth when we had our drug conversations; she was a pot-and-alcohol-only girl, she'd reassured me on numerous occasions, as though that were comforting. Should I be hauling my niece off to a drug and alcohol rehab? I asked myself. Any textbook or counselor would say so, I was certain. If I don't, am I turning my back on what could be a serious problem, refusing to acknowledge it, like Mary Tyler Moore did with her son's depression in *Ordinary People*? Just give it some more time, I told myself. Let's see how this year turns out. Tiffany has had enough upheaval for the time being. And so have you.

I put on Loreena McKennitt's *A Winter Garden* CD and decorated the tree while Tiffany slept. She's finding the same type of kids she ran with in Connecticut, I thought. But there's no way to prohibit her from seeing certain people. That approach hadn't worked for Megan; Tiffany always found a way to see the kids she wanted to, and prohibition only led to more lies, anger, and fighting. Plus I believe that telling a kid who's in full-blown rebellion she's forbidden to see a certain person only adds to that person's allure. I vowed to find something for her to do where she'd meet "nice" girls her age — girls who were involved in productive activities. Tiffany had dumped April — the punky one I admired — in early December, calling her "a selfish bee-otch," and she still hadn't found a way to get together with the sweet Sade on weekends. I'd arranged for Tiffany to start voice coaching again in January, but the lessons were private, so that wouldn't help. At least there's the TADA! Youth Theater audition in early February, I reassured myself. If she gets a part in their musical, she'll meet a ton of good kids and be plenty busy.

I finished decorating the tree alone, searching for several minutes to find the perfect place for each ornament. The repetition of it, combined with Loreena's dulcet tones, soothed me. I tried to focus on the fact that Tiffany had come home on time and was not planning to go out again after dinner. But as she slept, I couldn't escape the fact that Christmastime in the city was not going as Johnny Mathis had promised.

# Half Sick of Shadows

"Oh . . . my . . . God. *Uncle Eddy!*" Tiffany's scream came sailing down the hallway to where I sat arranging her Christmas gifts under the tree. She was always letting out high-pitched little yelps, like a small dog caught underfoot — when she stepped into a shower that was too hot or when she plucked her eyebrows or waxed her arm hair. But this was different; this was a scream of sheer terror.

"What's the matter, what's the matter?" I jumped up but she was already upon me.

"Look!" She pulled down her sweatpants to reveal a white-panty-clad butt cheek. With one hand she yanked half the material to the side and with the other she squeezed her ass hard.

"What? What? What are you showing me?" I feared a lump or some hideous sore.

"I have *cellulite!*" She was near to tears now.

I was relieved. "You scared the hell out of me, Tiffany."

"This is serious, Uncle Eddy! I'm only fourteen and I already have cellulite. It's all bumpy and disgusting!"

"Tiffany, let go of your ass before you bruise yourself."

She released her cheek and covered it up quickly, as if to get it out of her sight.

"Asses are supposed to have some fat on them," I said. "And that's how fat looks if you scrunch it all up like that."

"I bet your ass doesn't do that," she retorted with a challenging smirk.

"First of all, I barely have an ass. And I'm not about to pull down my pants and start squeezing my ass cheeks for you. You have a beautiful, womanly, curvy figure, Tiffany."

"I've got *cellulite.*" She dug her heels in. "Pleasepleaseplease, will you buy me some anticellulite cream tomorrow?"

"That stuff doesn't work *and* it's expensive. If you're worried about fat, then try to get some more exercise. Use the gym membership I'm paying for. Now, how about I put on some music and you open your presents?"

"Okay, but we have to talk more about this, Uncle Eddy. Exercise does not get rid of cellulite. It's just the way some *losers'* fat forms. And the only way to get rid of it is with special cream or liposuction, which I plan to get later."

"Enough about the cream. The answer is no. If you get some money for Christmas, you can buy it on your own." I lit the three white pillar candles I kept in the faux fireplace that my grandfather built back in the 1940s.

"I'm going to go get your gift." Tiffany walked off dejectedly.

I felt bad but I had to draw the line somewhere. If I indulged her every cosmetic whim, I'd be broke. Trips to Rite Aid were already killing me; between the expensive skin regimen Tiffany followed, the specialty shampoos, hair conditioners and gels, the nail polish, lip glosses, makeup, feminine and contact lens supplies, I never got out of there without dropping fifty bucks. (Since she'd moved in, Tiffany had gone through enough cotton balls for Christo to wrap a small country.) Plus if I encouraged her to battle cellulite, where would the body altering end? In addition to a tongue piercing and tattoos, she was already begging for a nose job, a boob job, and a foot job. Yes, a foot job; my niece hates her feet and wants new ones.

It was the evening before Christmas Eve, and Tiffany and I had just finished a delicious dinner of steaks smothered in mush-rooms and onions, with baked potatoes and broccoli. As we were leaving for Con-necticut the next day, we'd decided to cele-brate Christmas alone together before we left. I was not about to add the pile of gifts I'd gotten Tiffany to the already daunting number of shopping bags I'd need to lug on the train. I lit several votives and placed them on the coffee table.

"Ooooh, it looks so nice in here," Tif-fany said when she returned bearing a box and a flat parcel, both wrapped and tied with curling ribbon. "Here, I want you to open yours first." She handed me the thin package. "Merry Christmas, Uncle Eddy." She kissed me on the cheek and sat next to me on the floor in front of the tree.

"Thank you, sweetie," I said as I pulled the ribbon loose and opened the gift. Inside were twelve handmade cards of simple white paper, each representing one of the days of Christmas. "On the first day of Christ-mas . . ." the cover of the first card an-nounced in bright crayon colors. Inside, on the left side, the lyric continued, "My true love *said* to me . . ." Then, on the right, Tiffany had written, "I will never forget the times that we shared." She'd taped a paper door to the center of the page, like the

270

door in the Dream Date game I played with my sisters when I was little. (I'd secretly loved how every time you opened the door, a different boy would appear, each one cuter than the last.) Behind the flap, Tiffany had drawn two thin arms reaching toward each other horizontally across the page, the fingers just barely touching in the middle. The arms were impossibly long, giving the sensation that they'd bridged a great space to find one another.

"Oh, Tiffany," I whispered as I reached over, pulled her to me, and squeezed.

"Simmer down, Uncle Eddy," she whispered, impersonating me impersonating Cheri Oteri from *Saturday Night Live.* "That's only the first one; there are eleven more to go. We're gonna be here for a while." I laughed as I released her and proceeded to open the second day of Christmas. It took me a moment to realize, but the words on the cards were actually lines of a poem.

I will never forget the times that we shared.
I am eternally grateful, for you have always cared.
Without you I wonder, where would I be?

Living me without you, you without
   me.
And as much as I swear and I scream
   and I shout,
the true emotion I feel will never come
   out.
Something so true and so strong and
   alive
will quite often seek cover and quite
   often hide.
But I will let you know now
what I am feeling inside:
thankfulness, happiness . . .
and some joy on the side.

In the three months that Tiffany had
been living with me, she hadn't expressed
anything remotely like this. Behind the
door on the page that said "Living me
without you, you without me" was a simple
drawing of a house next to an apartment
building. The face of a crying girl peered
out from the house's single window, and
on the third floor of the building, a crying
man stared out. Tiffany understands how
devastated I'd be if she were to leave, how
mutual our need is, I thought. How does
she know? No other Christmas present
could have made me happier.

I opened the larger gift Tiffany had

brought for me. It was a white plaster angel, the kind that sits with ankles crossed on top of a shelf or bookcase. The angel was headless, but an angel all the same.

The weeks between buying a Christmas tree and celebrating the holiday had passed somewhat calmly. Tiffany's throat had healed up quickly and the family practice doctor we'd visited had confirmed that it wasn't strep. Dr. Mark Levine was a sweet, young gay doctor who'd taken a lot of time to speak with us and examine Tiffany. He'd even asked that I leave the room so he and a female nurse could discuss drugs and sex with my niece in private. When did doctors start being younger than me? I wondered as I walked back to the waiting room. "You should marry him," Tiffany said when she came out a half hour later. I appreciated the vote of confidence, but I was not about to put the moves on Dr. Levine.

Tiffany was putting a fair amount of time into her schoolwork and seemed to want to do well on her midterms. Her math skills were improving tremendously; watching her simplify endless polynomials was strangely moving for me. I'd often thought about becoming a teacher in the past, but this was the first time I had the actual joy of seeing a mind convert something completely foreign into second nature. We hadn't had any blowouts since before Thanksgiving, and our constant arguments about how late she could stay out and where she was allowed to go were tame by comparison.

Though some pressures felt lighter, I still found myself constantly worrying about my finances. My career was going well, but my monthly student loan payments were huge and Tiffany was proving more expensive than I could have imagined. Trying to keep the takeout to a minimum, I still made lasagnas most Sundays, but that only covered one extra night. With all of the Christmas parties added to my normal schedule of functions, I was finding it increasingly hard to find the time to cook. Megan's and my parents' monthly contributions helped, of course, but I was basically trying to support two people on my paycheck and it wasn't working. Each month I withdrew hundreds from my savings account, and every time I stood at the ATM, I wondered how Megan ever made ends meet.

After my sister had divorced Tony and he'd gone off to jail for driving with a suspended license, my father would often say things like, "Poor Megan, she has it so tough, raising those two kids on her own and working a job she hates." I'd often argue, saying things like, "She makes a decent salary, and it's only two kids; it's not like she has five." Or, "she makes three times the national poverty figure for a family of four." Since that figure was $22,000 or something moronic like that, I knew I was being an asshole. But I'd argue anyway, partially to stop the pity parties my dad always liked to throw — both for himself and others — and partially because I believed at least a little of what I was saying. "Zillions of people have it a lot worse than Megan," I'd say. Now, though, I knew just how difficult it was for her, and I felt bad for having said those things. Megan made less than I did, and the thought of having *two* kids constantly asking, wanting, needing, asking, wanting, needing made me shudder. If it wasn't a new jacket or sneakers, a Halloween costume or a Girl Scout uniform, it was money for a field trip, school pictures, a haircut, hanging out, a CD, a movie, whatever. It never ended, and Megan had been nothing short of heroic for how long she'd endured it. I knew she was saving a lot by having her daughter live with me, and that helped to assuage my guilt over how harshly I'd spoken of my sister, even if not to her face.

Before the holiday break I'd called Mr. Rodriguez to make sure that the cross-racial kissing wars hadn't resulted in any rumbles or deaths. All was quiet on the eastern front, he assured me, but he wanted to tip me off to another possible storm brewing.

"I'm not supposed to say this sort of thing," he began in a whisper, "but Tiffany has been hanging around with the worst girl in the entire school."

"Oh, my," I played along. "Who is she and what's so bad about her?" I was a bit taken aback that Mr. Rodriguez would speak this way about a student, but very curious to hear the details.

"Well," he paused. I imagined him looking from side to side over his specs to make sure the coast was clear. "Her name is Jenise. She's seventeen and this is her fourth high school."

"At least she'll graduate this spring and be gone," I jumped in, always the Pollyanna.

"Mr. Wintle, she's not going anywhere. She has successfully completed only one credit and is therefore still a freshman."

*"One credit?"* I was incredulous. "How the heck did she get into your school, then?"

"We were forced to take her. As long as a student claims to want to be enrolled in school, the system has to provide one, and in this case, we were chosen. That's how it works. She never shows up, though, and when she does, there's usually some incident. Jenise is bad, bad news."

"What sorts of incidents?" I asked, trying to milk him for as much information as possible.

"I really can't give you specifics, but I thought you should know."

"I can't thank you enough, Mr. Rodriguez. I won't tell Tiffany we had this conversation; I'll try to get her to tell me about Jenise on her own and go from there."

"I'm only telling you this because I care about my students," Mr. Rodriguez added. "Tiffany is a bright girl and she has the ability to succeed here. I want to help make that happen. It's too late for Jenise and she knows it, so she's looking for people to take down with her."

"I really appreciate it, Mr. Rodriguez. Please call me if there are any more developments."

When I took off my headset, I was grateful for the relative calm and safety of my office. Sure, there were political scuffles taking place in its halls — one would need a huge chalkboard to diagram all the resentments that flowed among employees at any given time — but Mr. Rodriguez's world was filled with more serious intrigue, and the stakes seemed so much higher. Though he was possibly even more of a drama queen than me, I couldn't have asked for a better ally at my niece's school.

"What is this music anyway?" Tiffany asked after she'd finished opening her gifts. "She has such a pretty voice."

"It's Loreena McKennitt, and she's singing 'The Lady of Shalott,' a famous poem by Alfred, Lord Tennyson."

"How do you know these things, Uncle Eddy? You know the name of every actor in every movie, and now you know about poetry too?"

"I do *not* know every actor's name, and I was a literature major in college. I wrote a paper about another poem by Tennyson — he's one of my favorites. Come on, I'll start the song over and we'll read along." From the shelf I grabbed an ancient volume I'd found in a used bookstore and we squeezed lengthwise on the love seat, facing the Christmas tree, the book balanced against our bent knees. In the dim light we did our best to read the words on the yellowed pages as they wafted gently over us:

> Or when the moon was overhead,
> Came two young lovers lately wed;
> 'I am half sick of shadows,' said
> The Lady of Shalott.

When the song was over, Tiffany turned to me. "So she dies in the boat?" she asked sadly. "She never gets to meet Lancelot?" I suddenly remembered watching *West Side Story* on television with my family when I was around eight. When Tony was killed, I ran screaming to my room and took to my bed, hysterical. My parents tried to comfort me through clenched smiles, but I was inconsolable. How could they possibly have been surprised when I told them ten years later that I was gay?

"No, she doesn't. But at least she left the tower, right? She was going bonkers up there."

"I guess. What does the story mean?"

"Well, I'm not sure," I answered carefully. "I think, for me, it's a metaphor for risking everything for the chance to love. It seems like the curse comes upon her when she falls for Lancelot, so you could argue that love is the curse. But I think the curse was sitting alone in the tower going crazy, seeing everything she was missing in her magic mirror. It's almost like she didn't even get to live at all until she set out in the boat to look for Lancelot."

"That is so *ill*, Uncle Eddy," Tiffany said, which meant that she liked it.

I saw an opening. "So, is Tommy Dash your Lancelot?" I asked innocently.

"No," she answered after a slight pause. "I saw him over Thanksgiving, but he hasn't called me since. He's forgotten about me, so I can't ever love him. I'll always be his friend, though."

"That sounds like a healthy attitude." My mind at ease, I returned to my pedagogy. "It's fun analyzing poems. They're like puzzles," I said. Loreena was now singing "Greensleeves" — believed by some to be by King Henry VIII — but I didn't mention it to Tiffany. "Think about it," I continued. "The Lady of Shalott can be every young girl who's protected by her parents, kept from the world. But she sees it all on television, in movies, and reads about it in books. It's when she first falls in love and leaves that protection behind that she loses her innocence. That part of her dies, and it's sad in a way. Maybe Tennyson is mourning that loss with the poem."

"Hmmmm," Tiffany murmured as she closed her eyes and rested her head against my shoulder. As the candlelight flickered on her sweet face, I knew this was a moment I would cling to in the years ahead. I wondered when Tiffany would fall in love for the first time, and with whom, and I wished there was a way I could protect her from the agony of losing that first love. I thought of the Sondheim musical *Into the Woods* and the witch's desperate, misguided plea to her daughter, Rapunzel, whom she'd imprisoned in a tower. "Who out there could love you more than I? What's out there that I cannot supply?" She had sung with a ferocity that only now could I fully understand.

Tiffany hadn't lived her life in a tower; she'd lived it down in the trenches, where her innocence had been taken from her long ago. But when it came to falling in love, Tiffany would be just as at sea as the Lady of Shalott.

# Acts of Contrition

"So, tell me everything," Orly said, after ordering a complicated assortment of steamed buns and dumplings from our Chinese waitress. She blew on her hands and rubbed them together furiously to try to get warm. We'd both gotten completely frozen on the short walk to the restaurant, and Orly insisted that the best recipe for defrosting was mountains of steamed dumplings.

Orly had been in Peru with her partner, Marisol, for the holidays, and we hadn't yet caught up face-to-face. I'd called an emergency lunch, which meant that I'd travel down to her office and we'd go from there. As I was in a state of high anxiety, I was lucky that Orly wasn't in court that day and had no witness interviews scheduled during her lunch hour.

"Okay, so Mr. Rodriguez calls me at the office at eleven o'clock this morning and tells me they just evacuated Tiffany's math class because she's thrown a couple of stink bombs in the middle of the lesson." I breathed deeply. "Orly, if she gets thrown out of this school, we're gonna be up shit's creek."

"Whoa, slow down, Eddy. First, what exactly is a stink bomb?" This is why I needed Orly. She broke things down into their components and helped make sense of them. At work she was the Master Interrogator.

"I went on the Internet and found out. They're these little glass vials filled with liquid ammonium sulfide. When you break them, they stink like rotten eggs. I can't believe she did this in *math class,* of all places. It's her worst class *and* I've complained about the teacher!"

"Okay, okay. So, these stink bombs are really just used for practical jokes and aren't dangerous. That should be a fairly minor infraction."

"Yeah, well, the school's penal code is a little different from yours. They're keeping her in the principal's office all day while they decide whether she'll get an in-school suspension or a superintendent's suspension." Just then our waitress placed a tremendous covered platter on our table. It looked like a bamboo flying saucer.

"What? They're going to suspend her?

Not even student arbitration like last time? What was the verdict on that, by the way?" Orly slid the platter in front of her and removed the lid. The steam wafted up toward her face, and she encouraged it by fanning her hands.

"Oh, that ended with her and Destiny having to apologize to each other. It was very informal." I eyed the dumplings longingly but, having burned my tongue once too often, knew they needed a few minutes to cool.

"And what's a superintendent's suspension?" she asked.

"It sounds like the school's equivalent of the Tombs, where they throw all the suspended kids from all over the city for the day." (The Tombs is the city's interim prison where all types of criminals are held together until they're arraigned.) "I can *just imagine* the friends Tiffany would make there. Did I tell you she's hanging around with, quote unquote, the worst girl in the school?"

"Yeah, you did." Orly laughed as she divided up the dumplings and slid one onto a big spoon with the help of a chopstick. I followed suit. "Was she involved in this?"

"No, Jenise isn't in Tiffany's math class, and when I spoke to Tiffany on the phone,

I asked her where she got the stink bombs."

"And?"

"Here's the kicker." I hesitated for effect. "She got them from *her father . . . for Christmas!* Can you believe what an idiot he is?" I nibbled off the edge of a bun and sucked the juice out of it.

"It's incredible, but yeah, given what I know about Tony, I can believe it. What else did Tiffany say?"

"Naturally, she said it wasn't her fault, exactly. She'd taken the bombs out to show a friend and he knocked them out of her hand."

"Spreading the blame. It never fails. Maybe she thinks they'll cut her a deal if she testifies against the other kid."

I laughed. "She said that her math teacher called Mr. Rodriguez on the phone, and within one minute, he came running in with the principal and assistant principal. They had towels for the kids with asthma to breathe through while they emptied the classroom."

"Wow. They sound like a regular SWAT team," Orly joked.

"Yeah, then they made every student in the class write a statement about what happened. Apparently Tiffany wrote that she had nothing to do with it, and every other student wrote that the bombs were Tiffany's. So now she's in trouble for lying too."

"So what do *you* think you should do?"

"Well, she has to be punished, so I'll take everything away *yet again* — cell phone, AOL, TV cable hookup — for at least a week. And she'll have to stay in this weekend. I guess I'll talk to her about what she has to lose if she gets thrown out of this school. But I feel like she's just not getting it, Orly. I'm getting more and more frustrated and angry with her."

"Of course you are, Eddy; you're only human. You've taken Tiffany in at her absolute worst possible age. You didn't have her for all those years when she was adorably cute and cuddly, like back when she sang us that song in the car. You've gotten her now, after her childhood went sour and she's filled with rage and crazy from hormones." Orly paused to make sure I'd really heard her. I had. "But you're doing everything you can, and the choices you're making in dealing with her are right and appropriate and come from your heart."

"I feel so powerless," I whispered, "and I can't stand it." There, I said it, I thought. The all-time champion Control Queen has met his match with this one, and it's going to be his undoing. I buried my face in my hands. "I can't get her to stop getting high," I muttered through my fingers. "I can't get her to behave in school, and I can't get her to pick better friends."

"Eddy, you couldn't possibly do any more." Orly reached over and rubbed my shoulder. "Really, give yourself a break. What you've given this kid already is immeasurable, but you can't force her to accept it. She may wind up blowing this whole opportunity, Eddy. And by God, if she does, it will *not* be your fault."

I'd not allowed myself to even contemplate failure. Hearing Orly say it now frightened me, as I didn't think I could survive it.

"You know what I think?" Orly asked rhetorically. "Her behavior at school has nothing to do with you or being in New York. It's a result of her having been back in Connecticut for nearly two weeks. She saw her father, hung with her old friends, fought with her mother, and was forced to spend time with that loser boyfriend of Megan's." She signaled the waitress for our check.

"I'm sure you're right." I lifted my head and sighed. "And there are two other little details I haven't told you yet."

"What?" Orly asked with concern in her eyes.

"Tony's girlfriend is pregnant. Sammy doesn't know yet, but Megan told Tiffany. So she's dealing with the idea of her dad starting a new family when he doesn't even contribute to the one he already has."

"What's *wrong* with his girlfriend? Actually, you don't need to answer that; I saw how some of the women up there are when we crashed Megan's twentieth high school reunion. I get the picture."

"Yeah, and it ain't a pretty one neither," I said in my best Susan Hayward.

"So, what's the *next* thing this poor kid has to deal with? You said there were two."

"Megan got fired two days after Christmas. When she went to work, her boss sacked her and they had security escort her from the building. After almost twenty years with the company, that's how they treat her."

"Was it related to her drinking?"

"No, at least not directly. Megan had complained to human resources about her old boss and was transferred into a new division. But apparently the old boss and her new one were in cahoots and determined to get rid of her. The official reason was for sending personal e-mails, which Megan does less than anyone I know."

"That's ridiculous. Is there any way she could sue them?" Orly began the long process of bundling up once again.

"She's going to look into it, but you know, unless there's some sort of gender or age discrimination or something, she's got no case. You can't sue because your boss is a prick and hates you."

I cracked open my fortune cookie as we headed out of the crowded little restaurant. "Your determination will bring great rewards," it read. I glanced upward and stuck the fortune in my coat pocket.

Christmas Day had gone smoothly *and* would be memorable, which didn't often go hand in hand. I'd been apprehensive about how I would respond to Eric, now that I knew so much more about him, but I'd promised myself I wouldn't be aggressive and would do my best to steer clear.

The holiday dawned gray, cold, and rainy, despite the forecast's calling for the biggest Christmas snowstorm in decades. Waking up at my parents' house, especially on holidays, always brings an enormous sense of security and comfort. Their little Maltese, Max, greets me at the bedroom door, practically having a heart attack with excitement over the fact that I've arisen. Though my parents keep their house at a frosty fifty-eight degrees, I'm greeted warmly by the smell of fresh coffee and the sound of classical music or old standards playing on the kitchen Wave. As Mom putters and Dad reads the paper, they offer hearty "good mornings" and never fail to inform me that Max had been waiting patiently at my door for at least an hour.

With the possibility of the roads icing up, I dallied over the paper and coffee no longer than an hour and got myself dressed to drive to the cemetery. My niece Heather had been buried in a woodsy graveyard about twenty minutes from my parents' home, and going there on holidays had become a ritual in the five and a half years since she'd died. I always went alone, as my mom could go anytime and, I'd gathered, my dad isn't big on visiting cemeteries. I never thought I'd be a cemetery-goer either, spouting the party line that you don't need a cemetery to feel close to a loved one who'd passed. But that had changed after Heather's death. Sometimes when I visited I felt simply sad and would crouch near the large rose granite stone, whisper a few words to her, and say a prayer. But other times the double-barreled grief and love that connected me to Heather's spirit would bring me to my knees. I'd sense her with me, comforting me, causing me to miss her more; it was only then that I could feel the full depth of her loss again. As I never knew which experience I would have, I was grateful to be alone.

This Christmas Day trip to the cemetery fell somewhere between the two. My sister Kathleen and her husband, Tyler, had laid a beautiful holiday "blanket" of greens and berry branches over the grave, and small potted pine trees surrounded the two permanent miniature firs that stood sentinel on either side of the headstone. Figurines had been placed on the stone's base, including a ceramic rottweiler — the preferred breed of the family. (They have *at least* one at any given time. Heather loved animals, as do her parents, and at one point their small home housed a dog, a ferret, a huge iguana, numerous birds, fish tanks, and, out back, a rabbit. Except for the fish and bunny, all the animals roamed — or flew — freely, so visiting was like walking into *Mutual of Omaha's Wild Kingdom*.) Today I'd brought along a small ceramic English bulldog to join the rottweiler, as Heather had gotten a fat, wrinkly, drooling one named Winston shortly before she died.

I didn't feel Heather's presence this Christmas morning, but I was acutely aware of how much I missed her. At every holiday dinner she insisted that she sit next to me — no matter who was on the guest list. I was only fifteen when she was born, and from the moment she could focus her eyes, we absolutely adored each other. Fifteen is a rough age for every kid but I doubt it can get a whole lot lonelier than it does for a closeted gay boy. Heather made me feel like a prince and a superhero rolled into one, and I thanked her for that before I kissed my fingers, touched them to the gravestone, and left.

Megan and Eric arrived at my parents' around one o'clock, after picking up Tiffany and Sammy from Tony's, where they'd spent Christmas morning with their father and his girlfriend, Donna. With a damp drizzle still falling, Eric made a chivalrous declaration that he'd carry all of the gifts and shopping bags in from the car, insisting that Megan and the girls go inside. I ran out to help, partially to make sure that the bundles included Megan's awesome chicken wings and stuffed mushrooms, which they did. Eric rattled on as he moved hyperkinetically around the car, opening and closing doors. He was like a windup toy or a marionette whose owner had not yet mastered his art; his head moved in every direction except mine, and he never looked me straight in the eyes. I caught bits and pieces of what he was saying and gathered that he'd bought Megan two DVD players for Christmas, no doubt angling for a stay of execution.

I'd given up a while back on trying to follow any thread that might exist in Eric's version of conversation. Usually it was a series of non sequiturs that required the listener to conduct an intensive post-mortem, with Eric's help, in order to construct some sort of narrative. And then there was always the chance that he would say something wildly inappropriate. On a previous holiday, in a room full of relatives, he'd suddenly said, "Why doesn't Chelsea Clinton have any brothers or sisters?" Realizing he was attempting a joke, a few of us muttered, "I don't know. Why?" "Because Monica Lewinsky swallowed them." If it weren't for Eric's laughter, you could have heard a pin drop.

Once inside, I kissed the girls and commented on how pretty they looked. Tiffany was rock royalty in a long, tight red dress and black, lacy bolero jacket. But it was Sammy who stole the show. For her entire life Sammy had hated wearing dresses and did so only if absolutely forced. (I'd gone to Megan's on Christmas morning two years before to give the girls a lift to my folks' house, as Megan was going to come later. When I'd arrived, Megan and Sammy were in a full-tilt war over Sammy's Christmas outfit. She'd refused to wear the green velvet dress Megan had bought for her. Attempting a compromise, Megan dug out a pair of black velvet pants and a white button-down shirt. But Sammy held firm, stating that she would only go to Grandma's if she could wear what she had on — shorts and a tank top. That's when I kneeled over her and pinned her arms down. Megan and I forced her into her tights and dress as she kicked and screamed, and then I carried her out to the car.) Now she stood before me in an outfit of her own choosing — a long, cotton, sleeveless dress of army camouflage, with a purple T-shirt underneath. On her feet were little black combat boots.

"Look who's developed her own personal style," I fawned. "You look fantastic! The hair, the glasses, I love it!" She'd pulled her long hair up loosely into a big clip and wore oval-shaped eyeglasses with avocado frames.

"Oh, get outta here, Uncle Eddy," she said as she blushed and threw her arms around me. At eight years old, Sammy looked like a miniature freshman at Smith or Mount Holyoke. I half expected her to whip out a book of Sylvia Plath poetry and start reciting.

"She picked out her glasses all by herself," Megan said as she sat down at the kitchen table. She crossed her legs at the knees and her top foot began bobbing up and down automatically. As she nervously chewed on her fingernails, I realized this would be Megan's first Christmas stone-cold sober and I felt for her.

Kathleen arrived around two, sans Tyler but bearing her famous spicy clam dip. Tyler was afraid to leave all the animals home alone should the storm hit. He'd never been very comfortable around his wife's family so we used to hear excuses like this all the time, especially after Heather died. But in the last couple of years he began showing up more often for holidays and sometimes actually seemed to enjoy himself. Tyler and I could not have less in common, but over the years we'd come to deeply respect and, I believe, love each other. Today he would be missed. As my uncles and their wives also begged off due to the storm, Christmas dinner would be an intimate one — just the Team of Five (as I call my immediate family), the granddaughters, and Eric.

My mother goes all out for every holiday, decorating the entire first floor of her house. If you happen by in March, you'll see cardboard shamrocks on the front door and a collection of miniature leprechauns in the foyer. On Thanksgiving, turkeys and carefully placed orange and brown leaves greet you. At Christmastime, not a square inch of space goes unembellished. The living room, home to a meticulously decorated artificial tree, was always the setting for appetizers and the opening of gifts. (Real Christmas trees had been abandoned years ago, after my father had one too many tempter tantrums over trying to get the tree to stand up straight.) In addition to the lights from the tree and its candle-holding, big-bosomed angel with Joey Heatherton hair, the room was aglow from a three-foot holiday doll that carried a lighted lantern (a silent caroler, I believe), a glowing plastic gingerbread house, an '80s fiber optics display, and several

Christmas candles. As we sat exchanging presents, laughing, and focusing often on Sammy or Max, Mom snapped away with her camera and we were all able to believe that, at least for the moment, everything was okay in our lives.

Outside, the temperature had dropped and the snow began to fall. And fall and fall. By the time we finished the delicious filet mignon dinner Mom had prepared, over a foot had accumulated, and through the frosted windowpanes, it looked like a veritable whiteout outside. With the exception of my parents, we all bundled up and headed out to shovel the steep driveway. When that was finished, Eric grabbed the old Flexible Flyer from the garage and I fetched my snowboard, which could double as a sled, and the six of us set out on a trek around the neighborhood.

Christmas is a cumulative holiday, which is perhaps why it can be so difficult. It carries with it every Christmas that went before, and you experience it each year as though you're all the ages of your life at one time. You're a child, an adolescent, and an adult simultaneously; people, places, and feelings that have gone or been left behind are with you again, bringing both great comfort and immeasurable sadness. As I watched Sammy and Tiffany chase each other through the snow, taking turns attempting to ride my old sled, this Christmas took on the mythic weight of my life, and my sense of joy combined inextricably with the knowledge of my mortality.

Having lunch with Orly always manages to calm me down; no matter what the task at hand, she makes me feel I can tackle it. Lately it seemed that it was Orly doing all the heavy lifting in our friendship, but I needed my friends now more than ever and vowed not to beat myself up over the amount of receiving I was doing.

When I arrived home from work that evening Tiffany was in her usual place — lying on the love seat in front of the television. In light of the day's events, one might think she'd be sitting at the table doing her homework in silence, but acts of contrition were never Tiffany's forte. I muted *The Simpsons* so I could properly confront her.

"So what are you going to do about this whole stink bomb thing? You know if you get thrown out of this school, it's going to be Humanities next, which would be disastrous."

"They're not going to throw me out, Uncle Eddy," she said without sitting up and facing me. "They're, like, totally over-reacting, as usual. I've gone through the Code of Conduct and am going to write an appeal arguing why I shouldn't be suspended."

"That's a good idea, Tiffany, but you've got to realize this comes on top of a series of incidents. I mean, you've only been in this school for a few months and you've been written up for insubordination, you've created a furor by making out with someone's boyfriend, and now you're exploding stink bombs in math class. Please tell me how you could possibly make such a bad decision as to bring those things to school with you to begin with. That's what really worries me." I'd worked myself into a nice lather but was determined not to raise my voice.

"I was just going to show them to my friends," she said defiantly. "Everyone gets in trouble in school, Uncle Eddy. It's not a big deal."

"Give me a break, Tiffany. Obviously the bombs were going to get broken at some point; it was just a matter of when. You should have known it would probably be while you were in the school building. And

I'll decide what's a big deal, not you." My voice, though not particularly loud, was taking on that edge that Tiffany hated — and that I liked even less.

"Okay, you're right. I shouldn't have brought them. But I still hate this F-ing school. Mr. Rodriguez and the rest of his retarded posse are a joke. They take themselves so seriously but everyone just laughs at them. And ninety-nine percent of the kids there make me sick. They try to be all ghettolike but they're just posers who can't see that it's not working for them." She got up and went over to the laptop on the dining table, presumably to begin typing her appeal.

"Let me know if you need any help making your arguments," I said as I took the AOL cord out of the computer. "I'll make us some Boca Burgers." I detached Time Warner's cable from the television, grabbed the cordless phone and headed into the kitchen. Tiffany's sentence had begun.

The appeal, which I helped turn into a mini legal brief complete with an eloquent summation, probably annoyed the school more than it helped. In any event, Tiffany wasn't suspended but rather received several more demerits toward the eventual suspension she would receive if these incidents persisted. She would, however, have to sit in the principal's office during math class for an entire week. I let Tiffany know that I didn't like this one bit and promised her that we would be spending our television- and AOL-free evenings factoring complex polynomials.

# Weapons of Mass Destruction

The morning of my hernia surgery I was beside myself with excitement. I — who can't even read a pamphlet about hepatitis in a doctor's waiting room without turning a pale shade of green — would, in just a few hours, be opened up with a knife for the very first time, have a chunk of flesh cut from my abdomen, and be sewn back up with a needle and thread. And yet I simply could not wait. The idea of not having to show up for my life for five entire days was a dream come true.

I had a running joke with my favorite colleague at work, Stewart Fischer, that involved my increasingly elaborate fantasy of becoming a "turban lady." Years earlier we'd driven up the California coast together, and during a quiet evening in Big Sur, Stewart and I had read aloud a bizarre proposal for a book about that unique breed of hatted woman. Ever since, when things have become overwhelming in our lives or at the office, we have recreated ourselves in various turbaned guises. In my current imagined incarnation I wore a white turban with matching terry bathrobe and reclined on an overstuffed lounge chair on the grassy grounds of an impossibly exclusive clinic. I wore giant Jackie O sunglasses to fend off the glare from the lake below, and in my lap lay open a thick, hardback novel, I was "taking the cure" and the book was, of course, upside down.

Beginning today, *in my real life,* I wouldn't have to drag my tired ass out of bed before dawn to get Tiffany off to school and then battle New York's record-breaking deep freeze the entire way across town to the gym and work. I wouldn't have to badger producers' lawyers to respond to my latest round of faxes or listen to clients proclaim, "This year is going to be *the big one!*" And, perhaps best of all, I wouldn't have to put Tiffany's needs before my own for a few days; she would have the opportunity to show her gratitude for all I'd done by waiting on me hand and foot. I'd bought a small, used TV/VCR for my bedroom and would spend all five days in bed on painkillers watching the pile of movies I'd borrowed from my parents and friends. It would be pure heaven.

When Dr. Garbowsky came to visit me

in the curtained-off little room where I was being poked and prodded by nurses until my surgery, he looked adorably rumpled in his green scrubs and gave me the sweetest smile. I noticed that his hands were even sexier than I'd remembered from our meeting: they were strong-looking and nicely veined, with clean, trimmed fingernails. (They weren't fussy, though; if they'd been professionally manicured and shellacked, I'd have run for the hills.) How strangely perfect, I thought. I feel incredibly attracted to this man who will be inside me in just a little while. Talk about intimacy; I wonder if he's even gay!

Apparently he'd come to tell me that he listened to an iPod in the operating room and to see if I had any special requests.

"Won't I be knocked out almost immediately?" I asked with urgency, momentarily losing my enthusiasm for being entered on a table.

"Of course, of course." His smile broadened. "But you might like to hear something specific to relax you when you enter the OR."

"Oh, I see. Entrance music, like the way 'Lara's Theme' plays every time Julie Christie comes on screen in *Doctor Zhivago*."

Dr. Garbowsky let go a deep, hearty chuckle. "I never thought of it that way exactly, but yeah," he said. "Like 'Quentin's Theme' on *Dark Shadows.*" *Dark Shadows?* Probably gay, I surmised.

"How about Bryan Ferry?" I asked innocently. "His voice really relaxes me. My favorite is 'Slave to Love.'"

"Of course I have that," Dr. Garbowsky responded, smiling slyly. "What record collection would be complete without it?" *Way* gay, I concluded happily.

An hour later I was being guided down endless corridors, dressed in only an ill-fitting hospital gown and rubber-bottomed socks. We turned a corner and up ahead I saw the bright lights and bustle of the operating room. What a production, I thought, and it's all for me! I felt like the ultimate turban lady — Norma Desmond in the musical version of *Sunset Boulevard*, when she returns to the studio soundstage for the first time in years. "Feel the early morning madness, feel the magic in the making," I belted out in my head. But then, as we got closer, I heard my own theme music playing and I prepared to make my entrance. I was an old pro, so my timing would be perfect and I'd strike just the right attitude; I would enter with the munificence of a beloved politician, and all the scurrying little people would think, *Ahh, the man of the hour has arrived!*

I only hoped that while going under from the anesthesia, I wouldn't make a pass at my surgeon.

Orly fetched me from the hospital an hour or two after the surgery and brought me back to the apartment in a taxi, stopping on the way to fill my Vicodin prescription. I was all goodness and light as she tucked me into bed and made sure I had everything I needed at my fingertips. Before she left to go back to work, she closed the drapes and popped a movie into the VCR. I'd selected *Sometimes a Great Notion*, an old '70s film starring Paul Newman and Lee Remick and based on the Ken Kesey novel. I'd always loved the title and had been meaning to watch the movie for twenty-five years. The '70s is my favorite decade in the history of film, and I was hoping for a searing relationship drama like *Coming Home* or *Five Easy Pieces*, movies I'd seen as a teenager that had made me frightened to grow up but determined to do it as fast as possible, and to try to be an actor when I did. I popped my first painkiller and promptly passed out.

I woke some time later to the sound of Tiffany's keys in the front door locks. When I looked at the TV screen, I had to stare for a moment to make sure that my foggy brain was actually processing the image correctly. Paul Newman was standing on a tugboat that was moving slowly down a river. That much made sense. But there, affixed to a pole at the boat's prow, was what appeared to be a disembodied human arm. And, even weirder, the disembodied human arm seemed to be giving the world the finger. I hadn't read the novel, but this was certainly vintage Kesey. Translating it to film so literally, though, seemed silly. Newman was obviously engaged in some act of supreme defiance, but to use a human arm to make a point was wildly over the top and just plain psychotic. Always the critic, I thought, even stoned on painkillers.

Just then Tiffany popped her head furtively into my bedroom doorway, as though she were both guilty of something and afraid of what she would find if she looked at me straight on.

"Are you okay?" she asked with a panicked strain to her voice. I wondered if she was high.

"I'm fine," I answered. "I was just

sleeping." I looked over at my alarm clock and saw that it was six in the evening. "Where have you been, Tiffany? I sort of assumed you'd come straight home from school today, since I did have surgery and all." My usual sarcasm was undiminished. "I might have needed your help or have wanted you to pick up some stuff from the store *with that extra money I gave you,* remember?"

She threw herself into my antique wingback chair and burst into tears. "I've had the worst day ever!" Oh, well, I thought, I guess my fantasy of being "off" from my life would remain just that — a fantasy. The turban would have to go back on its wig head for the time being.

"Why don't you put on that light and tell me what's going on?" I realized just then that I wasn't capable of sitting up but decided I would share that with Tiffany later. Despite the number of times I'd witnessed it, the sight of her crying still yanked at my heartstrings, so once again, her problems would come first. When she turned on the lamp next to the chair, I was relieved to see that she didn't look stoned.

"Well, I was with this girl Jenise that I've been hanging out with, and we found this wallet on the stairs, and when we opened it there was a fifty dollar bill inside. I was, like, tempted to take it before turning in the wallet but Jenise said we shouldn't, so we walked to the office together and turned it in. I mean, I know the kid whose wallet it was because his picture ID was in it, but I didn't know where to find him to give it back." She took a quick beat to catch her breath. "Then, later on, I saw him in the hall and told him I was the one who turned it in. He said, 'Thanks, but I wish I got my fifty bucks back too.' I couldn't believe he didn't get it back, and I felt like he was thinking that I took it, which I didn't, so I said, 'Let's go to the office and tell that bee-otch secretary to give it back to you.' So we went, and when we walked into the office, I told her to give him his money back. Well, the principal must have heard me because the skanky witch came out of her office and said, 'How dare you accuse my staff of stealing! You will apologize right this minute!' " Tiffany did the principal as highfalutin and self-righteous, with big arm gestures to match. "Well, screw that!" she continued. "Me apologize when that ugly loser took the money, not me? I got so mad that I started kicking the wall. So Miss Santiago made me sit in her office for the rest of the afternoon. She was going to call you but I told her you had surgery today and she said she'd wait until tomorrow. I swear I didn't take the money, Uncle Eddy!" She began sobbing again but managed to choke out, "Oh, and the extra money you gave me got stolen out of my backpack during gym class."

"That's quite a story, Tiffany," I said calmly. "Now, dear heart, could you hand me the glass of water that's sitting right next to me?"

"Sure," she sniffled. "You can barely move, huh?" She handed me the water and I sipped through a bent straw. "Aren't you mad about what happened?"

"In a parallel universe I'm sure that I'm furious," I answered dreamily, "but right now I'm floating on a cloud, and you're an angel who can bring me delicious treats. Why don't you heat up some of that lasagna for us, and we'll eat in here?"

"Okay." Tiffany looked at me quizzically and left.

Despite my semistupor, I knew instantly what had actually happened. Jenise had convinced Tiffany not to take the money so that she herself could pinch it on the way to the office. After all, fifty bucks is twice as good as twenty-five. Jenise had ex-

310

ploited my niece's naïveté; she knew Tiffany wouldn't suspect her of doing this in a million years.

Later, after she'd helped to prop me up and we'd eaten some gooey, heavily sauced lasagna, I told Tiffany I had two questions to ask her. I would need her to answer them honestly, as her answers would be important for my conversation with Ms. Santiago the next day.

"First," I began, "did you carry the wallet yourself all the way to the office?"

She thought for a minute, then: "No, Jenise carried it most of the way and handed it to me right before we went in."

"Okay," I continued. "Did you see the fifty dollars at any time while you were in the office to drop the wallet off?"

"No," she answered. "But I practically announced that there was fifty dollars in it when I walked in. Then, when I handed it to the secretary, she went through it to find out whose it was. If she didn't see the money, wouldn't she have said something then?"

"Not necessarily, Tiffany. That's an assumption you're making. She may have seen that there was no money but decided not to publicly accuse Jenise. She probably wanted to discuss it with the principal later, once it was confirmed by the wallet's owner that he did indeed lose the money. The secretary made some quick decisions right then, before speaking. Maybe you should have done the same before accusing her."

"Yeah, exactly. She decided not to mention the money so she could steal it and say later it was never in the wallet."

"All right then," I said with wide eyes and a fake smile as I took my second painkiller. "Please make sure to clean the kitchen, do your homework, and go to bed by ten thirty. I'm gonna watch *Oliver!*" And with that, I redonned my imaginary turban, rode deep into the Valley of the Dolls, and left my life behind once again.

I woke the next morning with my abdomen burning and my mind in a state of pure rage. I immediately took a painkiller, as Dr. Garbowsky had instructed, but it would've taken a lot more than one little pill to steer me off the warpath. I'd slept fitfully the night before, with nightmares tearing into my sleep like the vultures I'd once seen devour a zebra carcass while on safari in Kenya. Though I couldn't remember exactly what I'd dreamed, every nightmare involved Tiffany and resulted in my sitting bolt upright in bed, sweating and in pain, filled with terrible thoughts about her. What if she did steal that fifty bucks? What if she kept the extra grocery money too? What if she's been stealing from me this whole time? Has everything been a lie, an act? Is she actually beyond redemption and just playing me for a fool? What if I don't know this person sleeping in the next room at all? Maybe I have no idea how damaged she really is! For the first time in a decade I thought about a woman I'd once met whose face was half covered with hideous scars. She'd been sleeping in bed with her husband when their son attacked them with an axe. Her husband hadn't survived. Is Tiffany capable of doing something like that? I worried. Look at Patty McCormack in *The Bad Seed*: she had everyone fooled! By the time morning came, my fear had turned to anger and I was determined to continue fighting Tiffany's self-destruction. But to properly do battle, I first had to know the enemy.

I waited for the painkiller to kick in to hoist myself out of bed and begin ransacking my niece's bedroom. While halfway around the world Hans Blix and his team of weapons inspectors combed Iraq for weapons of mass destruction, I threw back Tiffany's purple silk curtains and began a search of my own. Despite my rage, somewhere inside I prayed that what I might find would not lead to war.

Like most teenagers' rooms, Tiffany's bedroom was her haven, her sanctuary. It contained all of her worldly possessions as well as her history; it both reflected her and helped to define her. Tiffany had spent many hours meticulously arranging and rearranging every little object and was always talking about things she wanted to acquire to make the room "even cooler." One week it was a beanbag chair, the next an exotic mosquito net for around her bed. The room had come quite a distance, though, in the few months she'd lived with me. What was once a pleasantly generic guest room (albeit with a gay man's sense of color — Hampton Sand, to be exact) was now the boudoir of an Arabian princess on acid. The color scheme was primarily purple (multiple shades) and midnight blue, with recurring motifs of crescent moons and stars. From the ceiling hung a tasseled Japanese *gohanzen,* as well as a brass lantern with blue glass and an oxidized copper mobile of — you guessed it — a moon and stars. The walls were covered with felt black light posters, and a bulletin board packed with photos of her friends, Megan, Tony, and Sammy, plus concert ticket stubs and other mementos. Next to her round mirror, with its thick purple and blue frame, Tiffany had hung a tiered brass potato and onion holder that she'd repurposed for her bracelets and necklaces. We'd bought tall bookshelves at Kmart to house her books, boom box, CDs, and a million other things, but its main purpose was to display her collection of jeweled picture frames and candle holders of every conceivable shape and size. Perched atop the shelves were her lava lamp and, on proud display, Kurt Cobain's *Journals* (another inappropriate Christmas present from Tony).

Tiffany's favorite area of her room was her Wiccan altar, which she'd created atop an old bureau that she'd entirely decoupaged with photos of her friends. On the altar's surface she'd glued dozens of polished little stones into the shape of a pentacle and surrounded it with incense holders, candles, and the collection of small glass bottles she used to store oils and herbs. On the wall over the altar were pictures of sprites and fairies, including the one Tiffany was determined to have tattooed on her lower back. She never spoke much about her Wicca, and I'd just assumed she claimed to be a practitioner so she could collect all the pretty accoutrements, but I saw now that she'd amassed half a dozen books on the subject; maybe she was more serious about it than I'd thought but preferred to keep it private, as many people do with their religion.

As I stood there on that bright winter morning, what I noticed most was the mess, and the toll Tiffany's residence had taken on the room. Melted wax covered the bureau and was splattered all over the carpet near her altar. Ashes overflowed from several incense holders and burnt incense sticks had spilled over onto the floor. On the carpet beside her bed was a stain a foot around, probably from some oil potion spilt by candlelight, as well as numerous burn marks. I'd stopped making Tiffany's bed months ago, and I saw now that I'd have to keep on her to change the sheets and wash the duvet cover more regularly. Bras, sweatshirts, shoes, and loose papers were scattered about. By teenage standards the room was probably a showplace, but to a neat freak like me it was a disaster.

I began my search with the shelves, methodically looking behind each book or tchotchke and opening up the little storage boxes that contained letters, notes, nail polish, and jewelry. I rifled quickly through each one without reading anything (controlling my urge to be even nosier) and kept my sights set firmly on contraband. Finding nothing, I moved on to the bureau. I was on my knees searching through the second drawer from the bottom — the one stuffed with panties and thongs — when I uncovered a gun. I stopped breathing, sank back onto my heels, and stared at the little black and gray pistol. I'd held my father's .22 caliber rifle once when I was a kid; other than that, I'd never held a gun or even been this close to one. It was a full five seconds before I realized that Tiffany's gun might not be real and ventured to pick it up. Though it was metal and fairly weighty, I knew instantly upon holding it that the gun was a toy.

Relief washed over me momentarily, but then the anger flooded back. Fake guns were completely illegal in New York City. Crimes were perpetrated with them all the time and it was not uncommon for the police to shoot a kid who wielded an imitation gun as a joke. This was serious. Plus Tiffany had taken the trouble to hide the gun in what she would consider her most personal drawer. She knew I'd confiscate it immediately. I furiously continued searching.

After I'd gone through the bottom drawer in the bureau and found nothing, I pulled it out completely. There, lying on the carpet in the empty space beneath where the drawer usually sat, was a small cardboard box containing a cache of drug paraphernalia. There were a couple of pot or hash pipes (which I hoped had not been used for crack), some rolling papers and two tiny plastic, Ziploc baggies. One contained what I guessed was about ten bucks' worth of very potent-smelling chronic, and another looked as though it might have held white powder but was now empty. Some other baggies were unused.

Though I knew I couldn't prevent Tiffany from smoking pot, I'd made it clear that she was not to buy it and certainly not to keep a stash in the apartment. And to make matters worse, there was now the possibility she was using cocaine or crystal as well. My search had proved my thoughts of the night before true; Tiffany was living a whole other life of which I was ignorant. She probably *had* taken that money from the wallet; how else could she afford to buy drugs? And what the hell is up with the fake gun? If she carries that with her when she goes to cop drugs, I thought, she is *totally fucked!*

Painkiller or no, my heart raced. *Jesus Christ!* I screamed inside as my body went slack against the side of the bed. So now I knew the truth, and it was as bad as I'd feared. But what about the loving girl who'd made me that magnificent Christmas gift less than a month ago? I sat there on the carpet for some time, wondering which girl was the *real* Tiffany and trying unsuccessfully to reconcile the two. Eventually, I scraped myself off the floor and climbed back into bed to call Orly.

"What if she's a criminal? Or worse, a schizo?" I asked, after filling Orly in on my eventful evening and morning. "At the very least she's a total narcissist and using more drugs than I thought. I mean, I'm lying here unable to move and she starts crying about her day. She's unbelievable! I've even been wondering if she could get angry enough to stab me in my sleep or something." I knew it sounded crazy, but I was glad I said it.

"Luckily, girls don't murder their parents. It just doesn't happen," Orly replied, humoring me. "I've seen elder abuse cases, and of course daughters steal from their parents. But they don't kill them."

"Oh yeah? What about Lizzie Borden and her forty whacks?"

"Okay, there was one exception and it was, like, a hundred years ago. And it was never proven beyond a reasonable doubt in a court of law."

"History repeats itself," I said. "Look at the two George Bushes." Orly laughed but I was dead serious.

"Oh, Eddy baby, you sound like a total wreck," she said with true concern in her voice. "You just had surgery yesterday, so you need to rest. Why don't you take a nice long nap so you'll be calmer when Tiffany gets home from school?"

"Yeah, you're right," I said weakly. "I'm useless like this."

"And you know, you don't have to confront Tiffany today about what you found, unless of course she discovers it's missing. But let's hope that doesn't happen. Why don't you just deal with the principal about the wallet situation and hold off on the rest until I have a chance to look at the baggie?" Orly had explained that when those little baggies are used over and over for pot, they can get all scratched up and look white, like they'd contained powder.

So there was a glimmer of hope on that front after all.

"It's going to be okay, right?" I was a whining child now, and I hated myself for it. How did I ever think I'd be able to handle this?

"You are going to get through this, Eddy," Orly reassured me.

"Yeah, I know," I sighed wearily. "I'm just exhausted and need to rest. Thank you for everything, Orly. I love you."

"Oh, baby, I love you too. Go to sleep now and give me a call later."

Employing my own version of reverse psychology, I decided to lull myself to sleep by watching Woody Allen's *Interiors*. Since each character in the film has a life more depressing than the last, I figured my current situation might feel like a cakewalk by comparison. I think I dozed off peacefully just as Geraldine Page walked into the ocean to take her own life. Is that a turban on her head, I wondered through squinted eyes, or am I just imagining it?

"Mr. Wintle, the type of behavior Tiffany exhibited in this office will not be tolerated." Ms. Santiago enunciated her words with precision, using a soft, preternaturally pleasant tone despite the subject of our conversation. It was as though she'd just told me there would be a bake sale at Thursday night's talent show and that I should stop by.

"I understand that, and I agree with you completely." I paced around the living room holding the cordless. Sitting down and getting back up took too much effort, and I'd decided this call should be made standing up. "I will call her school counselor, Judith Martin, to discuss the behavior," I continued, knowing that would be useless. "But this is the perfect opportunity for you to get Jenise out of your school. It's obvious that she took the money." I would never tell her I now suspected Tiffany as well. (Oh, no! I'm turning into one of *those* parents, I suddenly worried: "Not *my* little Johnny!")

Tiffany came running out of her bedroom and down the hall toward me. "Jenise did not take the money! That bee-otch secretary took it!" She'd shouted this so loudly I was sure Ms. Santiago had heard it.

"Shut the fuck up, Tiffany!" I screamed at the top of my lungs, forgetting to place my hand over the receiver. Then, into the phone: "Will you at least be conducting an investigation into the missing money right away?" I asked sweetly.

"The school will take whatever actions it deems appropriate," Ms. Santiago answered robotically. "I think we should end this conversation at this particular juncture."

Wonderful, I thought, now she thinks I'm totally nuts. Or worse, she's thinking, "Aha! Now I see where Tiffany gets her temper."

"Please, Ms. Santiago, I apologize for swearing. It doesn't happen often." Listen to yourself: how pathetic!

"Have a pleasant evening, Mr. Wintle. Perhaps we'll discuss this further in a few days." She hung up. Goddamn, I thought, if they ever use automated voice mail systems to give updates to families of people in the hospital, Ms. Santiago's their recording star. I could just hear her now: "I'm sorry, but your loved one passed away at one twenty-seven, eastern standard time. Please press three for the morgue drawer number containing the deceased's body." I hung the phone in its cradle.

"Good job, Uncle Eddy." Tiffany stood before me with her hand on her hip. "Why do you want them to start an investigation when it's obvious who took the money?" She looked at me like I was the village idiot.

"I am trying to clear your name, Tiffany." I spoke in a modulated tone, emulating Ms. Santiago. "If Jenise gets thrown out, that's just a positive by-product. Why are you so *against* the investigation if you didn't take the money?" I gave her my most penetrating stare.

"Okay, fine, I'm a thief. I have a mad crack addiction and I needed the money to buy drugs, okay?" She rolled her eyes at me for about the trillionth time since she'd moved in and headed toward her room. "This *gangsta* girl is gonna go do her homework," she said as she went, leaving me standing there feeling like I'd done every last little thing wrong, including being born.

"I'm going back to bed, so please make dinner in an hour or so," I yelled after her, my words halfheartedly trailing off to a tragic squeak, like Mary Richards's voice whenever she tried to assert herself with her boss, Lou Grant. Drained of all energy, I'd definitely be taking a rain check on the scene that would surely ensue when I confronted my niece about the results of my search. I slogged back to my room utterly defeated.

# Birds of Prey

How does her nose look? What will a casting director think of her voice? I'd popped in a videotape of Tiffany's work from her conservatory's previous summer session, and as I watched her perform a monologue in extreme closeup, these thoughts ran through my mind. I remembered how harshly I'd been judged, and I tried now to view my niece through the prism of expert discernment supposedly possessed by casting directors.

But then, suddenly, the fear in Tiffany's eyes hijacked my attention. In desperation she pleaded to the camera (or maybe to God?) to help her friends, who, one by one, were disappearing into the clutches of a malevolent force. Whether it was a cult or a prostitution ring or simply drug addiction, I couldn't be sure from her words. But as the tears of helplessness welled up in Tiffany's eyes and her voice tightened with fear, one thing became clear: I could not take my eyes off her.

Wow! I thought as I hit the stop button, fell back against my bed pillows, and stared up at the ceiling. That's how I feel about Tiffany — like she's being taken away from me, being pulled at by a dozen different forces, each more frightening than the last, all hell-bent on robbing us of the little girl who sang "My Heart Will Go On" while standing at the staircase railing waving good-bye with a white handkerchief as the *Titanic* left port. Megan's sense of loss must be devastating, too monumental to even imagine. Tiffany's performance had taken me there, to a place where her fear and powerlessness became my own. When she performed the monologue, had she thought about all of her friends who had been sent away? Or had she thought about her friends who were getting involved in guns, crime, and heavy drugs?

Then I realized that underneath the character's prayers for her friends was the fear that she would be the next to disappear, to be sucked into the darkness, but that she didn't want to plead for herself when people she loved were suffering or possibly dead. Her eyes, though, revealed her terror. As a former actor, I knew any performance that authentic was rooted somewhere in the actor's reality, especially when the performer was young and virtually untrained. Tiffany was frightened of what was out there. Though she seemed determined to try everything possible long before her sixteenth birthday, I was reminded now that a part of her ached for protection, not just from the scary world outside our home but from herself as well. And it was up to me to provide it, despite the conscious side of Tiffany that would fight me every inch of the way. As I lay in bed during my third day of recovery, my head a bit clearer, my thinking more rational, I questioned whether I possessed the energy and the fortitude for the job.

"Dude, your mom is a fucking psycho," I overheard Tiffany say on the phone. "She needs to be, like, seriously medicated." She must have come home while I was napping. Lately, according to Tiffany and her friends, everyone's parents were "psycho." I was sure the girls would love nothing more than to round us all up and lock us in some faraway asylum, like in that cheesy 1968 movie *Wild in the Streets.*

The time had come to confront Tiffany about the results of my search. I said a quick prayer for guidance, took a deep breath, and left the relative safety of my bedroom to enter the ring.

"Tiffany, can you get off the phone so we can talk?" She nodded and went into her room to wrap it up. The coffee table was littered with homework assignments and notes from every subject, as well as *Teen Vogue* and back issues of *Architectural Digest.* Textbooks, notebooks, pens, erasers, and other school detritus were scattered all over the silk area rug. Though I could now bend over fairly easily, I'd decided not to tidy up myself but rather to ask Tiffany to do it that night.

"What's up? How do you feel?" She plopped herself down on the love seat opposite me.

"Much better, thanks," I responded. "The pain is lessening, so I've cut down on the painkillers. It doesn't hurt as much to get up out of bed. Any mention of the wallet today?"

"No, and Jenise wasn't in school, as usual. So, what did you want to talk about?"

"I went through your stuff yesterday and I found your stash of pot and your fake gun." There was no dancing around it, so I just blurted it out. Orly had come over during her lunch hour and determined that the other baggie hadn't contained a white powder, so at least harder drugs were not at issue for the moment.

She bolted to the edge of the sofa. "You searched my room? What is your *problem?*" Her voice grew louder. "You can't just *do* that!"

"Yes, I can, Tiffany," I said calmly. "Your privacy rights are limited here, and I'm not going to get into a yelling match about it."

She sank back and folded her arms. "I can't F-ing believe this. I can *not* stand it here," she said, looking toward the window on the other side of the room, as though she might make a dive for it.

"You've been getting into trouble every other week and coming home stoned on weekends. I have no idea where you're going or who you're hanging out with. Now, after this week's wallet incident, I needed to see if I could figure out what's going on."

"So that gives you the right to search my room?"

"Yes, and I'm glad I did," I said defiantly. "Do you have any idea how much trouble you could've gotten into because of that gun?"

"It's a stupid toy gun. *Big deal.* And what did you do with my pot?"

"Orly's going to speak to you about the

gun so you can hear directly from law enforcement just how stupid it is to carry one of those. And I threw your pot away," I said. "We talked about this, Tiffany. I told you I didn't want you buying pot or keeping a stash in this apartment. Where are you getting the money to buy pot, anyway?"

"For the tenth time, I didn't steal that fifty dollars, and I'm not speaking to Orly or anybody else about that *toy*," she said with finality. Then Tiffany looked me straight in the eye. "You realize you can't control everything I do, right, Uncle Eddy?"

"Yes, I know that." But there are some things I must at least try to control, I thought.

"And you know you *have* to control *everyone* and *everything* around you, don't you? You know this about yourself, right?" She grew more empowered with each word. "You expect everyone to be perfect, like you think you are. Look at Kurt. You couldn't control him and make him perfect, so you dumped him."

"That's not true, Tiffany!" She knew where to strike, and of course it hurt all the more because I feared she was right.

"Yes, it is." She was standing now. "And

that's why you'll always be alone!" And with that, Tiffany ran into her bedroom and slammed the door.

"Let's face it, she's right," I whined to Stewart, my brother in turbanhood. He'd come over with a huge pot of his famous coq au vin, undaunted by its being a weeknight. Steven, Eugene, and Georgia had all promised to come by at various points over the coming weekend, but Stewart was intrepid and had traveled down from the Upper West Side on the subway, Corningware in tow. His rosy, apple-cheeked smile had cheered me, but dinner with Tiffany had been a largely silent affair. Afterward we'd retreated to my bedroom to watch a tape of *Thunderbirds*, a British sci-fi television series I hadn't seen since I was a little kid in the '60s. Stewart had a huge, unresolved crush on one of the puppets and had gone to great lengths to procure the video. But instead of watching, I was bending his ear about my argument with Tiffany.

"There may be a kernel of truth to what she said, of course, but it's a gross oversimplification," Stewart said dismissively.

I'd had my grandmother's antique wingback chair reupholstered in the mid-'90s, in a dark red damask with a gold fleur-de-lis pattern. I was sick to death of it but was happy now that I hadn't gotten around to replacing it; Stewart was born to sit in that chair. It was grand and it suited him perfectly, as he was like a count from a mysterious country, born a century ago. Indeed, his diction was so perfect and his vocabulary so refined that ordinary people often mistook him for a foreigner. And having read all of Jane Austen before he was eight, Stewart's sense of protocol was monolithic and his wit unparalleled. Though far too young, he was of the "old school," and when Stewart spoke, people listened.

"Teenagers are evil, vile creatures," he continued, not caring if Tiffany overheard him. "Their anger is such that no weapon in their extensive arsenals is too brutal to be deployed. If I were king, all children between twelve and twenty-one would be removed from society."

"No, seriously, Stewart. What if she's right?" I asked, frustrated. "What if I am too controlling to have a relationship? And what if I wanted Tiffany to move in with me only to have someone to control? What better project for a control freak than a child?" I was a hopeless case, I'd decided, driven by nothing but sickness.

"Oh, *pish,*" Stewart responded. "That's nonsense, Edwin. Don't you dare pathologize an heroic act of kindness. I won't allow it. You love her to the core, and everything you're doing stems from that love, not from a personality flaw." He paused for emphasis, but I knew he hadn't concluded. "She has many more poisoned arrows in her quiver, I'm afraid. What you must do is develop thicker skin."

"God, you're so right, Stewart. But I don't know how."

"Oh, you'll do it naturally; it will be necessary if you are to continue helping Tiffany. I have no doubt your hide will leather presently."

"Thanks for your confidence in me," I said. "But what should I do about this current situation?"

"It's simple," he answered decisively. "Tiffany violated the rules, so she must be punished."

"Ugh. The idea of keeping her in all weekend while I'm still recovering is a bit daunting. Maybe I'll let her go out but make her stay home *next* weekend."

"Absolutely not," Stewart responded. "The punishment must take place directly after the act or its meaning is lost. Would you like me to take her to the revival of

John Adams's *The Death of Klinghoffer* at BAM on Saturday? I hear it's even longer than Wagner's *Ring Cycle*."

"No, my parents took Tiffany on a cruise when she was ten, so she might actually like that," I joked. "I'll just keep her in this weekend. Maybe we'll get some quality time in — watch some good movies or color her hair or something. It's been since the fall that we've enjoyed a Saturday night together."

"Well, don't make it too much fun or it won't feel like punishment," Stewart warned.

"In truth, Tiffany is going to be furious," I said, "and I find myself feeling a bit afraid of her lately."

"Of course you do. Teenage girls are very scary. I don't know about you, but some of them were far worse toward me than the boys were when I was in high school. Especially the beautiful, cool ones — the girls who dated the handsome, athletic boys. They had so much already; their schadenfreude always puzzled me." Stewart was right. It was the *girls* who would scream "faggot" as I walked down the hallway, so everyone could hear. The boys were more subtle, mumbling their contempt or jabbing an elbow out here and there as they passed by.

Stewart came over and sat on the edge of my bed. "But you mustn't let her see your fear. If you do, all will be for naught," he whispered. "Think of her as a wild mustang. The first thing a cowboy learns is never to show his fear. Respect, yes. Fear, no. If she knows he is afraid, that cowboy will never tame her." He stared at me conspiratorially for a moment.

"Spoken like a true turban cowboy," I quipped. "I think I'll take your advice." A Wild West analogy was about the last thing I expected from Stewart Fischer, but then again, he has always been a man of hidden talents and interests.

After Stewart left that night, I spoke with Tiffany about my concern regarding her choice of friends, especially Jenise. I told her that I was worried she might be creating the same type of social circle she had back in Connecticut. Tiffany was not receptive to my thoughts.

The next morning when I awoke, long after she'd left for school, I found a piece of looseleaf paper slipped under my door.

I don't want to hear it again!! I don't want to hear how I failed horribly at being the person you fucking want me to be. I'm sorry I don't meet your standards. I'm sorry my friends don't meet your standards. Do you want me to just drop them because they don't take school as seriously as you want ME to? Well I won't. There was a period of time where I considered it. I considered dropping the only people who I ever cared about almost as much as I care about you. The difference between them and you is that they don't constantly point out my flaws. They don't pay attention to things like that, they make me feel good. All you do is help me to realize I am shit. All you do is complain about me and pretend that you are giving me valuable advice about life because it makes you feel more important. You think that because you are so "successful" that if you say it, then I will be influenced by your powerful words. Well, you are on a goddamn power trip, that's all I have learned from you, so get the fuck off my ass!!! I didn't drop my friends, I will never drop them for you. But I am a pathetic person, not because I didn't do what you required, but because I even considered it.

With each letter or poem, Tiffany was becoming more articulate at expressing her rage and frustration, making me wonder how I could encourage her to write without our fighting first. (She'd recently mentioned that there was going to be a poetry contest at school, and I'd been trying to convince her to submit some of her work. I even typed up her poems for her. "They're too personal," she kept saying. "It's too embarrassing." There's still time, I thought now.) As far as the substance of her letter went, it reconfirmed that I would be unable to control, or even influence, my niece's choice of friends. If I forbade her to see Jenise, Tiffany would go out of her way to seek her out. And as for the poisoned arrows, I'm not quite sure why, but this time they simply failed to pierce. After all, what teenager *doesn't* think every adult in a position of authority is bottoming out on a power fetish?

# Man, Interrupted

"Uncle Eddy, what the H are you doing?" Tiffany had come home from school and found me sitting on the floor of my bedroom surrounded by personal care products. I'd trained her to stop saying "hell," as it was a slippery slope down to "fuck." (Not that the plan was working.)

"I'm removing the price tags from all this stuff. I finally ventured out of the apartment — for a major Rite Aid spree." It was a freezing but gloriously sunny day and it felt good to join the world of the living again, despite my earlier fantasies of leaving it behind.

"So why are you taking off the prices?" She stood above me with her eyebrows furrowed, as though she was concerned that I might have finally gone insane.

"Because I own these things now and you don't leave price tags on things you *own*." Tiffany continued to stare. "I mean, you don't leave price tags on a pair of shoes or a new shirt, do you?"

"That's because you *wear* them, Uncle Eddy. We're talking deodorant and razor blades here."

"Okay, I'll try again. You wouldn't leave the price on a new lamp or a set of drinking glasses, would you?"

"I think you've been cooped up in here too long and your OCD is acting up." She wasn't going to let it go.

"I've always done this, Tiffany. I don't like opening the medicine cabinet and seeing price tags. It's just an idiosyncrasy." I knew it was obsessive-compulsive behavior, but I wasn't going to let her win. She'd busted me just two weeks ago after I'd tucked the shoelaces into every pair of shoes in the apartment. (I hate it when they hang out.) "That's an SAT word, by the way; it means 'quirky habit or character trait.'"

"Okay, if you say so, Uncle Eddy," she placated me. "Are you going to *venture out* again over the weekend?" I could tell she wanted to get rid of me and I couldn't blame her; I'm sure neither of us was thrilled with the idea of being alone together for two full days and three evenings.

"Definitely," I answered. "I'm hoping to go out tomorrow or Sunday afternoon to see *The Hours.* Do you want to join me?"

"Didn't you say that that book made you cry?" she asked. "Why do you want to see something that's going to depress you?"

"The book moved me," I said, "which is different from being depressed. Good art always stirs up my emotions, probably because I recognize some personal truth in it. Maybe I'll be sad, but it also feels good to know I'm not alone with that truth. Does that make any sense?"

"Yeah, I think so," Tiffany responded as she sat down on the floor next to me and leaned against the wingback chair. "That's why I feel so inspired when I listen to Nirvana. It's like they're playing to me." She paused. "No, I mean playing *for* me, saying what I'm thinking. I always want to write poetry or something after I listen to them."

"Exactly," I said, as I happily scraped the price off a bottle of Curél body lotion with my fingernail. "That's because you're creative, Tiffany, and you're inspired by other artists." When I smiled and looked into her gold-green eyes, I saw that my smile was returned.

I was glad Tiffany hadn't asked exactly what truth I'd recognized in *The Hours*. Though she knew I took medication for depression, she never delved into my history of battling it, which was probably just as well. Maybe she thought a person simply got sad for a long time, went to the doctor, and then began taking pills. I suppose that might be the case for some people, but it wasn't for me.

Virginia Woolf's losing battle with mental illness is the central thread of both the book and film versions of *The Hours*, but it was the fictional 1950s housewife Laura Brown's story with which I identified. Laura had been the odd, introspective high school girl who, in another decade, would have attended Smith or Vassar and become a writer. But it's the '50s, and on the day the story is set, Laura awakens (both literally and figuratively) to a life so completely alien to who she truly is that, by day's end, she has contemplated suicide and abandoned her husband and young son. Her life as the wife of the high school football star and decorated war hero, the mother of a beautiful little boy, and a homemaker in upscale suburban Los Angeles was the picture-perfect 1950s life — a dream come true for any young woman. But for Laura Brown it was a sentence worse than death.

My battle with depression began during my second year of law school. The first year had been all about proving to myself (and to my father?) that I could succeed in that cutthroat world of (mostly) heterosexual, conservative "One Ls" — young men and women who'd come of age during the Reagan years while I was smoking pot, acting, and participating in civil disobedience with ACT UP. After years of hiding out in the insular world of gay artists, cater waiters, and activists, I was now going to "play ball with the boys." And I succeeded — to no one's greater surprise than my own — and finished in the top 2 percent of my freshman class. But during my second year the reality of my life choice began to set in. I'd been accepted into a litigation clinic and spent a great deal of time working on real cases, much like a Legal Aid attorney would. The endless paperwork, mind-boggling rules of procedure, and the excruciating snail's pace of the cases left me frustrated and dissatisfied. As the pressures of law review, course work, and my caseload mounted, a creeping sense of anxiety began to gnaw at me. I started feeling that I was a fraud and became crippled by self-doubt. I could no longer speak up in classes or seminars, feeling that my every word, my every idea, would expose me as an imposter. When uncontrollable crying bouts followed, I sought out my ex-therapist and was quickly put on medication. By the end of second year I was functioning full tilt again and, after a glamorous summer as an associate at a venerable "white shoe" law firm, I accepted an attorney position for when I graduated the following year.

I know now that, like Laura Brown, I was entering the wrong life. The anxiety and depression were not caused by the demands of my workload (I'd always been a hard worker) but by the disconnect between my heart and my head. My mind told me that an intelligent, educated man of thirty *cannot* be a waiter, even if he's pursuing an acting career or writing a novel on the side. Whether my thinking was guided by societal or parental expectations, or both, I believed such a life would be a self-indulgent, shameful waste. So I ignored my heart, which held no passion for the law, and with a Band-Aid of psychotropic drugs holding together the schism inside me, I willfully marched forward. Swelled by the validation of guaranteed riches, a gorgeous new boyfriend, and my status as Big Man on Campus, I eventually decided I no longer needed the "crutch" of antidepressants; I stopped taking them by the end of my last year of law school.

Over the following summer I studied maniacally for the bar exam and, after I sat for it, took an amazing two-month trip to Africa, Greece, and Turkey. When I returned, I began my career as a hotshot Wall Street attorney, $90,000 in debt and raring to go, or so I deluded myself into believing. (I wouldn't have done so well in law school and landed this big job if it weren't the right thing for me, I'd convinced myself while watching the sun set over the caldera on Santorini.)

In just a matter of weeks I was closing my office door and lifting my chair up over my head, making sure I'd be able to throw it through the sealed window when I finally got up the nerve to jump the thirty stories to my death. Within a few months, at the urging of my therapist and boyfriend, I admitted myself to the psychiatric ward of a huge New York City hospital.

"I'm trying to understand your depression," my father said when he visited me there. We were sitting in the ugly, fluorescent-lit day room, where elderly lunatics milled about aimlessly among scraggly potted plants and unused game tables. (My anxiety level had been so high that the admitting physician had placed me in the senior citizens' ward; they were apparently quieter than the crazies my own age.) I was on multiple medications by that point and felt very relaxed, as long as I didn't think beyond the next five minutes.

"In my day," my dad continued, "we didn't think about things like 'personal happiness.' It was all so structured. You got married after high school or college, bought a house if you were lucky, and had children. There was no time to think about how happy you were or weren't."

"Yeah, but by the seventies you were living *The Ice Storm*," I said. "You drank martinis, swapped wives, and had no idea what was going on with your children." I'd figured all bets were off in the psych ward, so I could say anything.

"Well, I don't know about wife swapping, but I get your point. I still haven't been able to bring myself to watch that film," he said. "I guess I'm afraid to. Probably a little too close to home, you know?"

"Yes, I know," I responded.

"I think I've figured out what's caused your depression."

"I guess at this point it qualifies as a nervous breakdown," I said wearily. Since I'd first heard the term as a little boy — probably in relation to one of Elizabeth Taylor's many "collapses" — I'd believed that one lay in my future. There was a degree of relief in finally getting it over with.

"So what's your theory?" I asked. This ought to be good.

My father looked at me and concern filled his painfully blue eyes. "I think you're depressed because you've never fulfilled yourself as an artist, and you're afraid that time is running out."

No words came; only tears. My father slid toward me on the turquoise plastic-covered sofa and put his arm awkwardly around me, like a fourteen-year-old boy on his first movie date.

"How could you know that?" I asked.

"Because you're my son," he said, squeezing my shoulder. "I know you."

I was released in just two weeks, medicated and rested, but there was no going back to my mistaken life.

"So what do you say, Tiffany?" I asked as I gathered up my Rite Aid booty. "Will you go see *The Hours* with me? It's your one chance to get out this weekend while you're grounded."

"No thanks," she said, following me to the bathroom, where I began arranging the new products into still lifes on the medicine cabinet's shelves. "The story sounds a little boring to me. If I *were* to be allowed out, I'd see *House of 1,000 Corpses* instead."

That weekend, while I was mostly home recuperating and Tiffany was grounded, I never mentioned the lovely missive she'd left under my door. Instead I tried several times to start "meaningful" conversations with her. After an initial couple of hours of stomping around over being punished, she seemed to return to the old Tiffany I knew, dancing around the apartment with the phone glued to her head, emitting the occasional squeal of delight or horror (I often couldn't tell which), and playing both the TV and her stereo at the same time. Though my fear that Tiffany had no conscience had tapered off with the pain-killers, I attempted to discuss "values" with her. "My friends are the most important thing in the world to me," she said with a finality that ended the conversation before it began. When I brought up the issue of her father's starting a new family, she said, "If it makes him happy, then it's cool." And when I tried to talk about her mom's newfound unemployment, she only got angry: "She should sue those F-ing bastards." My niece never spoke to me of her Wednesday counseling sessions at school — except to say "I hate that lady" — but I hoped she was telling Judith Martin about these important developments in her family's lives.

Tiffany did speak repeatedly about her creative endeavors that weekend, though. It seemed that if I kept her in the apartment long enough, she would eventually work on her singing or jot something down in her journal — one of the few upsides to grounding her. She was studying voice privately with Ellen Foley, a former Broadway star and singer with Meat Loaf, and she needed to practice her scales as well as particular songs. (I'd spent many a night during my senior year of high school down by the reservoir with "Paradise by the Dashboard Light" blasting from an open car while my friends and I sat outside by the water, smoking joints and drinking beer. Though I screeched along with seeming glee, internally I lamented that it was only the straight kids who had access to that particular heaven. It was one of life's strange synchronicities that Tiffany was now studying with the woman whose voice I associated so closely with my own teenage longing.)

"I want to form an all-girl rock band,"

she declared after a grueling session of warbling along with Mariah Carey and Sarah McLachlan in her bedroom. "That would be mad cool."

"You absolutely should," I said. "I'm sure you'll meet other singers and musicians in college, if not before. With your voice, you can do Broadway, pop, or rock and roll." I wasn't so sure about the rock part, but I figured people who could sing in the other two styles could screech as well, if they chose to.

"But I want to do it now, Uncle Eddy. I feel like I can't wait." Tiffany executed one of her mock Britney Spears moves — spinning, then thrusting her hips, followed by a head roll. Her long hair punctuated the step with a flourish. "We'd have the best choreography and wear the sexiest outfits."

"Don't forget there's music involved too," I said, laughing. "And that's why there aren't too many bands of fourteen-year-olds around."

"I can't wait to start auditioning for real jobs next year," she said, performing pseudo ballet leaps down the hallway toward her bedroom. We'd agreed (or rather, she'd been told) that if she ended her freshman year with decent grades, she could begin auditioning for commercials and other acting work after school during her sophomore year.

One of my best friends in college had made a pile of money by doing commercials while in high school. I was envious of him and also resentful that my parents had not encouraged me to pursue acting professionally when I was a kid. Now that I had Tiffany, though, I realized how challenging the logistics of being a stage mother would be — and we lived right in the heart of New York City. But I'd often felt that I hadn't been given enough opportunities in high school to explore creative outlets. Though I found some solace (and self-esteem) by taking art courses as all of my electives, my afternoons were spent hanging out and weekends partying. I was trying to offer Tiffany more than that.

Besides logistics, there were also the vagaries of both failure *and* success to consider. I understood intimately the hazards of failure, but what if Tiffany were to succeed? Didn't most young actors and actresses end up with drug problems, having seen and done it all too soon? I comforted myself that since Tiffany was fourteen going on thirty anyway, at least the opportunities and life lessons that came with an early career would give these years some focus and depth — as well as maybe some income.

On Sunday afternoon, after I'd come home with my eyes all swollen from *The Hours*, Tiffany handed me a new poem.

What do you try to protect me from?
From love, from hate?
From the world's own realities?
Locked up, I cry
and I taste the sorrow.
It's sweet, it's salty; it hurts.
What do you try to keep me from
   knowing?
Your mistakes?
Your states of insecurity tell the truth;
they open up a gate, but close one as
   well.
In pain, I realize
the immaturity of another
shall instigate my independence.
It pushes me away,
but draws me in.

I read the poem, stunned. For a second I thought it was about Megan but then quickly realized it could just as easily be about me. Underneath the teenage emotionalism seemed to be an exact understanding of something I was just learning: I may have been opening up new worlds for Tiffany, but I would be unable to protect her from the pain they'd inflict. And unavoidably, I could only present those worlds to her through the soiled veil of my own experience.

"You must enter this into the poetry contest" was all I managed to say.

# Making Angels

"What . . . are . . . you . . . doing?" I bit my words out through gritted teeth, desperately trying to not scream, for Tiffany's sake. The nurse was on her third attempt to properly hook the IV up to the back of Tiffany's hand, and she'd failed once again. A stream of blood shot out of the needle onto the starched white hospital sheets, followed quickly by a splatter of droplets.

"Just keep looking at me, Tiffany," I said, seeing the fear in her eyes. She knew from my voice that something was wrong and squeezed my hand even tighter.

"I don't know why that keeps happening," the nurse said plangently. "Her hand is so small, with such tiny veins."

"Well, you obviously found one." Since I refused to take my eyes from my niece's, I threw the daggers with my voice.

"I'll go get the resident on duty," the nurse said, slinking out through the curtain. With my free hand, I quickly rearranged the sheets and blanket to hide the blood.

"She just had a little problem getting the IV in, sweetie." I dabbed at Tiffany's head with a cool compress. "The resident will do it just fine."

"That really hurt," she said softly as a single tear formed in the corner of her eye.

I leaned over and kissed her damp, ashen forehead. "It's going to be okay," I whispered. "You'll feel better soon, I promise."

On the Wednesday morning following the weekend that Tiffany was grounded, she woke up with a terrible sore throat. I grabbed my trusty *Rocky Horror* flashlight (no, I still hadn't bought a regular one, completely out of cheapness) and took a look. Her tonsils were indeed dark red — and as lumpy as always — but there were no visible white spots. I took her temperature with the digital thermometer I'd bought during her last bout of sore throat and, once again, was struck by her vulnerability as she looked up at me, waiting patiently. The raging young woman had slipped back inside the little girl.

"You have a slight fever." I pushed the moist, clammy hair from her forehead. "Go back to sleep for a while and we'll go to the doctor when I'm ready for work."

Though we had no appointment, Dr. Levine didn't keep us waiting long. I was grateful, as it was my first week back to work after my surgery and I'd barely dented the piles. Plus, Tiffany needed to be back in bed as soon as possible; that much was clear, no matter the diagnosis.

"I don't see any strep, and the swipe the nurse took came back negative," he said, "but it's not always accurate, so we're going to do a blood test just to make sure."

"Omigod, no!" my niece blurted out, alarm in her eyes. "Please, please. I can't stand needles."

"It'll be all right, Tiffany. I'll stay with you," I tried to pacify her. (I didn't tell her that I was twenty-seven before I stopped passing out during blood tests.) "It'll be good to know for sure whether or not you have strep." Or, God forbid, something else, I worried.

While the nurse drew Tiffany's blood, my niece and I looked directly at each other and I held her hand with both of mine. I described the giant, fluffy clouds that float over the crystal lake in the Adirondacks where we'd spent so many summer vacations. I reminded her how warm the wooden raft felt against your skin after climbing out of the chilly water.

My technique was a success; Tiffany remained conscious.

"We'll know the results by Friday," Dr. Levine said. "In the meantime, the usual — salt gargles, aspirin, and drink as many fluids as you possibly can."

"Shouldn't she start a cycle of antibiotics, just in case?" I asked. "That way if the test is positive, she'll be ahead of the game."

"I'd really rather not," Dr. Levine said apologetically. "Antibiotics are used far too often." He seemed to be asking me rather than telling me, which was probably his strategy for getting me to agree. Mensch that he is, Dr. Levine is also no dummy. I agreed.

Tiffany's throat grew worse over the next two days; I could actually see that her tonsils were swollen — something for which I'd thought a trained eye was required. Her fever grew too, though we kept it down with regular doses of aspirin. (I'd created a chart for Tiffany to fill out throughout the day, which she did; it recorded her salt gargles, aspirin, vitamin C, and fluids.) By Friday I was a sleep-deprived wreck from getting up with Tiffany during the night. People at work stopped me in the hallway to say, "Are you all right? You look ter-

*rible.*" I'd say yes and thank them when I really wanted to scream, "Of course I look terrible! I'm exhausted and I have been since last September. Oh, and by the way, you look fat!" But I didn't.

All day Friday I tried relentlessly to get the results of Tiffany's blood test, to no avail. Most times when I called the family practice, I wound up in a hellish voice mail labyrinth — that is, if I didn't get a busy signal. The few messages I left for Dr. Levine went unreturned. Between that exercise in futility and repeatedly calling each of Tiffany's teachers for the three days' worth of missed homework assignments, I lost almost an entire day's work. To add to the stress, every so often I called Tiffany to check in. Her voice grew coarser and weaker with each call, and she complained that the pain of swallowing was getting worse. Poor kid, I thought, and reminded myself to stop at the video store and pick up a pile of scary movies on my way home.

I hate leaving things unfinished at work, especially on a Friday evening. If phone calls went unreturned or paperwork went unanswered, I'd beat myself up about it intermittently throughout the weekend and never be able to fully relax. (Steven, also a "recovering Catholic," often chastised me for this, telling me to return my hair shirt to the rectory.) My neck and shoulders were tightly clenched as I left the office that night, my desk strewn with pink message slips and half-read contracts. All relegated to Manic Monday, I thought; that should be fun. As I walked along the north side of Washington Square Park, I gulped the frigid air to calm myself before arriving home to Tiffany. Instead, the icy air jumpstarted my asthma and I had to remove my gloves to dig through my briefcase for my inhaler. Instantly my fingers were frozen, *Goddamn that fucking doctor!* my mind screamed. How could he leave a little girl hanging like that? And goddamn this motherfucking cold! How much more of this can we take, for chrissakes? I sat down on the concrete steps of a stunning Greek Revival row house to let the Albuterol kick in and catch my breath.

After almost twenty years in New York, I'd developed a true love-hate relationship with the Big Apple (an idiotic nickname that falls on the hate side). And this was definitely a hate moment. I couldn't imagine myself living anywhere else, but sometimes life just seemed impossibly difficult here. The schlepping was endless: if it wasn't my gym bag, briefcase, or both, it was groceries, bottled water, manuscripts, or whatever else had to be taken from here to there. Life was spent unpacking and repacking bags, always organizing something to be slung over one's back and taken somewhere else. In the summer you're drenched in sweat within five minutes of leaving home; in the winter you're weighted down with even more bulk and are forever removing and redonning garments when going in and out of buildings. And when a day's toiling is *finally* over, you schlep home to your shoe box apartment to listen to your neighbors clomping around overhead.

I lifted my head from my hands and looked across the street toward Washington Square Park. Soft lantern light glinted on black wrought-iron fences, casting long shadows across the blue-gray night snow and the ample walkways lined with scores of empty wooden benches. It was an old black-and-white photograph come to life, timeless, and I remembered that Marcel Duchamp had once climbed atop Stanford White's huge marble arch to declare Greenwich Village the "Republic of Bohemia," or something like that. These days it felt more like Siberia than Bohemia, but I let go a long sigh and remembered for the eight millionth time why I lived in this crowded, grating nutcase of a town.

"You've really done everything you can do, Eddy," Megan advised me on the phone. I'd called her for the tenth time that week when Tiffany woke up on Saturday morning crying from the pain. "Children get sick all the time, especially Tiffany with her throat. Sometimes you just have to wait it out."

"Okay, but I'm starting to get nervous," I whined. "I've left a message for the doctor who's covering for Dr. Levine this weekend. We'll see what she says."

"I'm sorry you have to deal with this, Eddy," Megan said.

"Please, don't worry about me." I tried to assuage her guilt. "Let's just hope this clears up in the next couple of days. Tiffany is miserable."

"Well, it'll keep her out of trouble for a while, at least," Megan said, looking darkly at the bright side.

"Right?" I laughed. "So, what's the status with Eric?" I spaced out the conversations in which I broached this topic, and it had been some time since the last one.

"I've told him several times that we're no longer a couple, and I'm not having sex with him anymore. But he keeps coming over and shoveling the driveway every time it snows."

"Do you invite him in?" I was trying to get as clear a picture as possible.

"Well, just for hot chocolate or something." She sounded sad. "I feel so sorry for him, you know? He has nobody." Megan had a history of rescuing men who were weaker (and less intelligent) than she.

"Sounds like he's manipulating you. You're going to have to show some resolve here." I was moving dangerously close to criticizing her — something Megan feels is a habit of mine — and I didn't want to make her feel worse. "But I understand it's difficult," I quickly added.

"Yeah, it is." I could tell she wanted to get off now. "I'll check in with you tomorrow. And don't worry, Eddy, she'll be fine."

"I'll try not to," I said. "We're going to watch *The Exorcist* now, which should be nice and relaxing." Megan laughed her high-pitched staccato giggle, which was infectious and good to hear. "Give my love to Sammy," I said and hung up.

Tiffany spent a great deal of the weekend sleeping. Her fever never spiked, probably because of the aspirin (which I was now crushing for her), but she was pale and weak. I tried to get her to drink fluids at every turn, but I think the pain of swallowing was slowing down her intake. I'd stocked up on Jell-O, chicken broth, and Ensure shakes; at this point she wasn't having much luck with solid food.

When I looked into her throat on Sunday morning, I panicked. Her tonsils were almost touching her epiglottis, and they were covered with a white film. My first thought was, What if her throat closes up and she's unable to breathe? I'd never had an ill person, much less a child, completely entrusted to my care, and it was frightening. I shook off these thoughts, got a grip on myself, and gave my niece a sympathetic smile.

"It's that bad, huh?" she whispered.

"No, sweetie, but it's definitely gotten a little worse," I lied, grabbing a glass of water from her bedside table. "Take a sip of this for me." She took a tiny amount of water into her mouth and winced with pain as she tried to squeeze it down her gullet. The moment it went through, I could actually hear it, like the exaggerated swallow of a child imitating fear. Only this was real. Tiffany insisted on looking into the bathroom mirror with the flashlight, and there was no dissuading her.

*"Ewww!"* she screamed as best she could. "That is *sooo* gross!"

The covering physician returned my call that afternoon and advised me to wait for the results on Monday morning before doing anything.

"Is there any chance that she won't be able to breathe?" I asked sweetly. This was one situation where I would not get bitchy for the delay in having my call returned. Annoyed short-order cooks might spit in your food, but a vengeful doctor could kill you.

"No," the doctor answered definitively in her Indian accent. "Unless there is an allergic reaction, which isn't the case here, the throat will not close up completely. Swallowing may be difficult, but unless your daughter is complaining specifically about her breathing, she should be okay." I purposely hadn't bothered to explain that Tiffany was my niece; it prompted too many extraneous questions. I'd learned to simply say, "I have a teenage girl who . . ." Most people just assumed she was my daughter, and that was fine with me.

What the doctor said made some sense to me, but I couldn't help wondering. What if there's a moment where her throat actually closes and she's not able to complain about it? I called my sister Kathleen for her advice as a nurse, and then called my mom and at least six of my closest friends for their opinions. Everyone concurred with the doctor, saying to wait and see. It was only Orly who pointed out — in her lawyerly compassion — that since I'd called the doctor, Megan, and everyone I knew, there was no way the blame could fall to me if anything happened. "Gee, that makes me feel a whole lot better," I said, having the only giggle of the weekend. "You got all the angles covered, huh? What an attorney," I teased.

The previous three nights Tiffany and I had slept with our bedroom doors open, and I'd been awakened several times each night by a tiny voice calling out in the darkness. A soft, plaintive "Uncle Eddy?" would invade my anxiety dreams, which all featured Tiffany, of course. I'd lost her in a giant mob, or we'd be swimming in rough surf and suddenly her head would disappear. When I heard my name cried out, I'd search the water or the crowd until I woke up, realizing it was coming from the next room. Both relieved and anxious, I'd patter through the darkness to bring her water, aspirin, or Chloraseptic spray — whatever she needed. Sometimes she just wanted me to lie with her and rub her back until she was able to fall asleep again. I'd whisper that I understood how being sick was scary and lonely, but that I was there for her. "Draw an angel on my back with your finger," she requested one night. As I obliged, I realized I'd never felt more needed by another person in my entire life.

That Sunday night, though, the picture was not so sweet. Despite the doctor's (and everyone else's) assurances, there was not a chance in hell I would get a moment of sleep. Tiffany's breathing was far worse than Regan's had been in *The Exorcist.* (Which, by the way, had been a huge mistake to watch; I'd forgotten that the movie is as much about an hysterical parent who's powerless to make her child well as it is about demonic possession. *Perfect!*) Each breath Tiffany took sounded like the dreaded death rattle — like it could be her last. I lay there wide-eyed, listening intently, jumping up with the slightest pause or change in pattern. "The Lord is my shepherd," I'd start the Twenty-third Psalm for the umpteenth time but never finish. Instead, I thought about how I was always reading stories about some illness not caught in time. I remembered that someone I knew had lost his twenty-one-year-old son to a blood infection, after only a two-day illness. If they'd have taken him to the hospital sooner, would he have survived? If I made the wrong decision, so many lives could be affected, most of all Tiffany's. "Lord, make me an instrument of your peace." I tried the St. Francis Prayer, but that didn't work either. I was terrified, and no matter how hard I tried, I couldn't *not* think about my niece Heather.

At the moment my mother called to tell me there had been a crisis with my eldest niece, I was on the other line having phone sex with a medical resident in Washington, DC. I'd met him and his lover on a trip to Key West I'd taken with Eugene and Orly to celebrate my thirty-fifth birthday. The Washingtonians were my favorite gift to myself. Now the more handsome one was speaking to me from the resident's lounge at the hospital, which I thought was a bit odd. I excused myself and returned to my mom.

"She's in the hospital, honey. It's bad. You'd better come up right away."

"Was there an accident?" I asked.

"No, but she's very sick, Ed. Just come."

Her voice was quivering with tears. I clicked back to the resident and told him I'd have to take a rain check.

The ride on Metro-North through Westchester and into Putnam County was interminable. I desperately tried to concentrate on my prayers, but it was hard to do anything but say "Please God, please God, please God" over and over again.

When I arrived in Brewster, I took a taxi to my parents' house, where they'd left a note saying they'd gone back to the hospital in Danbury and that I could use their second car to join them. For some reason I called Kathleen's house, and to my surprise, she was home.

"I had to come home to feed the dogs," she said, her voice flat and affectless.

"Will you be there for a little while? I'll come there first," I said. "I don't even know how to find the hospital on my own."

"Yes, I'll be here for at least a half hour," she said, and hung up.

When I arrived at Kathleen's, she was sitting at the kitchen table drinking a cup of coffee and slowly folding laundry. She didn't get up to greet me with the usual hug and kiss but simply said, "Hello, Eddy," in the strange, dulled voice I'd heard over the phone.

"What happened, Kathleen?"

"It was an aneurysm. She began having seizures this morning at work and went unconscious immediately. A coworker heard her fall down . . . and she hasn't regained consciousness since. Her supervisor called me and I got to the hospital before the ambulance. When they wheeled her in on the stretcher, I could see that she was seizing. Her toes were curling inward, which isn't a good sign. It means brain damage, Eddy." She paused and I sat silent, stunned. "I can see the future," Kathleen said softly as she folded each article meticulously, pressing the fabric against the table to make creases. I stared at the repetitive movements, searching for comfort in them, but found none. Instead, I recognized some of the clothing as Heather's. "They performed surgery to relieve the pressure, but there's no prognosis yet. You can follow me back to the hospital."

Megan and Tyler, Kathleen's husband, were at the hospital when we arrived. My parents had left to grab a bite to eat. Within minutes, the doctor came to tell us they needed to run an emergency test, and then orderlies flew by wheeling a gurney holding Heather. I caught a glimpse of my niece's thick, strawberry blond hair streaming up the pillow, as well as the wide, white bandage that had been wrapped around most of her head. We sat there for an indeterminate amount of time, no one saying much, all of us pale and lifeless. Occasionally Megan reached over to hold my hand or I stroked Kathleen's shoulder. I refilled paper cups with water from the cooler in the waiting room and delivered them in silence. The doctor, whose face I have never been able to remember, returned after a long while and told us that all brain activity had ceased in my niece. She was being kept alive with a respirator and a heart pump. It was not a coma, as there was no chance she would ever wake up. Heather was, in essence, dead.

Kathleen seemed to fall into Tyler and they held each other. But Megan let out a wail and began to slide off her chair in my direction. I caught hold of her and held on, gulping in breaths of air to keep from imploding. She sobbed convulsively for a few minutes and then went limp in my arms. It felt like only moments had elapsed when a pleasant-looking lady approached us with a folder in her hand. She had come to speak with Kathleen and Tyler about organ donation. They went into a small, glassed-in room and sat at a table. I could see tears streaming down Kathleen's face as she nodded her head yes. Tyler had his arm around my sister but his face was expressionless, his eyes unblinking.

"Hello?" My mom's bell-like voice came from around the corner. Megan and I jumped up and went to her. When she saw our faces she knew. Luckily a nurse had been watching and wheeled a chair directly behind my mother just at the moment she went down. Megan knelt before her and, with Mom leaning forward, they held each other.

I went out into the waiting room and found my father standing at the water-cooler.

"What's happened?" he asked, seeing my colorless face. I pulled him to a quiet corner, near a window.

"She's gone, Dad," I said, disbelieving the words even as I spoke them.

"Oh no," he said, his face collapsing into grief. "No, no, no," he repeated as he sank onto the radiator in front of the window and fell against me. I rubbed my father's gray head as he held onto my waist, his body racked with sobs.

Dawn eventually came after that endless

Sunday night of lying awake listening to Tiffany breathe. I stared at the clock, waiting for it to be time to call my boss and tell him I wouldn't be coming in; there was no way I was going to leave Tiffany alone in her condition. I heard the thud of my *New York Times* hit my front door and was grateful that I'd now have a distraction for the next two hours, if I could focus my tired eyes enough to read.

Skimming through the Metro section, a headline caught my eye: "Search Effort off City Island Fails to Find Four Teenagers." Tiffany had heard from Aleksi over the weekend that their friend Peter's older brother had gone missing with three of his friends, and that it was believed they'd taken a boat out into the Long Island Sound from City Island on Friday night. I read now in disbelief that the boys were probably trying to row out to Hart Island, almost a mile away — in an eight-foot row-boat on a fifteen-degree night and in choppy, thirty-three-degree waters. I literally shuddered at the idea of such a horrible death and thought of Peter, the innocent-looking, blond, boy-next-door type — and how what remained of his childhood was now lost along with his brother. Though the article didn't mention it, I wondered if drugs or alcohol were involved, and if the boys' parents were thinking that they might have done something to prevent the accident, though I couldn't imagine what. Beyond that, I wouldn't allow myself to think about what those families were going through right then. Between the loss of Heather and being responsible for a teenager myself now, it was the unthinkable.

Finally, the clock struck eight thirty, a time my boss was likely to be at his desk.

"It's Tiffany. She's still sick." I felt my chin crinkle and my lips go white.

"Ed, are you still there?" he asked.

"Yes," I muttered, but that was all I could say. The stress of the last five days, combined with a lack of sleep, had worn me down.

"Ed, you've got to be strong for her," he said. "Don't let her see that it's getting to you."

"She's sleeping, and I'm in the living room," I choked out. After a few seconds I was able to describe her symptoms as well as my fears.

"I think you should go to the hospital," he said definitively. "Think about it; there's no downside and it will give you peace of mind, which you obviously don't have now."

"Thank you," I said with relief. "That's exactly what I needed you to say." My boss had two children, including a daughter Tiffany's age, and had been unbelievably supportive since my niece moved in. He wouldn't allow me to use personal time when I ran down to Tiffany's school for the afternoon or when I spent mornings with her at the doctor, and he understood when I ran out of work at six o'clock on the dot. "You're the best," I said. "I'll call you later to tell you how it went." I hung up and went down the hall to rouse the patient.

Tiffany and I waited only a minute before the resident came into our curtained-off section of the pediatric emergency room. He was scarily young and too handsome, with buzz-cut blond hair and sky blue eyes. In his tennis shoes, chinos, and short-sleeved polo shirt that matched his eyes, he looked like he'd just gotten off the plane from Iowa. Corn-fed, I couldn't help thinking. Yum. He reminded me of the roommate I'd fallen in love with during college who was now a married born-again Christian practicing medicine in Wisconsin. I still carried a tiny torch for Bill, and my heart melted for a millisecond.

"I hear the nurse had trouble with the IV," the resident said, kneeling down and picking up Tiffany's hand. "I'll take care of it." There were no introductions or bedside chat with the young girl who lay pale and frightened before him.

"Thank you," I responded.

The resident proceeded to have the same problem as the nurse, and Tiffany cried out in pain.

"Can we get a doctor in here?" It was not a question, and I'd said it loud enough to be heard beyond the curtain.

"I *am* a doctor," he said sternly, staring up at me with intense anger in his pretty eyes.

"Then get the IV in properly, *Doctor.*" I did not break eye contact.

After a couple more jabs, the resident succeeded in getting the IV in, hooked it up to a bag of liquid nutrients, and turned to me.

"The attending pediatrician will be in shortly," he said. "I've spoken with her on the phone and she ordered this IV — it should help with her dehydration. Within a couple of hours her coloring should be better and she'll perk up a bit." He left before I could say thank you.

The statuesque pediatrician was an attractive, older Swedish woman — Liv Ullmann with a stethoscope — and her bedside manner made the resident look like de Sade by comparison. She was kind and caring, and she touched Tiffany's face and showed her compassion. She said they would alternate the nutrient drip with a vitamin drip, so Tiffany would need to remain in the hospital for around six hours. Then she asked to speak to me outside the curtain.

"I spoke with Dr. Levine," she said in her *Autumn Sonata* accent, "and the blood test showed that Tiffany has mononucleosis. She also tested positive for a secondary strep — not the type that's usually treated with antibiotics, but a different one."

"Oh, Lord," I said, remembering to breathe. "Are either of them treatable?"

"Well, mononucleosis is not. The only way to get well is to rest. The symptoms of the illness — severe fatigue, dehydration, fevers, for example — can last from three weeks to several months. So enormous amounts of sleep, lots of fluids, and good food are the only remedies."

I couldn't believe what I was hearing. My mind reeled. Three weeks to several months? You've gotta be kidding! After all we've been through, now this! Any other curveballs you're gonna throw our way,

God? *Oh no, I sound like my father!* I immediately tried to focus on the fact that Tiffany didn't have anything more serious than good old mono, the "kissing disease." When the doctor informed me that 85 percent of all Americans test positive for mono by the time they reach adulthood, I felt a bit relieved.

"What about the strep?" I asked.

"I'll give you a liquid antibiotic, which may or may not help. But in any event, the throat should start clearing up. It looks like it's peaked. And cool things — ice pops, Jell-O, tepid pasta — are all better than hot stuff. Cool will help bring the swelling down." She wrote out a prescription and patted my shoulder. "You're new to this, I can tell," she said. "Tiffany's going to be fine. It just might take some time."

"Thank you so much, Doctor. You've been wonderful." My eyes welled up out of relief and gratitude, but I didn't allow them to spill over.

I saw that Tiffany was sleeping soundly, so I left the hospital to fill the prescription. As I ran around the wintry Village picking up supplies, I decided that, being a control freak with a type A personality, I was going to make sure Tiffany's recovery from mono would be one for the records.

# Mother, Do You Think They'll Drop the Bomb?

Marisol slowly moved the video camera closer and closer to Tiffany's mouth, zooming in as she went. Orly and I sat just out of frame, softly singing "Comfortably Numb" by Pink Floyd. "There is no pain, you are receding, a distant ship's smoke on the horizon . . ." Tiffany opened wide as Marisol used her free hand to shine a flashlight into her throat. Right on time — as the entire frame filled with the inside of Tiffany's gullet — Orly and I reached the creepily climactic "I-I-I have become . . . comfortably numb."

Contrary to Dr. Liv Ullmann's prediction, Tiffany's throat had gotten a bit worse since we'd left the hospital the day before. Her tonsils had formed a wall of flesh across the top of her throat and were now indistinguishable from her little punching bag. The whole thing was a startling yellowish white, like a dog's old bone found under the sofa. Tiffany had come up with the idea of videotaping it while Orly and Marisol were visiting. Marisol is a photography-based fine artist who'd recently begun to incorporate video installations into her work, so she quickly came up with a concept and a shooting plan. "You guys are so weird," Megan said when she called in the middle of our shoot to confirm that she was coming down to New York for a couple of days. I could've guessed that she wouldn't understand.

I'd been an OCD machine since Tiffany and I returned from the hospital, changing sheets, scrubbing the bathroom, doing laundry, setting up "nursing stations" in the kitchen and bathroom, calling Tiffany's school and everyone else who needed to know the results of our hospital visit, and generally doing anything I could to make myself feel I could control her recovery. Tiffany, thank God, had indeed perked up a bit from the six hours of intravenous medications. She looked more herself, though her voice was now reduced to a barely decipherable nasal honking. It didn't hurt her to speak, but she sounded so pathetic I encouraged her to remain silent. And her nighttime breathing had softened to a loud snore.

Megan left Sammy with our parents and arrived in the city the following day. A couple of times during Tiffany's most distraught moments, she'd cried out, "Mama! I want my mama!" I'd calmed her, moved that despite all the fighting and the abuse they'd hurled at each other, the primeval mother-child bond still existed. Though Tiffany slept most of the time during Megan's visit, I was glad that her mother was by her side.

Over the next two weeks Tiffany's throat healed, her tonsils slowly retreating to their respective corners. Her teachers sporadically faxed assignments to the apartment, as I'd requested, and I encouraged her to keep up. I was in a difficult position now, though, because all Tiffany had to say was "I'm too tired" and I'd have to acquiesce to her watching TV or sleeping. I was worried that when she started attending school again, she'd play the mono card all the time — with impunity. But I'd have to wait and see.

Tiffany had been excused from her second quarter exams because of her illness, but despite that, when her grades arrived, the news wasn't good. Except for an astounding 96 in math (stink bombs and all), she'd done worse than first semester. Though the A earned her twenty dollars, all the Cs and Ds pulled her report card payoff deep into the red. Tiffany didn't seem particularly disappointed about not earning extra pocket money, which made me question the efficacy of my bribery scheme. But she was thrilled with her A in math, as was I, and I repeatedly praised her for it. I also took advantage of our extra time together during her recuperation to talk about college, careers, and how important these few years would be to her future. If she went to college, I explained, she'd be the first woman on our side of the family to do so.

"Why didn't Mommy or Aunt Kathleen go to college?" she asked.

"Well, your mom didn't do all that well in high school. You need three years of a foreign language to get into college, and when Megan was failing Spanish II for the second time, our parents decided to steer her toward 'secretarial sciences,' which used to be offered as an alternative to college prep, especially for girls."

"Ew," she said, "just because of Spanish?"

"Well, there was definitely an element of sexism involved, I guess." I wanted to make my point about doing well in school, but I also didn't want to lie about my family's history. "You've got to remember too that going to college wasn't the norm in our family," I continued. "Grandpa, his father, Grandma's father, both Grandma's brothers — none of the *men* went to college, never mind the women. I was the first one. Even though there was never a question that I would go, it was a bigger leap for my parents to believe that my sisters should go, or that they'd be successful at it. It's hard to explain."

"Maybe they thought they'd have husbands to take care of them or something," Tiffany said.

"Exactly," I replied. "I think that was in the back of their minds somewhere."

"Boy, were they wrong as far as Mommy and Daddy go," Tiffany said sadly. "What about Aunt Kathleen?"

"Well, she was a good student, but she didn't score well on the SATs, so it was decided she would do a two-year nursing program at a technical school. She started it during her senior year. Aunt Kathleen has done well as a nurse, but she really wanted to be a lawyer. In retrospect, it seems pretty obvious that she could've gone to a community college for two years and then transferred to a bigger college or university. But then again, she and Uncle Tyler were crazy in love when she graduated — and college was not a part of his plan — so who knows what would have happened." I didn't tell her that they were pregnant with Heather even before Tyler — who was a grade behind Kathleen — had graduated high school.

"So why is everyone assuming that me and Sammy will go to college?" she asked.

"Because you're one generation farther along in the evolution of the family," I answered, "and we're catching up to the rest of middle class society. Plus, it's more clear than ever that there isn't a single interesting job that a young person can get without a college degree. *And* that a woman can't and shouldn't count on meeting a man to take care of her."

"I still want to be an architect," Tiffany said proudly. "I love designing cool houses and definitely at least want to design my own."

"Well, you got a ninety-six in math, so now you know you're capable of getting the grades that are necessary for you to become one. If you can improve your other grades, then the door will still be open and your dream still possible."

When I came home from work the next day, Tiffany asked me to sit next to her on the sofa so she could show me something. She'd dug out an old composition book that she'd started drawing in as a young child; she opened it now across our laps. Inside were dozens of designs for magnificent houses. Some had waterfalls in their foyers or wraparound decks with water slides down to gigantic swimming pools; others had only round rooms or rooms whose walls were floor-to-ceiling fish tanks.

"These are wonderful, Tiffany," I said. "If you get the right education, you'll be able to be or do anything you set your mind to."

Of course, if I had my druthers, she'd be a famous movie actress or recording star. But I didn't tell her that. Since getting Tiffany through high school and into college was priority number one, having her sights set on an architecture degree was just fine with me. After all, Gwyneth Paltrow studied art history at the University of California, Santa Barbara.

Tiffany's first day back at school was a Friday — also Valentine's Day — after she'd missed a total of seventeen days. As it was a few days shy of three weeks since we'd been to the hospital, I was thrilled that her recovery had come in on schedule. The day before she returned, I'd made an appointment for her to get a top-notch haircut, eyebrow waxing, and manicure at a fancy salon; it was both a Valentine's gift and a way to boost her confidence for her reentry. I knew she felt unattractive and spent, as everyone does after a long illness. We celebrated her recovery that Thursday evening by having Eugene over for dinner, knowing he would ooh and ah over Tiffany's shiny, bouncy new do. A bonus was that Eugene finally told Tiffany his story, in greater detail than I'd anticipated. (I'd previously given her the short, PG-13 version.) It was wonderful to watch her expressions as he described being a teenage runaway and transforming himself into "Natalia," followed by his addiction to drugs and alcohol, and his long journey back to "Eugene." It was almost Homeric — like a transgendered version of *Lord of the Rings.* The story left Tiffany virtually speechless, which was a rarity, but she smiled in admiration at Eugene like he was the coolest, most exotic creature she'd ever met. Thankfully, he didn't make his story as funny as he sometimes does, so I think my niece truly got the pain of my friend's life as well as the adventure.

"Are you guys going to the antiwar rally on Saturday?" he changed the subject suddenly. "It's going to be gigantic and might even get a bit rowdy." He smiled and raised his thin eyebrows expectantly.

"I'm planning on it," I answered. "I leave for LA on Sunday, so I've just got to make sure I'm ready. But Miss T here shouldn't be on her feet for that long yet, especially in this cold weather. You know how exhausting those things are."

"Yeah, it sucks for me," Tiffany chimed in. "It sounds so cool; I'm sure most of my friends are going." She looked downcast.

"Overdoing it could cause a relapse, and you've done so well." I moved her newly cut long bangs from her eyes. "We've got to be careful."

"And who's going to stay with Misty while you're in La La Land?" Eugene asked, recasting my "Miss T" as a new name for Tiffany. "You're not leaving her here alone, are you, Miss D?" ("Miss D" stands for "Miss Diagnosis," the drag name Eugene had christened me years earlier, but that's another story.)

"Of course not, Miss Gen-Natalia," I replied cattily. Tiffany giggled but looked completely confused. "Megan's coming for part of the week, then my mom."

" 'The mother and child re-u-u-union is only a motion away,' " Eugene sang as he danced around the table, clearing our plates.

We spent the remainder of the evening ranting about the evils perpetrated by the Bush administration. Remarkably, Tiffany stuck around for at least half of it; she may have been a somewhat captive audience, but she seemed rapt. I don't know if my niece understood much of what we were talking about, but she seemed to enjoy the sight of a couple of hyper queens ranting about politics from atop their high horses.

# Read My Apocalips

On Valentine's Day morning Tiffany handed me a greeting card that she must have picked up when she went to get her haircut, as that was the only time she'd left the house since we'd returned from the hospital. The front of the card said, "It's taken me a long time to understand you and interpret your actions and comprehend your motivations, but I think I've finally got you figured out," and on the inside it continued, "You're nuts! (But I like you that way.)" More importantly, though, she'd written the following inside the card:

Dear Uncle Eddy,
I love you sooo much. I hope you have a great Valentine's Day full of love and joy and fun!!
Love always,
Tiffany (The Eternally Grateful)

Since I had been alone for probably thirty-seven of my forty-one Valentine's

Days, it was not a holiday to which I particularly looked forward. Receiving Tiffany's card, though, certainly made me reconsider my attitude. I'd have to remember to pick up the curling iron I'd been meaning to get her from Kmart during my lunch break.

When Tiffany called me at the office on her first day back to school to ask if she could have Jenise over for a few hours that evening, my defenses were down. Like me, Tiffany had no real valentine and, since I'd planned to see *The Pianist* with a friend without realizing what day it was, Tiffany would be spending the evening home alone. I felt both guilty and sorry for her, so I gave her my permission, figuring she and Jenise would get into less trouble in our apartment than they might out on the streets. I would be proved wrong.

*The Pianist* left me feeling like I'd been pummeled by a meat tenderizer. I thanked God that my friend and I had had dinner before the film, as I don't think I could have eaten or carried on a conversation after it. My last good nerve was frazzled.

I arrived home after the movies to find Tiffany alone and watching television, Jenise having left hours earlier. Unfortunately, she had some bad news for me:

Jenise had taken my niece's cell phone with her when she left.

"She's going to bring it back, though," Tiffany said in her defense.

"Did she ask if she could take it, Tiffany?" I said, my voice tight.

"No," she answered. "I went to make a call and couldn't find the phone. So I called my cell from the regular phone, hoping the ring would help me find it. And Jenise answered it."

"What did she say?" I asked, helium-voiced with disbelief.

"I asked her what the hell she was thinking, just taking my cell phone like that, and she's all, 'What's up, yo?' Then she said she'd bring it back tomorrow."

"Yeah, right. Just like she brought the fifty dollars back to school." I was angry and couldn't help myself. "You were warned over and over about this girl, Tiffany."

"I hate it here!" she yelled as she ran down the hallway to her room. "Who steals from a friend?" She slammed her bedroom door.

"There is no honor among thieves, Tiffany," I shouted through it. "Remember how Luke turned on Toby? You hang out with criminals and you're going to get

389

burned. You've got to learn that!" Blinded by self-righteous anger, I couldn't see that behind the door was a lonely, brutally disappointed girl who'd thought she'd finally made a friend.

Filled with self-pity, I flung myself on the sofa in the living room and lamented that our sickbed respite had ended and Tiffany was back in action.

The day of New York's first big anti–Iraq War protest rally dawned sunny but bone-chillingly cold. I'd made no concrete plans to march with anyone, so I headed to East Midtown on the subway alone. This was a conscious choice, as I believe events like this can feel more authentic when you're anonymous and unencumbered by a group of friends; you can follow your instincts throughout the day, letting them pull you in unplanned directions. Alone, you can simply be absorbed into the humanity around you and be more a part of the crowd as a whole.

I left Tiffany curled up on the sofa, watching *Donnie Darko* for the hundredth time and anxiously awaiting Jenise's phone call. Apparently, when Tiffany called her cell phone that morning, she reached the new voice mail message the thief had stupidly recorded. That's not a good sign, I thought, but didn't say a word. Hoping against hope, Tiffany left a message imploring Jenise to call her and return the phone, as promised.

When I arrived at the protest march, the energy of the crowd was palpable and it swept me away. I was soon drawn by the sound of a deep but hoarse male voice chanting in a military, singsong fashion, with the crowd repeating each phrase after it was spoken. "Don't invade that foreign soil," the voice yelled out, followed by the crowd's echo. "We won't lose our kids for oil." Then, "If you keep on telling lies . . . You'll hear those children's mothers' cries." The leader was making up each verse as he went along. It was like he was channeling the words from his subconscious, much like I imagine rappers do when they get on stage and improvise. As I snaked my way closer to the voice, I saw a small group of men in fatigues and army jackets carrying a banner that read, "Veterans for Peace." When I saw the man who was shouting into the battery-operated megaphone, I immediately knew two things: he was a veteran of the Vietnam War and he was HIV-positive. He was tall and bearded, probably in his late forties or early fifties, and his face was ravaged from the side effects of HIV medications; his skin was mottled and bumpy and, more telling, the sides of his face just below his cheekbones were deeply sunken in — not emaciated, but actually indented. I imagined writing a prayer for peace on a tiny slip of paper, folding it up, and hiding it inside one of those crevices, just as I'd done at the Wailing Wall in Jerusalem. For at that moment, this man seemed to me an embodiment of the fight against all the injustices and ills the world suffered.

The Vietnam War and AIDS had been permanently linked in my mind for almost twenty years. When Reagan was elected president, I was an eighteen-year-old sophomore in college. "Stop Raygun" had been spray-painted all over campus, and shortly after he was elected, I was required to register for the draft in case the new president saw fit to take our country to war. As I couldn't imagine myself lasting a single day at boot camp, never mind in enemy territory, I remember giving thanks to God that I had escaped the Vietnam War by a narrow six or seven years. A year or two later, when I was home from school on break and driving my dad's blue Toyota Celica to my job at a French restaurant, I heard a radio report predicting that GRIDS (Gay-Related Immune Deficiency Syndrome) was likely to reach epidemic proportions in the coming years. They'd even given it a new name: AIDS. I had to pull the car over as I could no longer see the road. Time paused and, for a brief moment, history and my place in it all made perfect sense to me, as though I had jumped inside the head of the world's narrator. I had not been as lucky as I'd thought; AIDS was to be my generation's Vietnam. Thank God I couldn't know that, within a decade, AIDS would claim five times the number of American lives as the Vietnam War.

As I walked next to this soldier now, offering him bottles of water and bananas, yelling out the responses he begged, I felt that I'd been led specifically to these men who had fought in wars and knew whereof they spoke in demanding peace. Wearing the huge black fur hat Orly had brought me from Moscow and a long, army green coat, I imagined myself one of them and marched proudly in solidarity. We strode on through the valley of Third Avenue, surrounded by sheared walls of glass on either side. When I turned to look behind me, the sea of marchers stretched as far as

I could see. There were giant white doves, each kept aloft by a dozen protesters, and signs with slogans both funny and chilling. An elegant woman in her mid-sixties carried a poster of Bush with his typical vacant, pursed-mouth expression and the words "Read My Apocalips" printed boldly beneath him. A little boy who was perched atop his father's shoulders held a sign that said, "Regime change begins at home!" I kept wishing Tiffany was there with me to experience the incredible force of a united purpose. What would a fourteen-year-old think? I wondered. My first real understanding of any big political event was Watergate, which left me a disgusted and apathetic ten-year-old. They're all just a bunch of liars, I remember thinking. So why bother? Maybe if my niece saw this she'd feel a part of something, a movement, a cause. Maybe she'd feel hopeful that she could make some sort of a difference in the world. I knew, though, that had Tiffany been with me at the rally, I wouldn't have joined the veterans and my experience would have been vastly different.

"Did Jenise call?" I asked Tiffany when I arrived home, exhausted and frozen.

"No, but she answered once when I called and said she was on her way over." Tiffany spoke without averting her eyes from the television, which was tuned to a Japanese cooking competition. "But she never came."

"Okay, get dressed then, please." I tried not to sound too aggravated. "We've got to go to the police station on Tenth Street to file a report."

"Wha-tuh?" Tiffany sometimes stretched out the consonants at the ends of her words when she was angry, usually to stress her incredulity at my idiocy. This annoyed me to no end, but I was careful not to mock her.

"I'm leaving for Los Angeles tomorrow, Tiffany, so we have to fill out the police report today." It had been so long since we'd argued that I found myself nervous at the thought of an onslaught. "When a cell phone is lost or stolen, you have to fill out a police report in order to use insurance to get another one, which is still going to cost me at least fifty bucks. And we're not going to lie to the police and tell them it was lost, if that's what you're thinking."

"Why not-tuh?" She did it again, so as I sat down on the big sofa, I started counting to ten in my head.

"For a host of reasons, Tiffany." I tried not to get what my niece called "the voice." "First, we're not liars, so we're not going to lie to law enforcement about what happened. Second, there's no reason we should protect Jenise. She's not your friend; she's a thief who has to face the consequences of what she's done. Plus she obviously thinks she can get away with anything, answering the phone like that and changing the voice mail message."

"Oh, so you think it's *your* job to teach her a lesson?" Tiffany looked at me accusingly.

"She stole *my* cell phone. *I* paid for that phone!" I took a deep breath. "I'm not going to argue about this, Tiffany. Please go get dressed so we can get this over with."

The West Village precinct, which stretches clear through from Tenth to Charles Street, between Hudson and Bleecker, looked exactly like a movie set, with its fluorescent lighting and huge bulletin boards crammed with artists' sketches of "wanted" people.

"May I help you?" the female officer at the desk asked. She was a lovely Latina gal — not unlike J. Lo — with gorgeous skin, well-applied makeup, and dark shiny hair pulled back tautly into a ponytail. Who says police officers never *really* look like Charlie's Angels? I thought. Her name tag said Maria Espinoza.

"Yes, thanks," I answered quickly. "This young woman would like to report a stolen cell phone."

"Me?" Tiffany jumped in, "I thought you said it was *your* cell phone." She looked up at me with a slight smirk, one eyebrow raised. Good point, I thought, but I wasn't going to concede it.

"I paid for the phone, Tiffany, but it was stolen from you. So you're the complainant in this case."

"What happened?" Officer Espinoza asked Tiffany as she handed me some forms to fill out. With the policewoman's coaching, Tiffany relayed the salient events of the evening before while I penned in what I could.

"Has this girl been known to steal before?" the officer asked Tiffany, who paused and turned toward me.

"She was suspected of stealing some money at school recently," I said.

"So why would you *invite* someone like this into your home?" she asked, arching her perfectly shaped eyebrows.

"Because *someone* was being stupid," I said and looked toward Tiffany, who rolled her eyes, let out a loud sigh of disgust, and walked out of the precinct.

"So what happens now?" I asked.

"We'll call the school and get Jenise's home address and pick her up there. If the detective assigned to the case needs any more information, they'll call you at home. Otherwise, sometime after she's arrested, you'll hear from the district attorney's office."

"Thank you, officer," I said, taking our copy of the police report.

I found Tiffany outside, leaning against the brick wall of the precinct, kicking at something on the sidewalk. You shouldn't be out in this cold without a hat, I thought, but kept it to myself.

"You didn't have to call me 'stupid' in front of her," she said as we started to walk.

"I said you were *being* stupid," I replied, splitting hairs. "It was a stupid *decision* to have Jenise over to the apartment. I really hope you'll develop better instincts for picking friends, Tiffany."

"Whatever," she said as she turned her head away from me and pretended to look in the store windows along Hudson Street.

Tiffany was right. I shouldn't have embarrassed her in front of the officer that way; it was uncalled for. I knew instantly that I'd done it because I was ashamed that *I'd* made the bad decision to allow Tiffany to have Jenise over, and in an effort to save face in front of Officer J. Lo, I'd deflected all the blame onto Tiffany. But I couldn't find it in myself at that moment to apologize. I was too angry. Tiffany seemed hell-bent on finding the same kinds of kids she hung out with in Connecticut, and it had now cost me time and money.

"Why don't we pick up a video for tonight?" I asked, offering a twig of an olive branch. "And after I finish packing for my trip, we can order a pizza." We hadn't had pizza since before Tiffany had gotten ill, so I thought this might excite her.

"Me, Aleksi, and Liam are going to go visit Peter," she said matter-of-factly. "No one has seen him since his brother died." I guess Tiffany figured that her one day back at school meant she could now go out on weekend nights. And she was no dummy; she knew that of all the possible activities she could plan (or at least allege that she was planning), this was the one I was least likely to resist.

So this is my punishment for being mean, I thought. I would spend my last evening in New York alone, wondering where Tiffany really was and worrying that she might not be dressed warmly enough for this endless arctic weather.

# For What It's Worth

My business trip to Los Angeles left me completely rejuvenated. Even though it was only late February when I returned, for me the trip symbolized the end of a long and trying winter. I'd escaped the biggest snowfall since the blizzard of '96, having left the runway at JFK just as the first snowflakes were beginning to fall. Normally I'd hate to miss a snowstorm in New York, when the city's lifeblood pulses more slowly under the snow's blanket, its cacophony hushed. But not this winter. Not after nearly two months straight of subzero temperatures, constant code orange alert, my hernia surgery, drudgery at work, and of course the enormous pressures born of my taking in Tiffany.

I'd timed the trip to coincide with my niece's midwinter break so that Megan, Sammy, and my mom wouldn't have to get up at six thirty in the morning to get her off to school. The plan was for Megan and Sammy to come down for a few days, followed by my mom for the balance of the week, but the snow changed all that. Megan worried that she'd be trapped in my nine-hundred-square-foot apartment with two fighting girls for the entire break, so she'd decided at the last minute to whisk Tiffany off to Connecticut before any significant inches accumulated. I'd feared that if my niece went back to New Milford, running around and partying with her friends would lead to a recurrence of her mono, but apparently the snow prevented everyone from doing much of anything and the week went fairly smoothly.

Tiffany was home when I walked into the apartment the following Sunday, having taken the train down from Connecticut by herself that afternoon. She looked healthier than I'd seen her in some time, and she jumped up to greet me.

"How was it?" she asked cheerily as she hugged me and gave me one of her signature kisses, where she allows you to kiss her cheek but she kisses only the air.

"Great!" I said. "It was sunny and warm, and I met with zillions of producers. I must've driven on and off studio lots fifty times during the week, and I had lots of meals outside." I didn't tell her I'd ended the trip by sleeping with one of my best friends from high school and that it had been exactly what I'd needed. (Over Tiffany's Christmas break, I'd hooked up with a guy I met in a bar, but it had felt even more unsatisfying than I remembered one-nighters to be. Plus that was almost two months earlier; before Tiffany moved in I rarely went longer than two weeks without sex. In California it felt wonderful to be with someone who truly knows and loves me, even if it couldn't lead to a boyfriend relationship.)

"You know, I've been meaning to tell you this forever: you're supposed to actually kiss the person's cheek while they're kissing yours. If you don't, people might think you're a snob or superficial."

"You're kidding! Really?" Tiffany seemed truly surprised.

"Really," I replied.

"I never knew that, but I'll try it from now on. Here, let's practice." She did it perfectly on the first attempt.

"Very good!" I said, smiling. "When you get rich and famous, you can go back to the other kind." She laughed. "You look terrific," I added as I ran my hand through her shiny hair. "So, what are you up to?"

"Oh, I was just checking online to see if Freck chopped off his feet yet."

"Omigod! He hasn't, has he?" I feigned panic.

"No, the website looks the same as it has for months. No self-amputation is even *scheduled* at this point." Tiffany acted appropriately disappointed.

This was a running joke we'd had since the summer before, when Tiffany was still a visitor to New York City. Completely by accident I'd stumbled upon this bizarre website where a guy named Freck was trying to raise money to buy prosthetic feet. You see, his current legs were paralyzed from the knee down and his ankles and feet had atrophied (the photos were horrific). Because his health insurance carrier disagreed that it was "medically necessary" for his feet to be amputated and replaced with prosthetics, Freck decided he would chop off his feet himself with a homemade guillotine in front of a live online audience (presumably only those who'd chipped in for the prosthetics, a group to which Tiffany and I did not belong). Though I was fairly certain it was a hoax, when I found the site I immediately e-mailed the link to Tiffany, as I knew this was exactly the kind of macabre, darkly humorous stuff teenagers loved. Cutoffmyfeet.com had been a huge hit with Tiffany's friends, and every now and again we would check in on Freck's progress. Some people followed sports teams with their children, nieces, or nephews; we followed Freck's feet.

"How about that snow?" I asked. "Was it beautiful in Connecticut?"

"Yeah," she said with a sigh. "But I got kind of bored, all cooped up in the house, and Sammy drove me insane."

"She probably wanted your undivided attention because she hasn't seen you in a long time," I offered.

"Whatever," Tiffany replied, ending that portion of the conversation.

"Did you hear about the horrible fire in that Rhode Island rock club?" I asked. "A hundred people were killed." All week, every time I'd popped back to my hotel room to change or relax for a few minutes, the news programs were covering the tragedy.

"Yeah, and that band sounds like a bunch of losers. How retarded to put on a show like that in such a tiny space." She rolled her eyes in disgust.

"Promise me that when you start going to clubs, you'll always make sure you know where the fire exits are, okay?" In the past I would have ruminated endlessly on what it might have been like to die in that situation, but now all I thought about were the parents of the victims. I knew, though, that in the Great White fire, knowing where the exits were wouldn't have helped.

"I already *do* go to clubs, Uncle Eddy," Tiffany responded, batting her eyelashes at me in mock annoyance. "A lot of them have teen nights, you know."

"Well, I'm not so sure about that here in New York," I said and quickly decided to change the subject, though not to anything more pleasant. "Hey, did we hear from any detectives at the precinct?"

"Yeah, there's a message on the machine," she answered sadly. "They arrested Jenise and don't need us until we hear from the DA. Uncle Eddy, you know I'm gonna get my butt kicked, right?"

"I hope not, Tiffany, but if she tries to do something to you, I hope you'll handle it properly. How about we order some Chinese food? I'm jonesing for some hot and sour, and I *know* you've probably missed your scallion pancakes!"

Though several inches of gray, litter-strewn snow remained on the sidewalks and streets of Greenwich Village, I was determined to hang on to the spring I'd returned with and to make it my souvenir for Tiffany as well.

It was subtle, but in the weeks after I came home from Los Angeles, I began to sense a different current moving between us. My best guess was that my caring for my niece during her illness had somehow caused a shift in our dynamic. Maybe feeling her dependence on me so keenly enabled me to see her once again for what she truly was — a fourteen-year-old girl who needed my help. Sure, she'd brought heaps of baggage with her and was acting out up, down, and sideways, but she was still the Tiffany I'd always known: creative, sensitive, and big-hearted. Any paranoid worries that she might be bad to the bone were long gone. Seeing her as a kid again made me realize how much of her childhood had been stolen from her and reminded me that I couldn't possibly comprehend the anger and pain that the loss had caused. And perhaps having me by her side through her illness, battling demonic doctors, soothing her night frights, and simply providing the love, sympathy, and care she needed, made her finally see me for what I now truly was — her guardian and protector.

I think too I secretly harbored the hope that Jenise's stealing from Tiffany had frightened her just enough to make her realize (however deep in the recesses of her brain) that the world was indeed dangerous and that she just might not have it all figured out.

"Remember the word *Halliburton,* Tiffany," I said, taking her hand and looking directly into her eyes. She was sitting lengthwise on the love seat working on an essay for humanities about the pending war in Iraq.

"Omigod, what is it? A demon?" she asked, bulging her eyes out and trying not to smirk.

"No, that's Beelzebub, but you're close." I giggled. "Halliburton is an oil services company based out of Texas, and it's just been awarded an exclusive contract to handle Iraq's broken-down oil industry."

"So?" Tiffany looked at me like I'd just spoken in Swahili.

"Well, our vice president, Dick Cheney, used to be the CEO of Halliburton," I said. "And that company will make billions off of what's going on in Iraq."

"So the war will really be all about oil and not terrorism?" she asked. "Like the golf thingy in the nineties was?"

"That was the Persian *Gulf* War," I said as I stretched out on the big sofa, facing

Tiffany. "And yes, it will be about a lot of things, but oil and money are two of the biggest." This is fun, I thought suddenly, indoctrinating a child with my beliefs!

"That's disgusting," Tiffany replied, supremely indignant. "I'm going to add it to my essay. Everyone else will turn in papers explaining about weapons of mass destruction and al-Qaeda, then I'll hit Ms. Whitfield with this stuff. She'll think it's mad radical and I'll get an A." We both cracked up, but then I felt a wave of nausea roll through me.

"It sickens me to think that Bush and his cronies are exploiting September eleventh for political purposes," I said sadly.

"You were down near Ground Zero that morning, weren't you?" she asked.

"Yeah, I was at Orly's apartment, which had a ringside view of the towers."

"What happened?"

I paused before I answered, trying to figure out a polite, respectful way to say it, but there was none. "We saw a lot of people get killed." I hadn't spoken of that morning in a long time and it felt unreal, like I was lying — like it hadn't really happened. "That's all I can say about it right now, sweetie. Someday I'll tell you the whole thing." I didn't know when I'd be able to tell her my story of September 11, as just putting it into words seemed to trivialize it. Right after the attacks all the pundits encouraged everyone in New York to talk, talk, talk about it constantly, sort of like massive group therapy. But it seemed to me that people were always trying to one-up each other when they spoke of that terrible day at parties and functions, falling into the same competitive stances that New Yorkers take with everything. It had sickened me and I'd vowed to remain mostly silent about my experiences that day.

"Okay, that's cool," Tiffany said solemnly. Suddenly she brightened. "Ready to repeat everything you said, only more slowly?" she asked, pen poised to paper.

Much to my delight, March progressed rather smoothly. Tiffany seemed to be more focused on her schoolwork, even making an effort to have the television off when I arrived home in the evenings. She was feeling energetic enough to go on a three-hour audition for the TADA! Youth Theater's spring musical and had come home spiked from the experience. When she didn't get a part, she took it well, consoled by the fact that only two or three noncompany members were chosen from dozens. In the middle of the month Tiffany gladly went to Vermont with me and a friend, where she behaved politely toward our hosts and was a good sport about learning how to snowboard. I'd made the switch from skiing almost ten years earlier, and Tiffany had always admired my shredding as she'd tried to keep up with me on her skis. Pretty soon now we'd be catching phat air together. On the Saturday night of our ski weekend, we sat beside the fire reading *The Miller's Tale* aloud, as Tiffany was currently studying Chaucer in her humanities class. I was proud of my niece's poise and intelligence as we read and laughed at the poem's bawdiness. Our hosts, whose grown children were far flung and much missed, were charmed.

Then, on the evening of March 19, the United States began its war with Iraq. I arrived at work on the damp, dreary morning of the twentieth to the sight of bombs dropping on Baghdad as CNN blared endlessly from the conference room television. I knew as I watched that innocent civilians were surely being killed, and I felt ashamed.

Another antiwar rally was held on the following Saturday, the second day of spring and seasonably gorgeous. I encouraged Tiffany to go with her friends but I couldn't bring myself to march this time. Men and women, many half my age, were now risking their lives in Iraq, and I couldn't bear the idea that I'd be one of the thousands back home screaming that the whole enterprise was based on lies and that they weren't really fighting for freedom at all. At that moment in time, I actually hoped that George Bush had been telling the truth and that he was right about everything he was saying; horrible weapons of mass destruction would indeed be discovered in Iraq — nuclear bombs and whole warehouses filled with anthrax — and Osama bin Laden would be found sipping blender drinks on a balcony of Saddam Hussein's palace. I needed to hope that I'd been wrong about everything, if only it meant that people would not have to die for nothing.

While Tiffany was marching among hundreds of thousands of people on that glorious spring Saturday, I sat at home and wrote. I'd never owned a laptop until Tiffany arrived, and I loved that I could boot it up anywhere, including in bed. Not too long after she moved in, I started bringing it into my room on weekend mornings (while she slept late) and recreating some of the moments we'd experienced together. I realized quickly that I wasn't merely recording our life as a family but was also processing all that happened. I felt that a sea change was occurring within me, and I wasn't sure exactly how or why; maybe by charting our journey in words, I would better understand. Writing also became an outlet for a creative side that I'd long ago shuttered.

When I'd left acting, I instinctively knew the only way to come clean with it was to decide that I was mediocre and that, despite the fact that I'd been set on the profession since I was seven years old, it was no longer a calling and there were other things I could pursue. Creative writing was one of them. I'd studied fiction with John Gardner in college and continued to write stories, vignettes, and monologues during my years of pounding the pavement in New York. Reluctantly I decided I would give it a real try. It terrified me to put my energies into another creative field, but after I was accepted to law school, I deferred my start date by a year and moved out to Sag Harbor on eastern Long Island to study fiction with a novelist. For the most part, though, I found it excruciating to sit in a room alone at that point in my life, trying to corral my thoughts, and was unsatisfied with what I produced. And the idea of going from slipping headshots under doors to slipping manuscripts to receptionists was enough to make me look for the nearest tall building. Ultimately I decided to go back to the big city and prove myself in a "legitimate," respectable, and more secure profession: the law. Except for participating in a couple of staged readings, and writing one short story for my law and literature class, I ran from anything creative, frightened of both its pull and of my potential failure.

Now, thirteen years after I had left that workshop in Sag Harbor, I felt compelled to write. Ironically, my legal career had led me back into the world of authors and screenwriters, but I hadn't consciously planned to try my hand at becoming one of them. Then Tiffany came and awakened something long dormant. That sunny Saturday afternoon in late March, sitting on my bed and typing away, the laptop straddling me on a breakfast-in-bed tray, I began to understand what was happening to me. Tiffany's arrival had not only changed my day-to-day life but had somehow rearranged *me* as well, shaking free things I no longer knew I possessed. Living with a child whose entire life lay before her reminded me how to dream, how to believe again that anything was possible, and in working to build my niece's self-esteem through love and encouragement, I was discovering a new sense of my own worth. For the first time since my early twenties, when I faced a blank page on the computer screen, the old fears and listlessness were largely gone. In their place were focus, energy, and spirit. Plus Tiffany had given me a story to tell.

Around six p.m., while I was cleaning up my lunch dishes, I flipped the kitchen radio on to catch the news on 1010 WINS. Almost immediately I heard a report that the march had made its way to Washington Square Park but that the police couldn't get the protesters to disperse and there had been some trouble. Several policemen were injured and dozens of marchers were arrested. I'd loaned Tiffany my cell phone; she'd called me an hour or so earlier from Union Square, where she and her friends were hanging for a while before heading down to what was now the scene of the commotion. I quickly dialed my cell number, but it rang and rang until eventually my voice mail picked up. Oh Lord, I prayed, please tell me it's too noisy for her to hear the phone and that she's not downtown in some holding cell getting strip-searched by a mean version of Queen Latifah in *Chicago.*

I turned the television on to see protesters, empowered by their numbers, taunting the police, who in turn started getting rough. Sirens blared as red lights swirled and people screamed. "Battle lines being drawn," I sang to myself. "Nobody's right when everybody's wrong."

When I tried the cell phone again, my call went straight to voice mail without ringing, which meant it had been turned off. I quickly grabbed my sneakers, jacket, and keys and dashed out into the twilit streets of the Village, hoping that Tiffany had managed to steer clear of the melee. With her disdain for authority, though, a confrontation with police was just the type of thing she would love.

I could hear Washington Square Park long before I could see it. The sounds were not of sirens but of music. There wasn't just one loud, thump-thump beat, like when you approach a suburban disco from its parking lot, but rather many different beats and rhythms blended together in the evening air. I entered the park on the corner of Waverly and MacDougal. The irony of joining a peace protest while walking just feet from the Hangman's Elm — a huge English elm that was used for public executions until a mere century ago — was not lost on me. The wide pathways were filled with people of every color, age, and socioeconomic class. East Village punks rubbed elbows with aging bankers pushing strollers. Tourists chatted in foreign languages, their video cameras blinking, recording all. Many folks were gathered around a particular musician or two and were often singing along. I heard Crosby, Stills & Nash's "Teach Your Children" until it was overwhelmed by the next group's raw rendition of Lennon's "Imagine." I felt for a moment like I'd been transported back to the '60s counterculture that I'd been too young to experience, and I half expected to see Timothy Leary bouncing by on LSD or Janis Joplin ripping through "Me and Bobby McGee." Many of the people around me, I realized, had protested the Vietnam War just as they were protesting this one.

Everywhere the park sparkled with the flickering of candles, much as Union

Square had for weeks after September 11. As I approached the large amphitheater at the park's center — which is actually a giant fountain that spouts water only when the park's benefactor, NYU, is holding graduation ceremonies — tribal drumming, tambourines, and cries of ecstasy (or frustration or pain?) grew louder and louder. People danced, as if in a trance, some in circles with a lone dancer taking a turn at the center. Except for a few cops standing in small groups here and there with grins on their faces as they watched the "weirdos," there was no police action to be found. The skirmish must have ended, with the perps taken away in paddy wagons.

I was praying Tiffany wasn't among them when I saw her.

At first I thought the young woman dancing with another girl at the center of a group of young people — mostly boys — was a girl who simply looked like Tiffany. I stopped to watch for a moment before realizing that the girl was my niece. Her long hair hung down in front of her face and she swung it from side to side to the pounding drumbeat. Her arms were outstretched, as though she were crucified, and a cigarette glowed at the end of her right hand. My mind told me it was Tiffany; the girl wore the tight orange, brown, and white striped '70s shirt Tiffany had left the house wearing, her navel was pierced, and her low-cut jeans frayed over red and white Nike sneakers. But this was a girl I hadn't yet met, and I wasn't sure I ever would. She danced with abandon as the circle of kids passed around a blunt and drank from aluminum beer cans. I turned and slowly made my way out of the park, not wanting to interrupt a night I knew Tiffany would remember forever.

# Part Three

# Spring

# Cleopatra Rules

"Thank God Jack Nicholson's girlfriend isn't wearing that *hideous* tutu number she wore at the Golden Globes. That was a fashion felony!" Eugene screamed, simultaneously filling his plate from the buffet and keeping an eye on the television. The stars were slowly filing past the cameras on their way into the Academy Awards ceremony.

"Really!" I agreed. "And she's so skinny! As if being thirty years younger than him wasn't enough, she has to have the body of an adolescent boy too." Tiffany rolled her eyes and grinned at me. She sat erect on the sofa, between Marisol and Steven, carefully lifting small forkfuls of food to her mouth.

"She caught massive abuse from the press for that tutu number, believe me," added Julio, Steven's husband. "Though I must say she's got some major *cojones* between those toothpick legs to walk out of the house looking like that."

"I don't know if it's balls or delusions,"

Steven chimed in. "Remember, anorexics don't have a very realistic view of themselves."

"What a good psychotherapist you are," Eugene teased as he squeezed onto the love seat next to Orly, his plate piled high. "And that's coming from the former Queen of Distorted Body Image," he added wryly. Eugene was always more relaxed about his past when Tom wasn't around. Like Georgia and her husband, Connor, Tom thought the Oscars were about as fun as chewing glass. The group didn't hold this against him, though, as it was in keeping with his stalwart, landscape architect mystique.

"Well, at least we're already seeing *one* unexpected benefit of this five-day-old travesty in Iraq," Stewart piped in from the far end of the large sofa between mouthfuls of farfalle pesto. "The glitter has been taken out of the glitterati," he quipped. Stewart was referring to Hollywood's communal decision to dress more somberly this year and to keep red carpet chitchat to a minimum. "If you ask me, a return to simple elegance, which includes knowing when to keep one's mouth shut, is a welcome turn of events."

"I don't know about that," I replied from

my lonely perch on a dining room chair. "Tim Robbins and my idol, Susan Sarandon, are presenting. They may *look* toned down, but somehow I doubt they'll keep it zipped."

"Uncle Eddy is in love with that woman," Tiffany interjected. "If we watch *Atlantic City* or *Thelma and Louise* one more time, I'm going to drive *him* off a cliff!" The room broke out in appreciative laughter. "But I'm happy to watch *Dead Man Walking* over and over. Sean Penn might be old, but he is so hot."

"Very good, Tiffany," Orly said, still laughing. "Let's forget politics for a night and keep it to the movies." Being Israeli-born, Orly was doubly anxious about the situation in the Middle East.

"Oh, movies schmovies," Stewart jumped in. "Let's move on to the important stuff. What's for dessert?"

And so it went, Tiffany's first Oscar party. As I watched her giggle at my friends' antics, I wondered for a moment what she would have been doing on this Sunday night in late March if she were still living in Connecticut. Would she be down by the lake smoking cigarettes with her friends? Or would she be holed up in her bedroom, talking on the phone and listening to music? In any event, I was sure that this time a year ago, she could never have imagined she'd wind up in Greenwich Village cohosting a party for a television show — a party where guests competed by yelling out catty comments about every celebrity that flashed across the screen.

"Wow, that's intense!" I said on the following Wednesday after I opened the apartment door and walked into a solid wall of nail polish remover vapors. Tiffany had her suitcase-sized black vinyl nail kit spread open on the coffee table. At least a dozen little bottles of polish had been taken out and lined up, like benched basketball players hoping to get back on the court.

"It's a finger and toe day," she said with her back to me. She sat on the love seat but was bent over her feet, which were up against the table. Emeril was on in the background. "But you say that every time anyway."

"Yeah, but Miss Thing, today you've got the incense going too. You know how that turns my stomach, and the combination of the two is revolting." I moved down the hallway to close her bedroom door.

"Oh, I'm sorry," Tiffany called after me.

"I thought I'd closed it."

"Don't worry about it," I said as I threw my gym bag on my bedroom chair and headed back to join her in the living room. "So, you know I have parent-teacher conferences tomorrow, right?"

"Uh-huh." She didn't look up from applying sparkly purple to her big toenail.

"Anything I should know beforehand?" I asked, stretching out on the sofa to watch her at work. "Remember in the fall when I found out you'd been written up for a worse offense than you'd told me?"

"Yes, I *remember*," she answered sarcastically. "And, no, there shouldn't be any *offenses* reported this time. You've been hanging around with Orly too much; you make me sound like a criminal, with my *offenses*."

"You're right, I'm being a dick and I'll stop," I replied. "But speaking of criminals, any sign of Jenise?"

"Nope. She hasn't been back to school at all since she was arrested."

"Good. Maybe they got her out, *finally*."

"Let's hope so or I'm dead meat," Tiffany said casually as she sat back, wiggled her rainbow-hued toes and surveyed her handiwork. "I still hate my feet," she said with a sigh.

★ ★ ★

"Oh, you're Tiffany's uncle!" Ms. Robichon, the art teacher, said excitedly. "She is such a talented girl!" Is she kidding? I thought. Tiffany told me they'd had a huge fight when Ms. Robichon wouldn't give her the assignments she'd missed while out sick. "That crazy beeotch kept yelling at me, 'Not now, *Tee*-funny, not now!' " she'd said, imitating the teacher's French accent. "So I told her to go F herself, the tyrant." (Tiffany had started complaining about her art teacher's volatility back in September, so I always remembered her name as Ms. Robespierre. "How was the Reign of Terror today?" I would ask.)

"But I thought you and Tiffany had a big argument?" I now asked incredulously.

"Oh, you know how it is wiz teenagers," she responded, running her hand back through impossibly thick black curls. "Sometimes you have to do zis in order to reach ze next level wiz zem."

"I guess so," I said, shaking my head and smiling. Maybe she *is* nuts, I thought. After all, she is an artist. I couldn't help but immediately like this woman, though. First off, she was absolutely gorgeous. Tiffany had told me she was half French and half South American, but she'd said

428

nothing about beauty. And if Ms. Robichon was faking her enthusiasm for her students' creativity, then she was a brilliant actress.

"Tiffany is extremely expressive," she continued, her large black eyes shining brightly, "and she's not afraid to let her emotions into her work." Just then her three-year-old daughter's mop of dark curls appeared over Ms. Robichon's left shoulder. An exact miniature of her mom, the little girl had climbed up the art teacher's back and sprouted like an adorable growth.

"May I ask, then, why she got only a seventy on her last report card?" I didn't want to break the spell this woman had cast on me, but I simply had to know.

"Well, Tiffany got off to a slow start," she said. "She was socializing too much, flirting constantly wiz ze boys and not doing her work. But somezing has happened and now she does her work quietly by herself. It's like she's made some sort of decision to do zings differently, to try anozer approach." She paused to look in her grade book. "Zis quarter she has a ninety-five average."

"Well, that is wonderful news." I thanked Ms. R, who seemed anything but a tyrant, and said bye-bye to her little girl. Before I left, though, I promised to send her one of my clients' new scripts — about Modigliani, Picasso, Chagall, Soutine, and Rivera when they all lived together in the same building in Paris. She was thrilled.

I left that art room high, and not just because its smell of paint and wet brown paper towels took me back to my favorite hours of high school; it was the third positive meeting I'd had in a row, with each teacher noting a remarkable change since Tiffany had returned from being sick. But Ms. Robichon's perception of a conscious choice on Tiffany's part was the most exciting to me. I thought I'd detected a positive change in my niece over the last month, and now it had been confirmed by others — by her *teachers,* no less! I was ecstatic.

My last meeting was to be with Ms. Whitfield, Tiffany's humanities teacher. The course was two periods long and combined English and history. I'd always believed that the former was Tiffany's strongest academic suit. In middle school she'd done poorly in English because her in-class essays never stuck to the topic assigned. Tiffany had said that she liked to get creative with them but that her teachers were too narrow-minded. When I'd asked Megan to speak with them, she'd responded, "Tiffany's a C student, which is average. And that's fine. Not everyone can be a genius in school." I knew where this was coming from and it made me furious. Aren't parents supposed to want their children to surpass them? I remember thinking. But I said simply, "Tiffany is *not* average," and hoped that in time she'd have a teacher who would appreciate her imagination.

Ms. Whitfield was young, pretty in a plain sort of way, and extremely professional. She wore a gray pantsuit with a white blouse, and her blond hair was bobbed smartly just above her shoulders. I said hello, signed in, and sat at a small student desk facing her.

"Tiffany is an exceptional writer," she began. "Don't tell her this, but if she keeps it up, I'm going to nominate her for the freshman writing award." I couldn't believe my ears.

"She went from an eighty to a seventy in your class," I said. "How can that be if she's so good?" Tiffany's grade in humanities was of extra concern to me because it counted twice in calculating her average.

"The first quarter, when she was just settling in, she had an 80," Ms. Whitfield said, looking at her grade book. "Last quarter we did a lot of history and Tiffany didn't study enough for the tests. But this quarter we've done more essay writing and presentations. Did she show you the entry into Cleopatra's private journal that she wrote?"

"No," I answered as Ms. Whitfield handed me a piece of paper, which I quickly skimmed. Tiffany had entered Cleopatra's mind and brought her to life. The queen was eight months pregnant and complained of the intense Egyptian heat. She worried about the responsibilities of caring for a child while dealing with a treacherous court. And, most important, Cleopatra was anxious that her handmade gown wouldn't be delivered in time for that evening's affair.

"Wow, that really is good," I said, impressed. "I love how it all comes back to fashion."

"And her essay on Iraq was equally accomplished," Ms. Whitfield said. I looked away in guilt. "She did a verbal presentation of it and led the class in quite a rousing debate about the war. Her arguments were remarkably ordered and insightful. Tiffany has real leadership qualities, Mr. Wintle."

"I've always thought so," I said, and smiled, beaming with pride. I shook the teacher's hand and left her classroom walking on air.

Ari, the student Tiffany had described as the "nice Jewish boy next door," had introduced himself to me earlier in the evening, apparently after calling Tiffany to find out what I looked like. I imagined it wouldn't have been hard for him to find me, though; with the exception of Ari's father, I hadn't seen a Caucasian parent the entire evening. Ari had volunteered to help out with the open house, and every time I left a conference, I bumped into him. My humanities meeting was no exception.

"So how's Tiffany doing in Whitfield's?" he asked with more than a passing curiosity. He obviously had a huge crush on my niece — one that I wished was reciprocated. Ari was far better looking than Tiffany had let on, with his spiky black hair, fair skin, and red lips, and he carried himself with a mature confidence I hadn't expected. Does she really not see it? I wondered. I bet it's because he's too "nice."

"Ari, I'm stunned," I answered. "With the exception of gym, she's doing great in every class. Science included."

"Well, I think Jenise being gone is a good thing," he said.

"I agree," I answered, anxious to get going. I'd been there for hours and, as in the fall, the entire building was sweltering.

"She's going to make a small fortune this quarter," he joked. "Hope she doesn't break the bank." Okay, so maybe he is a little geeky, I thought.

I called Tiffany when I emerged from the West Fourth Street station to let her know I was almost home. I planned to wait till I was there with her to reveal the results of the conferences.

"Well? Tell me, tell me! What did they say?" she begged. For someone who was generally blasé about school, she certainly seemed anxious to hear. "What did Ms. Whitfield say?" There would be no waiting.

"Tiffany, you did it!" I squealed. "Your teachers raved about you," I said sotto voce now, trying to not be another annoying person walking down the quiet streets of the Village ranting on a cell phone.

"Omigod, omigod! I'm so happy!" And then Tiffany started to cry.

"Sweetie, what's wrong?" I stopped in my tracks on Perry Street and sat on the stoop of the building they'd used for

Carrie's house on *Sex and the City.*

"Nothing, I'm just happy is all," she said through her tears. "I've been trying so hard and I guess I'm relieved that it's actually paying off."

"Of course it's paying off, Tiffany," I said softly. "You're a smart, talented person. When you put your mind to something — anything — you can do it. And now you've *learned* that, once and for all, instead of just being *told* it."

"I love you," she said.

"Oh, I love you too." Tears now streamed down my cheeks too. "I'll see you in five minutes." As I folded up my cell phone, I realized that for the first time in the more than six months since my niece moved in with me, I now had a concrete reason to hope that this nutty, unorthodox arrangement of ours might just be working. I stopped on Hudson Street to buy a big bunch of yellow tulips for Tiffany and ran the rest of the way to the apartment.

# The Sins of the Mother

The next morning, after we'd celebrated in high style the night before by ordering in from our favorite pasta joint (Tiffany was nuts for their tortellini alla panna) and wolfing it down on the sofas in front of *Will and Grace*, it was business as usual. Tiffany was in the kitchen stirring her Carnation Instant Breakfast — yes, I'd repeated the sins of the mother — when I went in to get some coffee.

"Ms. Bernstein told me how much you've opened up in your Council for Unity class," I said as I poured boiling water through my single-cup filter.

"She did?"

"Yeah, she told me about the exercise the class did where all the students who had a parent with an alcohol or substance abuse problem had to go to the other side of the room."

"Well, since I have *two* parents who fit that description, I certainly qualified," Tiffany said matter-of-factly.

"Yes, but when people doubted you were telling the truth, Ms. Bernstein said you told them how you'd been feeling since you'd come to the school." I added two-percent milk to my coffee.

"Yeah, well, it's true. Just because I'm this little white girl who wears decent clothes and comes from Connecticut, they all assume that I've had it easy, like I'm some spoiled rich-bitch princess or something." Tiffany turned and leaned against the counter, sipping her Strawberry Sensation and grimacing. (It was the flavor she liked the least in the variety pack.)

"Then why do they think you came down to the city to live with your gay uncle, if everything was so great?" I asked.

"It seems like half the kids don't live with their parents, so it doesn't faze them," she said. "And everyone has a gay uncle, so they just think that's cool." Tiffany headed down the hall to her bedroom and I followed.

"So how did they respond to you? Did they cop to it?"

"Yeah, they sort of did," she said, braiding her hair in front of the crescent moon mirror. I sat on the bed. "Then we got into a whole discussion about how people get judged just because of the way they look. It was kinda funny because the topic was supposed to be how to deal with parents with drug problems."

"I'm sure Ms. Bernstein will remember to get back to that another day."

"She already did," Tiffany replied. "Is my part straight in the back?"

"Straight enough," I lied, since there wasn't enough time to fix it. "It sounds like a good class."

"It is," she said as she leaned in close to apply mascara. "It's just too bad there are only fifteen kids in it. That leaves about three hundred others who still think my biggest problem is what to wear in the morning."

"I also ran into Mr. Simpson last night. He told me you submitted your poem for the contest after all. He was quite impressed by it."

"Well, I didn't win," she said, pulling on her black Timberlands. "Is there anyone you *didn't* speak to?"

"I'm proud of you for entering, Tiffany. That took guts."

"Thanks, Uncle Eddy. Can I have an advance against my report card money?"

"Your sister Megan's on the phone," Rob announced to me from his desk. As I'd been in for less than a half hour, I was still leisurely eating a bagel and reading the Gotham edition of *Daily Variety.*

"Hey Megan, I have some good news for you," I said after donning my headset.

"Eddy, something bad has happened," she said, trying a little too hard to sound unemotional.

"What is it? What's the matter?" I asked.

"Eric broke into the house last night and attacked me with a baseball bat."

"What? Shit! Hold on." I jumped up and swung my office door closed. "What happened?"

"Well, I didn't know it was him because he was wearing a black ski mask. Luckily I woke up when he was standing over the bed, just as he was about to hit me the first time. So I was able to block the blow a little."

I was stunned, unable to quite process what I was hearing. This was the stuff of Lifetime Television for Women — a "woman in jeopardy" story I could sell to a producer — *not my own family's story.*

"So what happened then? Where was Sammy?"

"Thank God for Sammy, my little hero." Megan's voice cracked. "She heard me screaming downstairs in my bedroom and

439

called 911. Eric heard her yelling the address into the phone and got scared and ran out."

"How do you know it was him? Did you pull his mask off?"

"The police asked me if there was anyone I knew who might possibly do this, so I told them I'd recently broken up with Eric. They drove toward his house and found him walking on the side of the road with the bat and ski mask, plus a hundred dollars he took off my dresser. They picked him up and he admitted everything."

"Oh God, Megan, I'm so sorry. Are you okay? Did he hurt you?"

"Not really," she replied. "I spent the rest of the night in the emergency room, after I took Sammy to Mom's. We were worried that one of my knees was messed up but the MRI and X-rays didn't show anything. I'm just bruised up."

"How's Sammy?" The poor kid, I thought, hasn't she had enough to bear?

"She was pretty shaken up," Megan said. "But she's resting today at Mom and Dad's. She was shocked to find out that it was Eric." She paused. "I wonder if it's worse that it was someone she knows," Megan said sadly.

I thought of my eight-year-old niece's

sweet face, and how her big hazel eyes would now see the world as a place where no one could be trusted. I felt like I did that morning on the boat in Mystic, when Tiffany told me the awful things Eric had said to the children. My chest felt like an old suitcase forced shut with a leather belt, like it was being crushed and might explode at the same time. I reached into my bag for a Klonopin.

"What are you going to do now?" I asked my sister.

"I rented a movie on my way home from the hospital, so I'm going to try and relax and forget about it for a while."

"What did you rent?" I asked.

"*Hannibal*," she replied, laughing. "I know what you're going to say, but I figured someone being served their own brains for dinner will make my situation look like *Scooby-Doo* by comparison."

"Whatever you say, Megan." I wasn't going to touch that one. "Listen, I won't be seeing Tiffany before she gets on the train to go up there this afternoon, so I won't tell her anything when she calls me after school."

"Okay, I'll tell her when I pick her up at the station. Bye, Eddy."

"Get some rest, Megan. I'll call you tomorrow," I said before I removed my headset, folded my arms on my desk blotter, and laid my head down.

My cell phone rang just as I was walking past the beer-drinking crowd out in front of the White Horse Tavern on Hudson Street. As it was mostly a frat boy sports bar, I rarely entered the joint, but I was glad that the place where Dylan Thomas used to sit and write marked the turnoff for the street to my apartment.

"What the fuck? What the fuck? What the fuck?" Tiffany screamed into the new cell phone I'd bought for her during one of my lunch breaks that week.

I ducked around the corner on Eleventh Street and sought refuge in the doorway of the House of Sufism. "Try to calm down, Tiffany." I attempted a reassuring tone.

"Calm down?" she yelled. "I'm going to fucking kill that motherfucker! He hurt my mother!"

"I understand, honey, but he'll be going to jail for a long time."

"Well then I'll kill him when he gets out! I'll bash his fucking head in!" She was breathing hard so I knew she was pacing as she ranted.

"Where are you, Tiffany?" I asked.

442

"In Grand Central, waiting for my train." Her voice lowered a decibel or two.

"Oh, God. Why did your mom tell you this over the phone?" I felt anger rising up inside me, filling the space where sadness and anxiety had resided all day.

"That's not important!" She was yelling again. "I knew something was wrong when I spoke to her, so I made her tell me. It's not her fault!" How typical, I thought, you *made* her tell you. That's exactly why your relationship doesn't work!

"Okay, okay. Just find your platform and get yourself settled on the train." I had no idea what to say. "You have a bottle of water and something to read, right?"

"Yes," she said, sounding calmer.

"Okay, try not to think about it too much. In an hour and a half, you'll be with Mommy and Sammy, and that's the most important thing." It took great effort to not tell her to stay off the cell phone during the trip, as the minutes were prime time. She would need to call her friends, I knew, and Tiffany's taking care of herself at this moment was more important than my wallet.

As I walked the two remaining blocks to my apartment, my brain started spinning inside my skull. I knew this guy was crazy! Why didn't the rest of the family see that?

How could Megan have been attracted to someone like him? And then, instantly, my thoughts froze on the image of someone hurting my sister — my sweet, funny, well-meaning sister with her giant heart. The commingling of fury and sadness made bile rise up in my throat, and I quickened my step. I didn't allow myself to think what might have happened to Sammy if her mother hadn't managed to cry out, or to Tiffany had she been there.

Knowing my niece would be away, I'd planned a hookup with a guy from the gym for seven o'clock that evening. I'd seen Jordan around the city for years and had been lusting after him for almost as long. He'd bartended shirtless at one of the city's hot spots forever, and a couple of years back, I'd seen him at a swanky Upper East Side holiday party where he'd been hired to be a Tom of Finland version of Santa Claus (again, shirtless). Guests posed for photos on his lap, but I'd declined, as I sensed his attraction to me and had bigger plans for him. Shortly after that, he slipped me his number at the gym, but I'd just met Kurt so I never called. Now, after all these months and years of waiting, I was finally going to have that gorgeous specimen alone in my apartment, all to myself. It never occurred to me to cancel our tryst in light of my family's crisis. In fact, I was raring to go more than ever. For a couple of blissful hours my mind would be gone, my sentient self obliterated by something primal, unthinking. The despair, pain, and rage that vibrated through my skull would be quelled, even if only temporarily.

Plus I figured that after Jordan and I had had sex, I would finally have earned the right to ask him who (or what) had bitten off half of his left ear.

# Longtime Companion

Tiffany returned to Manhattan midafternoon that Sunday, as she wanted to leave herself a couple of hours to do homework before our Sunday evening ritual of dinner and *Six Feet Under.* When she arrived, I was sitting on my bed sorting medications by putting them in a plastic container with seven compartments — one for each day of the week.

"Hi, Tiffany," I yelled, "I'm in the bedroom." She dropped her bag outside my door, threw herself onto the foot of my bed, and began to cry.

"What is it?" I asked, reaching over to push aside the hair that had fallen across her face. "Sammy's okay, isn't she?" I'd spoken to Megan on Saturday and she'd said they were fine, though no one except Tiffany was really talking about what had happened.

"It's not that," Tiffany managed to squeak out. "Brooke's mom, Janet, has liver cancer and is dying. I feel so bad for them." She curled tighter in the fetal position and sobbed.

"Oh, gosh, I'm so sorry, Tiffany," I said, as I jumped up and went around to sit behind her and rub her back. I'd met Janet almost two years earlier when she brought Brooke and another friend down for an overnight visit during the summer. She seemed nice enough, but she drank a six-pack of Zima while watching a video with the girls after they'd returned from shopping. Tiffany told me after they'd gone that Janet was an alcoholic but that she'd managed to kick a long heroin addiction a few months earlier. What? I remember thinking. That makes her alcoholism okay? Tiffany's friendship with Brooke seemed to taper off in the year that followed; after Tiffany moved to New York, I'd never heard Brooke's name mentioned again. I wondered now if Janet's illness might have driven home the knowledge that Megan could have been killed by Eric.

When she finally got up, she looked me square in the eye and said, "You're not going to tell me you have a fatal disease one day and then die a few weeks later on me, are you?"

"Of course not, honey," I said, hugging her tightly to me. "I'm not going anywhere. Well, not without giving you a lot of advance notice," I half joked. "I promise."

"Thank you," she said and headed off to her room to listen to Coldplay's "Yellow" again and again while she unpacked.

I sat motionless for a moment, staring at my assortment of pills. So she knows, I thought. I'd suspected so, but now I knew for sure. We obviously needed to have a real conversation about my health sometime soon. I'd been putting it off for a couple of years now, waiting for things to get better in Tiffany's life so as not to add to her burden. Now was not the time, though, as her slender shoulders already seemed to sag under the weight of so much bad news. At least Tiffany had gotten me to say exactly what she needed to hear; hopefully, I would be able to live up to my promise.

I'd tested positive for the HIV virus almost fifteen years earlier, when I was twenty-six years old. In the days following my diagnosis I went for on-site counseling at the Community Health Project on Thirteenth Street. The skinny, chain-smoking queen with whom I spoke told me I wouldn't live to see thirty. He said I'd better make a living will and a regular will and designate a healthcare proxy, and do it all quickly. He also told me to start reading up on AIDS because everything was going to start to go — my eyes, my skin, my lungs, my muscle tone. Everything. I'm sure that counselor from the A Team is long dead, may he rest in peace, but none of the awful things he predicted came to pass.

I'd already decided to leave acting and had taken the Law School Admissions Test before I tested positive. If I had any doubts, though, the deal was now sealed: being a gay actor was tough enough; being a gay actor trying to conceal a fatal illness would be impossible. Law school seemed better than ever. I could die doing something decent and respectable; I would study to be a civil liberties lawyer and everyone, including my parents, would be proud. (Going to my grave a waiter or an unemployed actor was simply out of the question.) Plus I wouldn't have to work a demoralizing and exhausting job to put myself through school; massive loans were available to law students, so I could live well while I studied. And I'd *never* be around long enough to have to pay a dime of the money back!

I thought I had it all figured out, but of

course, life intervened. Further testing showed that my immune system was in working order, and my new HIV doctor said it could be months, even years, before that might change. New drugs were being invented and, with the help of groups like the AIDS Coalition to Unleash Power (ACT UP of which I was already a member), the FDA approval process was being streamlined and a whole system of human testing had been put in place. Thus I'd been granted a stay of execution. So now what?

Like many people diagnosed with a fatal illness (which HIV was at that time; it was just a question of *when* you would die), my next step was to get reacquainted with God. I'd been brought up as a nice Catholic boy but had turned my back on religion as a teenager, largely because of the hypocrisy and intolerance of the Church. Organized religion and faith, I declared, were for those not strong enough to face life on their own, existential as it might seem at times. Now I was one of those people, but the way I rediscovered my connection to God didn't involve going back to mass.

The day after I tested positive, I called a close actor friend of mine. I was crying hysterically and barely able to speak, so he told me to meet him at a particular address in a half hour. I donned big Ray Ban sunglasses to hide my swollen eyes and slogged across town to Perry Street in the West Village (I was living with Beth on Avenue B at the time). When I arrived, I found this little curtained storefront packed with people sitting on metal folding chairs in near darkness. Immediately my friend jumped up and guided me to an empty seat. After he sat down next to me, I realized that to my left sat another good actor friend. The three of us had shared a dressing room while doing a play just months before. They each put an arm around me and the proceedings began.

In the center of the room an attractive heterosexual man sat on a raised platform, behind a tragic little podium covered in kitchen floor linoleum. Someone dimmed the lights further and the man began to speak. I felt safe and cozy sandwiched between my friends, and it was a relief to have something other than my own misery to focus on. The man said things I'd never imagined anyone saying to a group, much less to a group of strangers. He spoke of how, when he reached his twenties and later his thirties, he kept expecting to feel the way he thought a grown man was supposed to feel — in command, capable, wise. But he never did. It seemed to him that other men were given something that he wasn't — a set of instructions, a key, something. He admitted to feeling like he was never "enough" and frightened that he never would be. And then he spoke of how God had helped him to heal from all of this self-torment, and how he realized he was not alone with any of these feelings.

I had always thought only gay men felt this way but that we're too competitive to ever admit it to each other. We're too busy butching it up, acting like we have all the answers and nothing fazes us. But hearing this man testify to all these feelings, and watching as everyone clapped and shook his hand when he finished, I felt like I had finally found a home — a place where I would be accepted as I was. Because those two dear friends had invited me to that address on that specific day, I would spend the next ten years of my life attending meetings of Alcoholics Anonymous.

Law school was not for another year, so I was able to study and sit for the LSAT a second time, prepare all of my law school applications, and practice the principles that the program of AA was teaching me.

Not drinking alcohol or smoking pot was a small sacrifice for admission to what seemed to me a combination of group therapy and spiritual guidance. Plus I figured it would help keep my immune system in good shape for even longer, as well as eliminate one brand of time-wasting temptation while I attended law school. I even gave up coffee too. Over the course of that healing year, I decided to defer my acceptance to law school and to face my fear of writing. Nine months after I tested HIV-positive, I moved out to Sag Harbor to confront that blank page. Though the writing didn't go as well as I'd hoped, I met a man who would become the spiritual mentor for whom I'd been waiting without ever being consciously aware of it.

Peter Hallock was a tall, elegant, charismatic man fifteen years my senior. A Renaissance man of sorts, he was a painter and a writer, and deeply spiritual. Peter was also a Vietnam War veteran and HIV-positive. He introduced me to numerous metaphysical texts, including those of Ernest Holmes and Thomas Merton, which we often read together and discussed. He also comforted me when I was overcome with fear and anxiety, led me through prayer, and taught me how to meditate. We spent many hours walking along the ocean or hiking in the Mashomack Preserve on Shelter Island, sometimes praying together or talking, and sometimes just being happily silent. In short, Peter taught me how to trust in the universe again, which gave me the courage and strength to return to New York and attend law school, knowing that, no matter what happened, I would be okay.

Peter died of AIDS two years after I left Sag Harbor. I had visited him as often as I could, and the moments we lay wrapped in each other's arms on the bed where he would soon die, expressing our gratitude for the three short years we had together, were among the most transcendent of my life.

At my second meeting of Alcoholics Anonymous I'd met Eugene, who'd very recently made the transition back from being Natalia. (I had, in fact, mistaken him for a very butch lesbian.) Though it seemed that Eugene and I couldn't have been more different, at heart we were the same: two creative men searching for our voices. And it was upon this shared struggle that we built our friendship. When I reminded him ten years later that alcoholism is a self-diagnosed disease, and explained that I had fudged that requirement a little in order to continue on the healing path upon which AA had set me, Eugene gave birth to my drag name before my very eyes — Miss Diagnosis! By the time I left Alcoholics Anonymous, though, I was keenly aware of my addictive personality and knew that I had to keep vigilant watch on all of my obsessive-compulsive behaviors, whether they centered around substances (including food), sex, work, cleaning and organizing, relationships, or even spirituality.

After Tiffany left my room that Sunday afternoon, I wondered whether my entire journey had been for the purpose of preparing me for this: being my niece's guardian. Could it be that I've been spared so that I would be able to help another? I asked myself, looking down at my array of HIV medications. I knew it was a question that could never be answered, but one worth asking all the same.

# By My Side

The day that Saddam Hussein's statue was toppled by Iraqis and dragged through the streets of central Baghdad, Tiffany and I were scheduled to meet with an assistant district attorney regarding Jenise's case. I told Tiffany the news when she met up with me at my office after school.

"That is so ill," she said happily. "So maybe the Iraqi people really are glad we're there."

"I hope so," I responded, leaning back in my desk chair. "I hate to sound cynical, but it seems like too perfect a photo opportunity for the Western media. We'll see, though; time will tell, I guess."

We rode the 6 train downtown to the Brooklyn Bridge stop and worked our way back up Centre Street toward the criminal court building. It was a route with which I was very familiar after ten years of visiting Orly at work.

"I want to ask you something, Uncle Eddy," Tiffany said out of nowhere.

"Why don't we make a deal?" I asked, ever the opportunist. "If I say yes, then I get to ask you something too, okay?"

"All right," she said without hesitation. Tiffany often made deals without really considering beforehand her end of the bargain. "Last year, on the night before your birthday, did *you* call security on me?"

Totally busted, I thought. I guess I'm the one who should've thought harder about striking this deal. I figured there was no getting out of this one while being honest at the same time. "Yeah, actually, I did," I said simply.

"I knew it!" she shrieked. "I knew it that night, even! How could you do that? That is so whack!" Luckily she was smiling, as I would have hated to go into the DA's office in a fight.

"Well, think about it from my point of view, Tiffany," I said. "I was afraid you were hurting yourself and I wasn't able to calm you down. I figured the sight of two uniformed security guards would do the trick."

"Okay, whatever," she said abruptly, raising an eyebrow and glancing sideways at me. "But for the record, I think it was a bit extreme of you."

We'd arrived at the Hogan Place entrance, so my question for Tiffany would have to wait until after her interview with the assistant district attorney, which she handled beautifully. "An open and shut case," ADA Hector Rios said. Tiffany's statements were consistent with the evidence he'd gathered, and he was certain of conviction. As Jenise had no prior record, he said she was likely to be sentenced to only a few days of community service but that he would also seek restitution for the phone. Tiffany and I were both surprised when he then asked if we wanted an order of protection against Jenise. Much to my niece's chagrin, I told ADA Rios about an obscene phone message Jenise had left in which she pretended (badly) to be a boy asking to schedule a blow job from Tiffany. After some discussion, we all decided the order wasn't necessary, especially since Jenise had not shown up at school even once in the nearly three weeks since the theft.

"I can't believe you told him about that nasty phone message," she whined after we left the building. "I was so embarrassed!"

"Well, he asked what the message was, and I wasn't going to lie to him," I said.

"But he was so hot!" She covered her face with her hands and moaned.

"Oh, now I get why you're so embarrassed!" I teased. "Well, I agree, actually." He *was* adorable, but I hadn't planned to mention it. "Isn't he a little old, though?" I felt compelled to add. "Plus I wouldn't have thought he was your type; he was so preppy with his gelled hair, navy suit and shiny black shoes."

"Yeah, but he was really a hottie, you could tell," she said laughing. "He looked like he'd be more comfortable in a hoodie and Tims."

"Tiffany, he has to be at least twenty-five years old to be an ADA. You're scaring me!"

"Why?" she asked indignantly. "Tom Cruise is, like, forty, and everyone thinks he's hot. And it's not like I'd get with him or anything."

"Well, that's good to hear," I said with mock relief.

"Look at *you*," she said, turning toward me as we walked. "You're Tom Cruise's age and some of my girlfriends think you're hot."

"Get out of here!" I screamed. "First, you can't compare *me* to Tom Cruise, and second, don't let your girlfriends talk about your uncle that way!" We both giggled. "Okay, so now it's my turn to ask you something, remember?"

"Yeah," she said with a sigh. "I was hoping you forgot."

"No such luck," I replied. "So, what I want to know is: what's the story with you and Tommy Dash? Did you see each other this past weekend?"

"What do you mean?" she asked. "Why are you bringing up Tommy all of a sudden?"

"I think you're carrying an Olympic-sized torch for him," I said frankly. "You're not interested in any of the guys at your school, or in Aleksi or any of his friends. Not that that's a bad thing, though I do think Peter is very sweet."

"Oh, so you think it's weird that I don't have any boyfriends?" Before I could answer, she continued, "The way I look at it is this: the only difference between being good friends and going out with someone is sex. And since I'm only in high school, I might as well just be friends with the guys."

"So you're telling me you don't plan on having sex until you're out of high school?" I didn't believe it for a second.

"Well, at least not until more of the boys have cars and I'm able to stay out later." Well, that's a little more honest, I thought, though I didn't see why either of those two things were necessary. But I wasn't about to argue.

"You still haven't told me about Tommy," I said gently.

"I'm sort of confused about him," she said. "I know I love him, but I think it's more like you'd love a brother, or a really close girlfriend."

"You mean it's platonic, where there's no desire to have sex involved?"

"Well, we've made out before, and he *is* looking really fine these days. But yes, I think I want to be just friends with him. And no, I didn't see him this weekend because he has a girlfriend now, and she's really threatened by me." What girl wouldn't be? I thought.

"That sounds like a good plan, Tiffany. Especially since he has a girlfriend," I said as we walked under the steel and glass subway gazebo at West Broadway.

"Oh, she's a stank ho. I don't care about her," she declared as we descended the stairs.

"Look, Tiffany!" I exclaimed when we reached the corner of Eleventh and Greenwich Streets. It was a spectacular spring morning and overnight the Bradford pear trees that lined many of the Village's

461

streets had popped. Billowing clouds of white cotton now overhung Greenwich Street for as far as the eyes could see.

"It's so beautiful," Tiffany said with reverence. "Let's walk underneath them."

"Of course," I replied. "Then we'll turn up Charles Street, where the canopy completely blocks out the sky."

"I don't remember these trees being white last summer," she said as we walked, the morning sunlight warming our faces.

"They're only white for about a week every spring. The little buds blossom, and then the blossoms turn to green leaves."

"Cool," she replied.

"All good gifts around us," I sang softly, "are sent from heaven above, so thank the Lord —"

"It's a little early for *Godspell*, Uncle Eddy," Tiffany interrupted, teasing me, but I was glad she at least remembered the song. A few years earlier, after Megan had taken the girls to see a production of the play, the four of us had danced, acted, and sung along with the entire soundtrack from the movie. I'd played Jesus, of course, though Sammy tried to muscle in a couple of times.

"It's just so hard *not* to sing on a morning like this," I said, "and I always want to acknowledge God when I see such amazing beauty."

"Well, I'll just acknowledge the flowers," Tiffany said. She was exactly where I was with God when I was fourteen, so I decided to change the subject.

"You have to know which streets to walk down during different times of the year," I said. "Next month we'll have to switch from Waverly to Christopher because there's the most magnificent wisteria vine covering an entire tree in front of the puppy store. You'll like that: wisteria is purple."

"Okay, but who says 'magnificent'?" She looked at me and smiled.

"I do," I said proudly. "Adjectives are fun, and there are a ton of them besides *cool, whack, ill,* and *fly.*" Tiffany laughed.

"Have I told you lately that you're crazy?" she asked.

"Since Valentine's Day? That was almost two months ago, so I'm sure you have," I replied. "Listen, I hope you're talking to Ms. Martin about all the stuff that's happened. You know — the attack, your dad's new family, Janet's illness. That's what she's there for."

"No, that's what my friends are there for," she said. "I don't like that lady, Uncle Eddy. All she wants to talk about is *drug*

463

*abuse* and *having sex.*" Tiffany's eyes widened as she whispered the mock scandalous words. "Therapy is still retarded," she added, echoing the opinion she'd expressed months before.

"I've been seeing my therapist for over a year," I replied. "He gives me wonderful support, especially when I'm going through changes. You're going through so much right now, Tiffany; I'd be a bad guardian if I didn't insist you talk to a professional. Maybe we can find someone better."

"What I'm going through is called *life,* Uncle Eddy, and there's nothing to do but to live it." She walked on sadly, her gaze to the ground, oblivious now to the bounty overhead.

Right through dinner, Easter Sunday at my parents' house went relatively smoothly, with everyone cautiously avoiding discussion of world events. At the end of the meal, though, I found myself alone at the table with my uncle Tommy and his wife, Patricia, who insisted that little mobile anthrax factories had been found buried in Iraq. I pictured New York City hot dog carts with yellow and blue umbrellas touting fresh chemical weapons instead of all-beef frankfurters. Just as my uncle's face was turning crimson and my aunt's voice rose three octaves, my mom came swooping in.

"Okay, clear out, all of you," she said, coffee cups dangling from her fingers. "I need the space to set up for dessert." Always on her social toes, Mom knew how to defuse any potentially volatile situation — a talent not uncommon among matriarchs and eldest siblings, I supposed.

"We love ya, kid," Aunt Patricia whispered in my ear as she squeezed my shoulder on her way out of the dining room. "But you'll see."

Everyone had assiduously avoided another topic that day as well: Eric's attack on Megan. His name, in fact, seemed to be verboten. I'd been cornered several different times for the story, but always in private and never within earshot of my sister. My uncle Barry, Mom's middle brother, had offered to get some of his old friends from the Bronx to come up and "break the motherfucker's kneecaps" until I assured him that Eric was safely behind bars. His wife, Crystal, on the other hand, had gotten choked up when I told her that Sammy had saved the day.

"I see a real difference in Tiffany," my

465

mom said now, placing a platter of mini Italian pastries on the table. "She really seems to have matured."

"Oh, I hope you're right, Mom. We've had a good little run lately, culminating in the glowing reports I received from her teachers." I was spiral-fanning paper napkins, a residual talent from my cater waiter days. "There's so much for her to deal with, though. I wish things would just *stop happening* for a while, so she could catch up, you know?"

"You're not kidding, hon," she said, sighing. "I'm really worried about Megan again. Your taking Tiffany was supposed to give her time to get things together, which she seemed to do. But she's been unemployed for over three months and now this thing with you-know-who." She leaned on a dining room chair, her body heavy with the weight of it all.

"It's going to be okay, you'll see," I reassured her. "Megan's smart. She knows she has to start looking harder for a job. She spent twenty years at a job she hated, so she just needs a break is all." Nothing Mom was saying was incorrect, but my role has always been to fight against the Irish gloom that could so easily pervade our clan. "Let's have a hug," I said, holding out my arms.

"What would we do without you?" she asked as she pulled me firmly to her, the familiar smells of perfume and hair spray enveloping me. After all I've put you through, I thought, you still have such faith in me. Don't you see that it's *I* who couldn't get along without *you?*

My mom had been my biggest cheerleader since Tiffany moved to Manhattan. Inspirational cards arrived regularly in the mail, and hardly a day went by that her name did not pop up on my computer screen at least once. If she could only know how much I needed those e-mails, the purpose of which she pretended was to fill me in on this or that— "Max was groomed this morning and he looks adorable" or "I've had it up to here with that hospital auxiliary!" — when really she was checking to make sure I was okay and to let me know she was there for me.

Tiffany spent the week following Easter in New Milford, as her school was closed for spring break. I was looking forward to the time off, as well as hoping that since Megan was out of work and Sammy would be in school, Tiffany and her mom might spend some solid quality time together.

I was also anxious to have a second date with yet another guy I'd met at the gym — a handsome, blond ex-actor ten years my junior named Brent Smolinski. (Jordan was already ancient history; the next time I saw him he'd told me that he and his boyfriend had gotten back together. I doubt they were ever apart.) Every Saturday for months now I'd seen Brent at the branch of my gym closest to my apartment, where he spent at least two hours on the Stair-Master. Thus I spent my entire workout, which never lasted that long, staring at his gorgeous ass in motion. The combination of caring for my niece, feeling creatively virile again, and good old-fashioned spring fever had my confidence running high, so I worked up the courage to ask him out. To my surprise, Brent accepted, flashing perhaps the whitest teeth I'd ever seen and momentarily softening a jaw to rival Luke Wilson's.

Our first date consisted of a long, romantic walk around the Village on a warm spring night. Brent seemed a bit awkward and the conversation was jumpy. It felt like work but I didn't want to give up too easily; I'd waited a long time for this date. Even though we never really found a connection, the date ended with us making out for over an hour in the vestibule of his apartment building on Cornelia Street. When it came to kissing, there was definitely chemistry and Brent was hardly ill at ease.

Our second date, though, was an unmitigated disaster. We met for dinner at a cozy Italian place on the corner of Jane Street and Eighth Avenue. I could tell that Brent was trying hard to make small talk and show an interest in me, but it became painfully obvious that the stunning young man who sat before me was an utterly miserable human being. He seemed soured from having had no success as an actor, speaking bitterly about the careers of his fellow NYU graduates, and he hated his current job of planning special promotions for on-site concession stands. To make matters worse, it was a humid evening and he kept complaining that his hair hadn't come out right, checking the mirror next to our table every so often, and he spoke of feeling fat even though he did his gym routine religiously seven days per week.

I knew by the end of dinner that I wouldn't go out with Brent again, but I couldn't let go of the idea of getting him into bed. Years of experience told me that sex was only good if you really cared for someone (as I had Kurt and my friend in California) or if your partner was a fairly blank slate on whom you could project your fantasies (as was the case with Jordan). But Tiffany's away, I thought. It could be months before you get another chance like this, and it definitely *won't* be with Brent. Somewhere inside I knew this was simple self-justification and that I was just jonesing for the brand of ego feeding I used to crave so often. But I pounded back that knowledge and asked Brent over to my apartment. Despite his being physically perfect in perhaps every way, sex with him was about as fun as waiting in line for two hours in ninety-degree heat to ride a roller coaster that lasts forty-five seconds. And that's coming from someone who *hates* amusement parks.

Unfortunately, I would later learn, Tiffany's and Megan's time together didn't go much better.

# The Scion, The Witch, and The Earlobe

"Uncle Eddy, can I take a workshop at Morgana's a week from Saturday?"

Tiffany and I were having a Thursday night dinner of delicious homemade tacos; I'd seen an El Paso kit in the store and remembered that Tiffany missed the "Mexican nights" she, Megan, and Sammy had had at least once a month. The last time I'd served ground beef was in the form of Hamburger Helper Beef Stroganoff, and Tiffany had pleaded, "Please, Uncle Eddy, no more ground cow." But it had been a while now, and she seemed okay with this variation.

"What's the workshop and how much does it cost?" I asked. Morgana's Chamber is a Wicca shop on West Tenth Street that carries all the supplies the modern witch could possibly need. Every time I ventured in with Tiffany, I'd gone into immediate allergic meltdown from the two large black cats that slinked around, shedding their hair all over the merchandise.

"It's on how to make amulets and talismans, which sounds really cool," Tiffany replied, spooning more Paul Newman salsa over her taco. "I'm not sure what it costs yet."

"That place is creepy," I said, scrunching up my face. "Last time I was in there I almost stepped in cat puke, and you should have seen the e-mail addresses on the workshop sign-up sheet. One was Mother's milk runs black today at Earthlink dot net."

"Eww, that's nasty," Tiffany responded. "I just remembered Kitt's coming down next weekend anyway. She's not a witch, so we'll just hang out."

"Don't forget I'm getting us all tickets for a midnight movie on Saturday at the TriBeCa Film Festival, okay? It's about a bunch of girl rock and rollers, so I think you'll like it. And we'll have dinner to celebrate your grades first." Tiffany's report card had arrived, and it had cost me $105. A small price to pay, I'd figured, to a student who'd gone from "at risk of failure" to the honor roll.

"Yeah, that sounds really cool." Tiffany cleared our plates, and I followed her into the kitchen with the salsa and sour cream. She began to wash the dishes while I enjoyed putting all the uneaten taco components into separate little Tupperware containers. I no longer had to ask Tiffany to do the washing up, pots and all. (Now I occasionally offered to do them *for* her, especially if her homework load was heavy.)

"Uncle Eddy," Tiffany began in her tell-tale cadence. "Tomorrow night a bunch of us are going to hang out up in Niko's neighborhood."

"What neighborhood is that?" I asked, spooning ground beef into blue-tinted plastic.

"I think it's called Washington Heights," she said, never pulling her focus from her yellow-glove-covered hands.

"Sorry, Tiffany, but you can't hang out in that neighborhood. Not now, not ever." The fact that I'd never met Niko was irrelevant.

"Wha-tuh?" She shut the water off and turned toward me, a look of disgust on her face.

"It's not a safe neighborhood. Orly told me that around seventy percent of all the crimes committed in Manhattan happen in Washington Heights. There are going to be certain places I am not going to allow you to go, Tiffany. I get to decide what's safe and what's not."

"I'm going to be with my *friends,* and they *live* up there. I'm not afraid to hang out up there if I'm with them." Her tone grew strident. "They're not going to let anything happen to me, Uncle Eddy."

"How are they going to protect you from a stray bullet, Tiffany?" I asked. "Look, I'm sorry, but just because you're not afraid doesn't mean you're not in danger. There are so many reasons you can't go up there, not the least of which is that I don't want you riding the subway home from that part of town at eleven o'clock at night, even if you're not alone." Tiffany brushed past me into the hallway.

"You can't control where I go, Uncle Eddy," she said, growing more shrill with every word. "And it's ridiculous! What's the difference if I'm hanging out in Washington Heights or Washington Square Park? You think crimes never happen *there?*" Tiffany was pacing the hallway now, winding herself up for a full-scale tantrum. It had been several months since the last one but the pattern was familiar, as was the constriction in my chest. Don't engage, I told myself.

"You're doing this because of what happened in New Milford last weekend, aren't you?" she asked accusingly, standing next to me now, her hands on her hips and her face only a foot from mine. "You haven't mentioned it all week, but *now* you're deciding to punish me."

"No, Tiffany," I said calmly. "This is simply one of those judgment calls that I get to make and that you have to accept. You cannot fight me like this every time I make a decision about what is appropriate and what is not." If you do, you're going to have to leave here, I wanted to say, but fought back the words. *You mustn't threaten her, Ed.*

Tiffany had made her curfew the previous Saturday night, showing up in a car with a boy Megan didn't know. She asked Megan if he could drive her over to Jackie's house, where Tiffany wanted to spend the night. When Megan said no, they began to argue and Tiffany called her a "fucking bitch," got in the car, and drove away. I'd only heard Megan's side of the story, but it didn't matter; Tiffany had left the house without permission, which was the bottom line. Megan and I decided that I wouldn't punish Tiffany when she came back to the city but that she wouldn't be allowed to return to New Milford for a couple of months.

"You're driving me crazy, do you know that?" she screamed at me now. "I feel like a trapped animal and you're doing it on purpose."

"Tiffany, you need to go into your room, okay? I'm not going to argue about this."

"Oh, *you* don't want to argue about it, so that's it?" she taunted. "You just don't want me hanging around with Dominican boys, and that's *your* problem." She waited for me to respond but I didn't. "You want me to hang around with nice little rich kids here in the West Village because that's who *you* would hang out with. You think you can control every single thing I do, who I make friends with, and where I go. And that's *sick!* You need to talk to your therapist about it. Why can't you just be more chill?"

" 'Why can't you just be more chill?' " I imitated her, wiggling my head from side to side like a cool hip-hop girl. I knew it was wrong as I did it, but I was enraged that she didn't appreciate any of the freedoms that I *did* give her. I let her run all over Manhattan, from Midtown down, often having no idea where she was or whom exactly she was with. I didn't forbid her to go into apartments where no adults were home, or to smoke pot or drink a little, as long as she remained in control of herself and promised to call me if she needed help. I hadn't told her she couldn't hang around with the criminally insane Jenise or with Aleksi, who I knew was a pothead.

"Go . . . to . . . your . . . room . . . Tiffany," I said through clenched teeth, each hand on an opposite counter of our galley kitchen. I wasn't using the counter for support so much as trying to gain strength from the building itself.

"I fucking hate it here!" she shouted as she ran into her room and slammed the door hard.

I tuned the living room stereo to a classical music station and lay on the sofa with my *New York Times.* I didn't want to hear the inevitable sounds of Tiffany ranting to her friends about me. One night, after a relatively minor argument, I'd asked her if she still wanted to go out for Chinese food. She'd reluctantly said yes, but before we left, I heard her talking on the phone to a friend: "Now he expects me to sit across a table from him and watch him eat? He's disgusting!" I vowed now that if I heard her yelling about me — through her bedroom door, down the hall, and over the music — then she was basically yelling *at me,* and I would have to take some sort of action. But what? The only sounds that emanated from Tiffany's room, though, were those of Tupac, and my anxiety was tempered by a hope that this incident had ended relatively quickly.

I lay there for more than an hour, eating ice cream and reading the newspaper. Finally I heard Tiffany leave her room for a moment and go to the bathroom. When next I got up, an envelope lay on the floor at the entrance to my bedroom. With great hesitation I picked it up and opened it.

Dear Uncle Eddy,

I'm sorry this is not a stupid poem expressing my deep dark sorrow that I wrote halfway to express myself and halfway to kiss your ass. I want to start by saying that I absolutely *love* it when you fucking mock me because it makes me feel all warm and tingly inside. I'm sorry that since I'm not "old and wise" like you are we can't have a fucking conversation. Oh yeah, that's right, *I'm 14.* That must mean that nothing I say matters!! Why can't I have the goddamn choice to make myself happy at no one else's expense but my own? Contrary to what you and Mommy may think, I am not stupid and did not waste 8 months of my life in this shit hole city just to go back and do the same stupid shit I would have done before I came down here in the first goddamn place. It's human nature I suppose, well, at least in the Adeletta-Wintle/bro-sis duo, to think that everything is all horrible and worse than it actually is! Is it that hard to let things fucking go and not blow shit completely out of proportion? Have you taken a look at the standards you set for people lately, because they are way too fucking up there. Maybe that's why I'm not the only one who lives my "secret life" alone. Should I try to analyze your life a little more? Maybe after you read this letter we can sit together with a stopwatch and talk civilly about our feelings, then you can put all your notes in the file labeled "Tiffany." Or an even better idea: how about I go to therapy on Wednesday and talk about my ever so fucked up perspective on the world? Then you can pretend that I am actually changing how I feel. I try to be a pretty happy, uplifting person, but for some reason it's not working. Maybe it's all that nasty "Mr. Superior" negativity you bring around all the time. I think that it's about time to climb off that high horse and join us humans here on the ground. You know what? I am absolutely, positively fucking done with this bullshit. I am done grieving over, and tearing myself apart over, two people who obviously give a shit about my future but couldn't give two shits about my state of mind right now. Oh, no, I spilled my guts on these three little sheets of paper and explained to you exactly how I feel. What do you think of me now? *AM I A HOPELESS CASE?* Maybe you should just send me to boarding school and get me out of your hair so you don't have to spend another 5 minutes reading my obviously extremely meaningless letters. At least you can go spend time with Sammy when you want, or up and go to the theater every other night and not worry if I'm home smoking pot and eating all the leftover Chinese food.

Love,
Tiffany

I sat on my bed, stunned. Despite Tiffany's behavior at her mom's over spring break, I'd thought things were going much better between us. Somehow I believed I'd earned her respect as a guardian by the way I'd handled her illness, by the way I'd become involved with her education, and simply by the way I lived my life. Have I been deluding myself? I now wondered. Has she simply been playing along, placating me, while none of her underlying feelings or beliefs about her life and herself have changed? The pure venom of Tiffany's letter also shocked me. She'd never spoken to me like that, except maybe the night she was punching her bed the autumn before. Had I not established a strong-enough boundary? Had I been too much of a friend to her, so that she feels she can speak to me this way? I remembered that the night I'd called security Tiffany's tantrum had been over being told she couldn't stay an extra day in Connecticut on her birthday weekend, and now she was in a fury over being told she couldn't hang out in Washington Heights. When she was at Megan's, she was told she couldn't sleep over at a friend's house. She was still constitutionally incapable of accepting no for an answer. But did she really think New York was a "shit hole" and did she truly see me as such a condescending asshole? Of course all the stuff about Megan and me conspiring against her is classic teenage thinking, I thought, but what does she mean by "secret life"? I guess she means "sex life," but if you're doing it *alone* it can't really be called that. Very clever, but she's only fourteen; she shouldn't be lamenting the lack of a sex life!

I reminded myself of all the signs of Tiffany's progress — the turnaround she'd made at school, her dedication to performing and writing, and the way she seemed reconciled to staying home on weeknights — as well as of the fact that teenagers have the market cornered on rage and persecution complexes. And besides being the scion of a histrionic old former actor like myself, Tiffany has a preternatural talent for squeezing every ounce of Sturm und Drang out of any situation. Plus it's progress, not perfection, I thought. You can't expect to erase almost fourteen years of conditioning in seven months. It's the same as your feeling better about yourself but still being unable to stop yourself from sleeping with Brent. As they say, old habits die hard. Just as my reaction to her letter was softening, Tiffany came running into my room and threw herself on my bed and bawled.

"What is it, Tiffany? What's happened?" I slid over and gathered her up into my arms. Her face was awash in tears and the skin around her eyes was the color of watery beet juice.

"I called Mommy and she was drunk," she wailed and fell back against my chest sobbing.

"It's going to be okay, sweetie," I said, kissing the top of her head and squeezing her tight. "Everything's going to be all right." You poor, poor kid, I thought. How many different bad feelings can you possibly endure all at once? As I held her, I remembered seeing *Splendor in the Grass* on *The 4:30 Movie* as a little boy and how shocked I'd been by Natalie Wood's horrific battle with the teenage crazies. (Every afternoon I'd race around the block delivering my newspapers so I could make it home by 4:25. I'd close the drapes tight to black out the den, grab a lemon and a salt shaker, and tune in to WABC. My heart would race with excitement as the graphic of the film camera spun around and grew larger and larger, accompanied by the familiar theme tune, *da na na, da na na, da da duh da.* Sitting alone in the dark, sucking on salt-covered lemon quarters, I'd been unwittingly indoctrinated into the cults of *Valley of the Dolls, Whatever Happened to Baby Jane?, Hush, Hush, Sweet Charlotte,* and many other "classics.") I'd witnessed teenage girl madness again with Megan, albeit to a much lesser degree, and now I was living through it with her daughter. At the moment, though, what I felt more than anything was gratitude; a mere hour after Tiffany had written me such a vitriolic letter, she'd come running to me for comfort.

"Shhh," I whispered, as her breathing slowed and became more regular.

"Sometimes my thoughts are so loud, I feel like everyone around me can hear them," Tiffany said conspiratorially as I stood over her and Kitt, her friend from New Milford, on the 2 train heading down to Chambers Street. We were on our way to see *Prey for Rock & Roll* at the TriBeCa Film Festival. The girls had spent a good two hours blowing out their hair, trying on different outfits, and putting on makeup. I sat on the sofa writing on the laptop, available for consultation at each stage of the process. "Does this shirt make me look like a whore?" Kitt had asked. "No," I'd lied, "but it's so tight it looks a bit tacky."

Having spent years watching my two big sisters apply eyeshadow and don platform shoes, the comfort of something familiar but long forgotten had washed over me.

"You're so crazy, Tiffany," Kitt now teased, flashing an adorable metal-mouthed smile.

"No, seriously," my niece continued earnestly. "When that happens I look at someone in particular and I think real hard at them, 'If you can hear me, touch your earlobe.' "

"And does it ever work?" I asked, my face floating above them like some perverse deity.

"No," Tiffany admitted a bit sadly.

"I'm sure there are people who can read your thoughts telepathically," I said, trying to sound reassuring. "But you just don't know who they are."

"Of course, Uncle Eddy," she said with a ring of impatience in her voice. "Kitt and I read each other's minds all the time. Don't we, Kitt?"

"Absolutely," Kitt said, playing along. "Like right now, I bet you could go for some cheesy potato skins with bacon."

"Omigod!" Tiffany squealed. "I can't believe you knew that!"

We had dinner right next to the theater,

at TGI Friday's, a chain I'd heretofore managed to avoid. (And it's in TriBeCa of all places — the last bastion of cool in Manhattan!) The girls packed away the food like sumo wrestlers trying to bulk up, with Tiffany satisfying her potato-skins craving and all of us enjoying ice cream sundaes for dessert. The film, which stars Gina Gershon as the leader of a group of aging girl rockers who stick together through thick and thin, was a bit edgy to be watching with fourteen-year-olds. (At least they look sixteen or seventeen, I reminded myself with relief.) The music was fantastic and, as I watched, I imagined Tiffany being a part of the glamorously sleazy world of rock and roll, maybe even as the lead singer in a band. Why did I thrill at the thought, despite the disappointment and heartache that inevitably comes with the territory? Because when the music soars, I thought, it all becomes worth it — every single struggle and every defeat.

"What did you think?" I asked the sleepy girls when it was over.

"I liked it," Tiffany answered. "But the music sucked," both girls said in unison, reading each other's minds once again.

# Take A Sad Song
# and Make It Better

"Mr. Wintle, we have a bit of a situation here, I'm afraid," Ms. Santiago said in her robot voice. "Jenise came to school today and told Mr. Rodriguez she's been in jail all this time, since Tiffany had her arrested."

"That's preposterous," I said, immediately on the defensive. "The assistant district attorney told me she'd been convicted but that she'd been sentenced to only a few days of community service and restitution. What is she doing there? Didn't you have her officially removed from the school's roll?" I signaled to Rob to hold any other calls that came in.

"Why weren't we informed of any of this?" Ms. Santiago asked pointedly.

"Jenise hasn't been in school for almost three months," I replied. "It seems to me that it would be the school's responsibility to find out why. Besides, I called Mr. Rodriguez the week after Jenise stole Tiffany's phone and told him that she was going to be arrested. I would have thought he would have contacted the district attorney's office directly."

"In any event, I have Tiffany here in my office," she said. "I can't have these girls bumping into each other in the halls of my school."

"How long has she been detained in your office?" My computer clock told me it was almost noon.

"Since Jenise arrived this morning for school."

"What?" I practically yelled into my headset. "This is outrageous! I want my niece in her classes. She hasn't done anything wrong. You've got a convicted criminal roaming the hallways, and Tiffany is being punished? You need to get Jenise out of that school *now* —"

"Excuse me, Mr. Wintle," Ms. Santiago interrupted, her tone not changing by even half a note. (She sounded as wooden as Madonna had in *Speed the Plow* on Broadway. I'd gone to the manager and asked for my money back, to no avail.) "There are procedures to be followed. We'll have to apply for an involuntary transfer for Jenise, but just so you know, the superintendent's office could decide

488

that it's Tiffany who will be transferred."

"Over my dead body," I said slowly and with finality, like a bad actor in a B movie. "I happen to know that this is Jenise's fourth high school. And Tiffany is doing very well in *your* school, so *she* will not be the one to leave." I wrote down the name Gail Cohen on my notepad, my nerve bolstered by our Friend in a High Place. "I'll fax you the paperwork I have from the assistant district attorney who prosecuted Jenise, and you can go from there. In the meantime, though, I want Jenise in your office and Tiffany in her classes."

"I'll watch for the documentation," Ms. Santiago responded pleasantly while somehow implying that she didn't quite believe our side of the story.

"It will be there pronto," I said and hit the headset button on my phone to terminate the call. What is her problem? I wondered. Had Tiffany alienated her so much with the stink bomb incident that she couldn't distinguish between the two students? Or was it Tiffany's kissing the Puerto Rican boy? Or maybe the incident with the wallet? Okay, so there had been a number of problems, I thought, but maybe Ms. Santiago doesn't realize how well Tiffany is now doing in all of her classes. I'll

489

have to call Mr. Rodriguez and ask him to inform her.

Every evening from that day forward I asked Tiffany if Jenise had been in school that day. The answer was always no.

I had little success in discussing the Washington Heights argument with Tiffany after Kitt went back to New Milford. "I didn't think you and I spoke to each other that way," I'd said, referring to her letter.

"I treat you with as much respect as you treat me," she'd responded. "Not trusting me and not letting me go where I need to go is not treating me with respect."

There was no making her understand that my decisions relating to her freedom — her curfew, her ability to move around the city — had nothing to do with how much I trusted or respected her but rather all to do with what I felt was safe and appropriate for a fourteen-year-old girl. For her entire life Tiffany had been able to argue and harangue her way into getting what she wanted with Megan and, I guess, Tony. Like any small child, if she met with resistance, she screamed, thrashed around, threatened, and basically made her family's life miserable until they gave in. And for some reason, Tiffany's parents were unable to hold firm. So "wear down and conquer" had become her MO — one she never outgrew — and I wasn't going to fall prey to it.

But what's going to happen next year, I worried, when she's a little older and has some close girlfriends to hang out with? How am I ever going to keep any controls on her behavior? I'd hoped that the respect she'd had for me since she was a tiny girl, when we were friends more than uncle and niece, would carry over to my guardianship. And I'd believed that the progress Tiffany had made with her self-esteem — she could no longer deny that she was smart and talented — would somehow give rise to an ability to respect authority. Was I trying to connect dots drawn on different pieces of paper? It seemed to work at school; as the teachers said, she'd chosen to do things a different way, to achieve rather than to disrupt, and her behavior in her classes had changed considerably. Why wouldn't the same hold true for our relationship? Wouldn't her love for me, combined with her increasing trust and admiration for all I'd done, enable her to accept that I might know a little more than she does about the world and about what's good or bad for her? Hadn't I earned the right to tell her what to do? I feared that I might never earn that right, and that disaster lay ahead if she continued to fight me on every limit and to disrespect me when I held firm to those limits. But I could only move forward, hour by hour, and hope for the best. Our latest argument hadn't ended with her hurting herself or my calling security, so maybe progress was being made after all. The words of her letter echoed in my mind, though; the insults, the cursing — they were the language of her relationship with Megan, not with me. Now that Tiffany had committed those words to paper, was it only a matter of time before she said them to my face?

As a teenager, I had certainly been no angel myself. Like Tiffany, I'd begun experimenting with alcohol and pot before I even hit thirteen, and when I was in high school, the trouble got more serious. At fifteen my best friend Joey and I took an older girl's car from a party. She'd passed out, and Joey wanted me to teach him how to drive. I'd been obsessed with driving since I was old enough to walk and had hounded several older girlfriends into letting me drive their cars long before I was eligible for a learner's permit. I'd decided it was safest for Joey to practice in a big parking lot, so I drove the Plymouth Duster over to a strip mall in a neighboring town. We were behind the stores, with Joey at the wheel, when we saw the taillights of a police car up ahead, doing a routine patrol. "Quick," Joey said. "You drive, and let's get out of here." No sooner had I executed a perfect three-point turn and begun speeding away than I saw the cop car in my rearview mirror. He was gaining on us, so I sped up. We were now in the wide-open section of the lot, so I stepped hard on the gas. The cop's lights flashed and his siren blared as the distance between us narrowed. Realizing it was ridiculous to think I could outrun a police car, I began to slow down. Just then the officer pulled up on my right side and cut his wheel toward us, crashing into the front right fender of the Duster, bringing both cars to a halt. I sat rail straight in the driver's seat, my entire body numb, while the officer pulled Joey out of the passenger-side door. I heard yelling but was too frightened to turn to see what was happening.

Minutes later, in the backseat of the squad car, Joey turned to me and said,

"Eddy, I think I've been shot." He took my hand and put it to his shoulder. I jerked it away and looked at it under the strobe of the passing streetlights. It was red, black, red, black, red, black, and I knew I was seeing blood.

I was terrified of the trouble I was in, not just with the law but with my parents as well. My early childhood had been a fairly happy one, yet they'd managed to inculcate in me a healthy fear of their anger. When I went before the judge several weeks later, my knees buckled and my legs shook uncontrollably. As rehearsed, I told the judge that I didn't plan on being back in a courtroom until I'd earned my law degree. Joey was already sixteen, so his case was more serious, but because the officer had had his gun drawn when he pulled Joey out of the Duster, the charges were dropped. The gun had gone off accidentally, its muzzle resting on Joey's shoulder, causing a serious burn, and the officer was suspended from the force. Within four years, though, Joey would have a high-speed encounter with a utility pole, leaving him with a reconstructed arm, a metal plate in his skull, and mild brain damage.

I would have two more scrapes with the law before reaching adulthood, one my senior year of high school when I was caught with pot on a school ski trip and another upon graduating from college. My parents had given me a cruise to Bermuda as a graduation gift, and my girlfriend and I were arrested there for possessing small quantities of assorted narcotics. We were fined a hefty sum, which my parents paid and I had to work off before being able to move to Manhattan to begin my acting career. My father admitted to me before I left that he feared I would be found running naked down Christopher Street, out of my head on some substance. That never happened, though I did chase a boyfriend with whom I'd argued down Bleecker Street one night, wearing only a raincoat and work boots.

I understand now the enormous pain I was in as a teenager, and how much I would have benefited by having an adult to whom I could have turned for advice. Though I had friends in high school, my inner life was a secret, as well as a source of great shame. And it was the gnawing loneliness and the low self-esteem born of that shame that caused me to anesthetize myself with substances. Parents didn't speak to their kids the way they do today, and I carried the gulf between my parents and me into my relationships with teachers and, later, professors. Adults would not understand me, I was sure, and existed simply to judge. As a result, I avoided them. I was jealous of the students who became friends with their professors, and resentful that no one had taken me under their wing. Of course it was I who pushed them away, frightened that I wasn't worthy of their attentions.

I wish now that I'd had an Uncle Eddy, someone to encourage me to explore my creativity, help me sort through my feelings and, most of all, to tell me that I was amazing and could do anything. I'd tried to be that person for Tiffany throughout her life, but would it now be possible to be that *and* an authority figure? Are they mutually exclusive? I wondered. Or is it simply too late to change the dynamic from one thing to a hybrid of that and another? Only time would tell, I knew, but just in case, I decided to call Georgia, my cool guitar-playing girlfriend, to see if she could help out.

I treated myself to a Vinyasa yoga class during Georgia's and Tiffany's first guitar lesson. I'd been trying to make the seven thirty class on Wednesday mornings but often decided to read the *Times* in bed, blowing off both my regular gym routine and walking Tiffany to the subway. But on this Monday night in May I luxuriated in an hour-and-a-half, sweat-drenched class that ended with fifteen solid minutes of *savasana,* a yoga relaxation pose.

When I walked into the apartment, the smells of Georgia's home-cooked vegetarian dinner permeated the air and I could hear the lesson in progress down the hall. Georgia must have brought over two guitars, because she'd play a chord and then Tiffany would immediately repeat it. I listened for a minute before knocking on the bedroom door.

"Whatchya doin'?" I asked after being given permission to enter.

"Falling in love with your niece," Georgia said, smiling ear to ear. Tiffany glanced my way briefly but remained intent on getting the chord right.

"Join the club," I responded, secretly glad that I wasn't the only adult who'd succumbed to the teenager's charms. "How's it going?"

"Amazing," Georgia said. "Tiffany's going to have this down in no time. She's musical to the core." My niece looked up from her guitar long enough to roll her eyes and grin; her concentration was not to be broken.

"Just as I suspected." I smiled proudly. "Dinner smells yummy, Georgia, thank you. I'll help myself; you guys keep playing."

Tiffany had taken to Georgia right away the first time they'd met, which had been nearly two years earlier. She loved that my friend was an ex-songwriter for a major record label who'd gigged with her own rock band, not to mention Georgia's "No Blood for Oil" button and her penchant for alluding to people like W. B. Yeats and Kurt Cobain in the same sentence. I asked Georgia if she might be willing to spend some one-on-one time with my niece and maybe develop a closer friendship. I was hoping that Tiffany might confide in her about boys and sex. In essence, I recruited Georgia to replace the old Uncle Eddy, and she was totally game. When I mentioned that Tiffany had always wanted to learn the guitar, Georgia saw it as the perfect way for them to bond.

Now, as I sat eating the delicious mushy green stuff Georgia had prepared, I recognized the chords of "Hey Jude" wafting down the hallway. I thought of Uncle Tommy and how he'd encouraged Megan to learn the guitar as a teenager. She was the only one on the Team of Five who was musical, and she had a gorgeous voice. It was deep and smoky, and when she sang "Leaving on a Jet Plane," it brought tears to my eleven-year-old eyes. Megan had long since stopped playing, declaring that she was no good and couldn't sing. Does she still have that old guitar? I wondered, as Tiffany's and Georgia's voices blended for the epic *naah, naah, naah, na, na, na naahs.* Though I wasn't thrilled that Tiffany's first song on the guitar was one rumored to be about a heroin addict, I felt my entire body settle into that deep-gut comfort of knowing the passing decades had brought life full circle.

# No White Knight

"I've got it," I practically shouted across the table. "*You've had brunch at my apartment!* Nine years ago. You were a friend of my ex's from Harvard." Eugene had been trying to fix me up with his new friend Trevor for some time, and I sat now with them and Tom, Eugene's boyfriend, in a small seafood restaurant on Bedford Street. I knew Trevor was no stranger the minute I saw him, and when he mentioned he'd lived in Boston until recently, it all came flooding back.

"Really?" Trevor asked with a smile, his cheeks morphing into sexy creases. "I don't think so. I only recognize you from the train two years ago." Apparently, when Eugene had told Trevor my full name, he'd flipped; two years earlier Trevor had spotted me on a MetroNorth train and gotten my name and address from the delivery label on the *New York Times* I'd left behind. He'd written a poem about me but never summoned the courage to send it.

Other people might find this a bit scary or odd, but I loved it, not just because it was flattering but because it was exactly the kind of thing I would do (though *I* would have sent the poem). Back in my dating (read "cruising and boffing") heyday, I'd left my phone number under bread plates for waiters, stuck notes on car windshields, and placed "I saw you on the F train" ads in the *Village Voice.* In the mid-'80s, I'd even left a phone message on then-Oscar-nominated actor Tom Hulce's home answering machine, pretending I was calling someone named John with important news and imploring him to call me back *immediately.* I figured the sweet-faced Hulce would surely call to tell me I'd had the wrong number, whereupon I'd charm him with my sultriest phone voice and we'd end up on a date. (He never called.) So obviously Trevor's romantically aggressive behavior was both familiar and endearing to me. And for once I was the stalkee, I thought happily. Too bad I didn't know it, though; if only he'd sent the damned poem.

"No, I'm sure of it now," I said with a knowing grin. "You were in town for the '94 Gay Games and you came to the brunch my boyfriend Rick and I threw. I have group photos from that day and you're in them. I also remember because my friend Don was visiting from London and he thought you were totally hot. I did too, but I was jealous because I had an unrequited crush on *him*." When Eugene's eyes bugged out of his head and his thin, permanently electrolysized eyebrows arched almost to his hairline, I realized I'd just told a potential boyfriend that I'd been lusting after two other men while I was in a relationship — not the most brilliant move on my part. "But of course I didn't act on either infatuation," I quickly added.

"Okay, right. Rick's boyfriend. I'm starting to remember now," Trevor said, squinting one eye and nodding at me. (He spoke with a slight Boston accent — "stahting to remembuh nahow" — which was charmingly upscale, not trashy like the guys in P-Town who said "Bawb" for "Bob.") "I was out of my mind back then, drinking and drugging like a maniac," Trevor continued, "and you're much more handsome now too, *ahn-cha?*"

"God no," I said. "In '94 I still had the cutest little bubble —"

"But-cha ahh, Blanche, ya ahh," Eugene barked breathily at me, doing his awesome Bette Davis *and* poking fun at Trevor's accent. "Seriously, though," he said, taking

Trevor's hand, "Edwin here is only getting better as he gets older." He shot me a "shut up" glare, as if he thought I was actually going to tell Trevor that the HIV drugs I was taking were making my ass disappear and my legs turn into a living diagram of the circulatory system. *Nevuh!* I thought. "We're all teddibly jealous," he added, now doing Gwyneth doing British.

"*You* look great," I said to Trevor, taking Eugene's cue to change the subject. "You remind me of Steve McQueen in *The Towering Inferno*, with those rugged dimples and blue eyes." I wasn't lying a bit; changing "creases" to "dimples" was simply a matter of diplomacy. And Trevor really had aged in a naturally masculine way, sort of like Kurt — and unlike so many gay men who enter middle age looking self-consciously preserved.

"Oh, you're sweet . . . I guess." Trevor paused. "But wasn't Steve McQueen, like, fifty when he made that movie?"

"Okay, so *The Blob*, then," I offered, enjoying our sparring.

"That's better," Trevor said. "I'm only thirty-eight. Well, almost thirty-nine." I was surprised to learn this, as he looked older to me. Sure, his hair had thinned on top since '94, but so had his face: hence the sexy folds when he smiled. I wondered for a moment if he was HIV-positive, as so many of us had lost fat in our faces from the combination drug therapy, but instead I chalked it up to my denial about how old I looked; I thought *everyone* was my age or older.

"I've been through the wringer since then," he continued. "I had a disastrous nine-year relationship where I was drunk and my partner was high the entire time. I found out I was HIV-positive just two years ago, and when we split up last year, I had a total nervous breakdown and wound up in the hospital for two months." *Red flags! Red flags!* I could hear Steven's therapist voice screaming in the back of my head. *Less than a year out of the mental hospital! Danger, Will Robinson, danger!* Despite my nagging thoughts, I found Trevor's honesty refreshing and felt relieved that for once I wouldn't have to hide anything about myself. Certainly it was a bit strange for him to tell me all of this on our first meeting. But why shouldn't he? I thought. He's going to have to tell me most of it at some point, so why not lay his cards on the table? I'd never told Kurt about my visit to the psych ward, deepening the shame I felt about the incident. I decided to tell Trevor right then and there what had happened when I'd begun working at the law firm — even though it was really none of his damned business — and it felt good. And since I'd spent only two weeks in the ward, I figured it didn't seem like I was trying to one-up him in the maladies department, an extremely annoying habit of many New Yorkers.

"It wasn't like you lost nine years of your life, either." I changed the subject back to Trevor. "You managed to get your MSW during that time and start your career in social work." We'd both been prepped beforehand about each other's jobs; Trevor worked with low-income folks with HIV, helping them manage their healthcare and welfare benefits. "And look at you now. You've got an important job doing what you love, you're clean and sober, and to top it all off, you've met Eugene and Tom."

"And he's the best sponsor a guy could hope for," Trevor said, taking Eugene's hand in his. *What?* I almost fell off my chair. *Your sponsor?* Eugene had told me Trevor was in AA, but not that he was sponsoring him. You idiot! I wanted to scream. How am I going to complain to you about my dating neuroses while you're hearing everything from the other guy too? It's not fair to me, to our friendship, and it could be detrimental to Trevor's sobriety. I made a mental note to kill Eugene the next time I saw him.

As I smiled across the candlelight into Trevor's dangerous, sparkly eyes, I knew that no complicated twists in this little group's dynamics would prevent me from seeing him again. Neither would all the red flags in China.

"How beautiful, Tiffany!" I shouted down the hall from the living room, referring to the little hacienda she'd built for her Spanish class. The elaborate model was displayed atop the dining table, which was covered in newspapers, and the hanging light fixture spotlighted the red fluted tile roof she'd created by cutting drinking straws in half. She'd cleverly cut up the long, thin strips of balsa wood I'd bought her into tiny tiles, painted them in bright colors, and created mosaics to decorate the exterior walls and serve as a festive trim for the windows and doors. "It's like a Mexican gingerbread house," I yelled. "I can't believe you did all of this today." Before I'd left work to meet Eugene, Tom, and Trevor for dinner, I'd called Tiffany to remind her that the project was due the next day. She'd detected that I was way more stressed about it than she was and said coolly, "I've got it under control." She obviously did.

"How does building a house help you learn Spanish?" she'd asked when the project was first assigned. "Don't ask me," I'd answered brusquely, knowing that shopping for supplies would fall on my shoulders. (I would later be even more annoyed when it wound up costing me fifty bucks.) Now, though, as I admired Tiffany's attention to detail and her sense of design — the conical bushes she'd fashioned from green construction paper, the cactuses made of pipe cleaners — I saw the more abstract, non-language-related value of the project: Tiffany had taken a vague, seemingly senseless assignment and run with it. She'd designed a house and built its model with raw materials, from the ground up, and it had turned out splendidly. I pictured her riding the crowded F train to school the next morning, holding her hacienda tightly on her lap, and I felt the pride I imagined only a parent could know.

"I'm glad you like it," Tiffany said as she came skipping down the hall wearing a pink muscle T and gray sweats that said

507

'Angel' just below the waistband. "Building it inspired me to start another project in my bedroom. Come see," she said, grabbing me gently by the arm and leading me away.

"Look," she whispered as she slowly opened her bedroom door. "It's the dreaded letter." I didn't remember at first what letter she was speaking of, but my eyes were immediately drawn to the two lines of color that now striated three sides of the room. Intrigued, I turned to my left and drew closer. On irregular-shaped strips of purple and black construction paper Tiffany had glued sentences she'd cut from the letter I'd sent her nine months earlier, when the entire family had reached out in an attempt to pull her back on track. She'd affixed the story of the girl who rose above her circumstances on purple paper, while the sadder story of the girl who was doomed to repeat her mother's mistakes ran lower around the wall, against a black backdrop. On the periphery of the colored strips, Tiffany had taped snippets she'd cut from magazines or greeting cards — things that complemented or personalized the story for her. Beneath the black-backed sentence "After the divorce her mother's drinking got worse" was a small piece of white paper that said, "Hope you have a great 14th! Eric." Then I noticed that above the purple sentence, "She remembered all the people who loved and believed in her, and found the courage to express her pain and grief through her creativity," Tiffany had placed an illustration of a knight in full armor riding a white horse. I felt my chin quiver, so I squeezed my lips tightly together, turned toward my niece, and held up my fist so we could knock knuckles.

"It's totally *fly,*" I said, forcing myself to smile when I wanted to cry. I just hope I rode in on time, I thought, and that my mettle has proved up to the test.

Tiffany and I had begun sharing a journal several years earlier, when she was around ten or eleven. It was a tacky-looking book covered in pink roses, and I can't remember where we got it or even whose idea it was to begin with. I suspect it was Tiffany's, though, as she was always thinking up ways to keep us connected when miles apart. (To my delight, Sammy was currently following suit by braiding matching anklets for us to wear from one summer to the next.) The journal had a little padlock and we each owned a key, and every once in a while one of us would write about an experience we'd shared together. I kept my key in the center of a rock Tiffany had given me long ago — a rock she'd bought at the Natural Stone Bridge and Caves gift shop in the Adirondacks. It was the souvenir kind that they cut in half and polish, with a center that's hollow but jagged with sparkly, quartzlike crystals. I'm sure Tiffany had proudly told me the name of the stone when she presented it to me, but I'd long since forgotten. I did remember her instructions, though: "You keep one half and I'll keep the other half," she'd said in her singsong Mouseketeer voice. "Then, whenever we see each other, we'll bring them together to make the rock whole again." Years later, when we began sharing the journal, I wasn't surprised to find that the key fit perfectly inside the rock's core.

During the course of our nine months of living together, I'd made several entries, only now they were less about events in our collective life and more about how I felt the arrangement was working out. Each time I opened the journal I couldn't help but go back and read passages written when things were far simpler between Tiffany and me. Tonight was no different. As

I sat down to write about how moved I was by Tiffany's turning my letter into an expressive work of her own, the book flipped open to one of her earlier entries. She was visiting New York for the weekend and we'd gone to see M. Night Shyamalan's film *Unbreakable.* Apparently we'd concluded that the movie's main theme was that inside all of us lurks a superhero, if only we can believe in ourselves enough to let it emerge. "I don't need to find my inside superhero," Tiffany had written, "because my Uncle Eddy is a superhero to me. I know that when I am with him he will protect me from everything bad and that he believes in me more then [sic] anyone else ever could. Even me."

I hadn't read this in years, and even though I felt good that I'd stepped up to the plate to help make Tiffany's life better — indeed, to "protect" her — it made me sad to read the entry now. Sure, I hoped that the white knight on her wall was me, but I knew that most of the time she saw me as her adversary. Gone was the uncle she'd once idolized, replaced now by this uptight, controlling man whose mission in life was to deprive her of everything that makes her happy. It could be a decade or more, I thought, before she has any idea what's really gone on here and how purely my intention has been to help her.

I decided then to make certain that Tiffany knew about my HIV status, to have that long-delayed real conversation. If she was going to believe that she knew and understood the human being I truly was — rather than the superhero she'd thought I'd been — then it was important for her to know some of the other battles I was waging.

# Crazy in Camelot

"So, what did you think of Trevor?" I asked Tiffany as I set a heaping stack of steaming pancakes down in the center of the table, right next to the plate of low-fat sausages I'd meticulously browned. It was a stunning Saturday morning in June and we were both in visibly good moods — me because I'd had a thermonuclear date with Trevor the night before, and Tiffany, well, probably just because she was young, gorgeous, and living in Manhattan. On a morning like this, breakfast with Tiffany could only be a pleasure.

"He's pretty hot," she said, stabbing a couple of large cakes with her fork.

"Well, I *know* that," I responded. "But what did you *think* of him?" I asked, and quickly added, "Didn't you think he was funny?" Objection, I thought, leading the witness. Sustained.

"I thought he was trying too hard," Tiffany said matter-of-factly as she cut a sausage in two with the side of her fork.

"To be funny?" I asked, my curiosity fully piqued by such a nuanced observation, especially coming from a fourteen-year-old. I was aware that kids, like dogs, often pick up on cues that adults miss, especially bedazzled ones.

"Well, yes, but not only that." She chewed thoughtfully for a moment. "He was trying too hard to get me to like him, which made him seem very insecure."

"Very interesting, I can see why you would say that." I took a whopping bite of pancake to slow the conversation down so my mind could catch up.

I'd flattered myself that Trevor's nervousness was due to what I perceived as pyrotechnic chemistry between us. I too had felt a bit on edge, especially at the beginning of both solo dinner dates we'd had since Eugene fixed us up. I'd melted into each evening, though, both lulled and ignited by the freedom of our laughter, our openness, and the way we each kept insisting on turning the floor over to the other, only to take it back a second later. They were the kinds of dates where the words can't come out fast enough, where responses trip over new thoughts, where you both have to work hard to lasso the conversation back onto something remotely resembling a linear track. And all the while you're lost in the ocean of his eyes, impatient to earn the next smile and scarily gratified each time you're rewarded. The restaurant has long since disappeared; you don't notice a thing about the food, the waiter, or the couple sitting only inches to your left. You're outside of space and time — the ultimate escape — and you want to experience it unequivocally, so you fight, battle, wrestle the desire to fast-forward through time to find out how it all ends. Because you know when it's this good, it almost always ends badly.

Despite all of the red flags thwacking me in the face — how Trevor's hands shook from the lithium he was taking for his bipolar disorder, how he was still seeing someone else (which Eugene had told me the first time he'd mentioned Trevor but which I'd promptly and conveniently forgotten), and how he sometimes seemed scattered among twenty places at once ("It's my ADHD," he'd offer apologetically) — there was a gravitational pull exerted by Trevor Knapp that I could not resist. Maybe because British Don had wanted him and not me nine years earlier. Maybe because, like Kurt, he represented that masculine ideal I sought out —

strong, capable, worldly wise (but what the *hell* was I basing that on?) — or maybe it was his good, old-fashioned Kennedyesque mystique. Trevor was raised in the family mansion overlooking the sea on the coast of Massachusetts. His father had built a business empire and later became a regional politician (the Knapps actually knew the Kennedys). Trevor had degrees from Harvard and Columbia and had eschewed lucrative opportunities in favor of doing service to society. His sisters sat on the boards of important charitable organizations, he had fresh flowers delivered to his apartment once a week, and the latest family crisis involved his brother-in-law's surviving a shark attack while diving off an exotic South American island. In short, Trevor was impossibly glamorous, smart, and funny, and when I was with him I felt glamorous, smart, and funny too. I'd barely dated a soul since Kurt and I had broken up fifteen months earlier, much less felt this strongly about anyone, and over the course of the last decade and a half I'd been rejected innumerable times because of my HIV status. I'd be damned if I was going to let Trevor slip away simply because there were warning signs portending what *might* happen. If I were so easily daunted I'd have thrown in the towel at twenty-six and left New York City to die in the suburbs.

And now, more than ever before, I had the sense that my life was complete; I had an established career, I'd rediscovered my passion for writing, and thanks to Tiffany, I had a family of my own. It was a life I'd fought hard for, and one that was worth sharing. But it was a life that would never take second position to a man, no matter how chivalrously he swept me off my feet. As long as I kept that in mind, I knew I'd be able to keep my budding romance with Trevor in perspective and take things relatively slowly.

"Tiffany, you know that I'm HIV-positive, right?" Her forkful of pancake hung in midair, a string of syrup dripping down to her plate.

"You did not just say that, Uncle Eddy," she said softly without moving a muscle in her entire body or face, as though she'd been flash-frozen.

"Yes, it's true," I said. "I'm sorry to spring it on you like this. I thought you already knew, and there's no good time or easier way to say it."

"Oh . . . my . . . God," Tiffany's hand free-fell to her plate. Her fork dinged the china loudly and sent a fine splatter of syrup out over the polished cherry table. Tiffany seemed not to notice; her watery eyes stared at me unflinchingly.

"It's okay, sweetheart. I've been this way for fifteen years and I'm in good health. I've never been sick from it. Not once. That's why I take all those pills, to fight it, to keep from getting sick. Really, it's going to be fine." I hadn't rehearsed for this moment — there was no way that one could — and I found myself searching for words that were not to be found.

This was only the second time that I'd personally told a family member about my HIV infection, and the circumstances were vastly different from the first. For two weeks after I learned my status, I avoided all calls from my parents. I was afraid that the sound of either of their voices would send me into an hysterical crying jag, and I had no intention of telling them what had happened — at least not until I got a handle on it myself. After a couple more weeks passed and I'd survived one or two phone conversations with them, I decided I was strong enough to pay my parents a visit for my mother's birthday. The three of us went out to a pleasant, uneventful dinner at a local restaurant to celebrate. What I couldn't have anticipated, though, were the profound feelings of loss I would experience the next morning, when I woke up in my childhood bedroom.

As I'd been gone for only four years, my mom had not yet fully redecorated. Reminders of the teenager who had lived, dreamed, and suffered in that room were everywhere, from the bright orange I'd insisted on painting the walls to the Yes sticker on the back of the door to the one ski poster left hanging. This had been the private sanctuary of a sensitive, dream-filled young man who, like Tiffany, had his whole life ahead of him. The grief of awakening in this room now, a failed actor with a fatal illness — an illness that could have been avoided — was too much for me to bear. Desperate, I ran to the bathroom, turned the radio up loud and the shower faucet on full force. I stripped off my clothes and jumped behind the curtain just as my head and heart exploded with sadness — a sadness I thought would kill me.

My mom had left for work earlier that morning, but my dad was already retired, and when I finally emerged from the bathroom I could hear him puttering around downstairs. I was determined to avoid him for the remainder of the morning, as I didn't want him to see that my eyes were swollen nearly shut. I made coffee while he was in the shower and drank it in the living room while he read in the den. Whenever I heard him coming, I'd duck behind an easy chair so that when he'd pop his head in he wouldn't see me and would continue on up the stairs. "Eddy, where are you?" he called down at one point. "In the living room, Dad," I answered. "I was in the bathroom before." This went on for at least two hours.

Finally the time for me to catch my train back to the city approached.

"Eddy, why don't you have a sandwich before you go?" my father yelled, having given up looking for me.

"Okay, Dad," I shouted from the living room. "I'll come make it."

He sat at the kitchen table with his crossword puzzle before him, his reading spectacles perched near the end of his nose.

"Can I make one for you too?" I asked, making sure my back was to him as I made my way to the refrigerator.

"Sure," he said. "What's a five-letter word meaning 'between'? There's an 'Fr.' in the clue, so I think it's French."

"Entre," I replied, thinking, This is obviously not the *Times*. "Like the Miou Miou film *Entre Nous*, or 'Just Between Us.' "

"Mew *what?* You've grown too sophisticated," he said as he looked up at me and smiled. "A real city guy."

"Well, this sophisticated city guy is going to join you for a bologna and American cheese sandwich, since those are the cold cuts in stock."

"What? Something wrong with baloney?" he asked, not looking up from the puzzle.

"No," I replied as I reached for the mayonnaise and iceberg lettuce. "I just haven't had it in years. Probably not since I moved out." And with that, the dam burst again. I dropped the baloney on the floor — on the floor of this room where my father sat in his usual spot and the cheery midday sun streamed in through the yellow-curtained windows, this room where I was kept safe and warm and fed for so many years. I grabbed the edge of the Formica counter with both hands to keep myself from caving in as I sobbed.

My father jumped from his chair and ran to me. He grabbed me to him and wrapped his arms around me, holding me up as I cried on his shirt.

"What is it, my boy?" he asked over and over as I wept. "What is it, my baby boy?"

I'd never been held by my father like that, and he'd certainly never spoken such words to me before. Comforted though I was, I cried even harder. I couldn't have known then that in nine years' time, when we'd lose our Heather Ann, I would hold him in almost exactly the same way.

My father didn't share the news with my mother for at least a year because he didn't think she could handle it. I'd finally insisted. My parents, in turn, told my sisters and my uncles, sparing me the terrible anguish those moments would have wrought. With Tiffany, though, the news had to come from me directly.

"But having HIV hasn't been any picnic, either. Believe me, Tiffany." She'd resumed eating, finally, but didn't know what was expected of her beyond that. "I started on medications seven years ago, and some of the side effects have been difficult to deal with."

"How do you think you got it?" she asked timidly.

"Oh, I *know* how I got it. I trusted someone I was dating when he told me he'd tested negative twice in the previous six months. But it's not his fault," I added. "He may have lied to me, but only *I'm* responsible for me. I owed it to myself to *always* be safe, and I let myself down. You can't rely on someone else to take care of you, Tiffany. Ever."

"Do you think you'll write about it in your book?" she asked.

"I imagine I will," I replied. "It's part of my story and, though I regret not being safe, I work hard at not being ashamed that I'm positive. I'm not always successful; maybe writing about it will help." She nodded and wiped the tears from her eyes. "Speaking of my book," I continued, "now that you've won the freshman writing award, maybe you'll consider writing some chapters for it, telling our story from your point of view."

"That sounds cool," she said, "but I think I want to write my own book, if that's okay."

"Of course it is. It's great, in fact." I reached out and took her hand. "Hey, why don't you call it, *I, Tiffany: What Uncle Eddy Doesn't Know?*"

"You're nuts, you know that?" she said and giggled. "If I write it, then I'll have told you."

# Huckleberry Friends

For our walk along the Hudson River, Tiffany wore a form-fitting beige and pastel blue tank minidress with high cork-platform slip-ons. Judging from the looks on the faces of every man we passed (gay, straight, and otherwise), she must have looked at least eighteen, if not twenty-one. A head turner at fourteen, I thought. We're in deep shit. To the more observant, Tiffany's walk would be the most revealing clue to her true age. Not yet practiced in the art of walking four inches off the ground, she kept her head and shoulders unnaturally still as she carefully measured each stride one by one. To those of us in the know, Tiffany's coltish awkwardness added immeasurably to her charm.

It was one of those early June evenings that promises hot summer nights just ahead, but your skin is still surprised by the feel of warm air, reminding you that you're just a creature who has lived through another winter on the planet. The joy of that simplicity made me want to roll around on spring-soft grass, gulp honeysuckle air, and feel sand between my ghostly white toes. And, of course, jump on anything male with a pulse. Tonight I was doing a heroic job of not gawking or sighing after the many shirtless gods flying by on foot and wheels, probably because the inuring process had started in May, when a mere flip-flopped foot could send me into a tizzy.

Living with a teenager on a school schedule made me more aware than ever of the approaching summer. Finals were coming, along with a Regents exam in science, and Tiffany's excitement at successfully completing her freshman year of high school was almost palpable. She'd been talking about the family vacation in the Adirondacks for months now, and how one of the girls she knew there would be old enough to drive this year, so they'd be off cruising every night. (As if! I'd thought, but a girl can dream.) I understood all too well that in teenspeak *car* and *freedom* were the same word. Later in July, when she was back in New Milford, Tiffany was determined to build a fort with her girlfriends in the woods on Kitt's property. She'd sketched out the design and even called her uncle Tyler, who worked as a manager at Home Depot, to see if he could start putting scraps aside. I tried to be as encouraging of her plans as I could, knowing how seldom such grand schemes came to fruition. (I never did build that raft on which I was going to spend the entire summer floating around the reservoir, entertaining my friends.) Plus Megan and I had decided that Tiffany would be spending very little time in Connecticut over the summer, but we hadn't told her that yet.

On this warm June evening I'd come home to the surprise of a full "gourmet" meal prepared by Tiffany, along with a beautifully set table. She'd cleverly cobbled together ingredients she'd found in the house and spent a few of the emergency dollars I kept in my bedroom on the items she'd needed to buy. For a first course there were delicious stuffed mushrooms that were neither soggy nor dry. The main course of penne with chicken and (frozen) broccoli florets in a creamy sauce couldn't live up to the standard set by the mushrooms but was perfectly fine. As we smothered our heaping plates with grated cheese from the Mouli, I told Tiffany in five different ways how sweet it was for her to have done such a kind thing for me.

Afterwards I'd suggested we go for a walk along the river, where the fences had recently been removed to reveal the brand-spanking-new Hudson River Park. Though it was early on in the six-year project, we were fortunate to live adjacent to the first section to be completed — the stretch of riverfront from approximately Barrow Street north to Gansevoort.

"Maybe we can find some Good Humor," I'd said as I cleaned up the very messy kitchen.

"What do you mean?" Tiffany had asked with complete sincerity. "I'm already in a good mood."

"It's a brand of ice cream, sweetie," I'd said, chuckling. "Though I probably haven't said that in thirty years. When your mom, Aunt Kathleen, and I were little, we called the ice cream truck the 'Good Humor Man.' I think there might be one down by the river now."

"Cool," she'd said. "You scared me for a second; it sounded like a code word for getting high."

"That'll be the day," I'd said, and meant it.

Now, as we strolled along the river, me gnawing dutifully away at my vanilla Hood bar, anxious to get to the chocolate fudgy hard stuff near the stick, neither of us could quite get over how stunning the new park was. (I suspected Tiffany had declined an ice cream so she could focus primarily on walking.) What twenty years ago was a wasteland of broken pavement, ten-foot-high piles of sand, and city-owned sanitation trucks was now a verdant ribbon of a park with narrow, rolling grass meadows, a paved biking and Rollerblading path, and a promenade with benches and poplar trees just along the river's edge. Three new piers had been built out over the water, two of them with huge expanses of grass and sail-like tarps rigged at interesting angles to provide shade for the chairs and tables beneath them. And everywhere we turned there were huge beds of multicolored lilies.

"Omigod!" Tiffany whispered so as not to scream. "I can't believe they did this all right in our backyard!" Our backyard, I repeated to myself, and smiled broadly at my niece.

"That's right," I said. "And it's absolutely magnificent. This summer you and your friends can bring a blanket and a boom box down here and hang out. The park stays open late — way past your curfew."

"That will be so cool," she replied, not questioning my assertion that she'd be here during the summer. "My friends from New Milford have got to see this. Can I have a few of them down at once, Uncle Eddy?"

"Well, two shouldn't be a problem," I said, turning my face toward the cool breeze blowing off the river. "But let's take it day by day and just enjoy this moment for now."

People were all around us, running, biking, blading, throwing Frisbees, lounging on the grass playing Scrabble or reading, practicing tai chi, pushing strollers; one man was even flying a small kite to the delight of his tiny daughter. And yet there was a churchlike hush over the park, a strange calm, as though everyone was experiencing the same reverence as Tiffany and I.

We stopped to chat for a few minutes with a producer I knew, a handsome ex-model who walked arm in arm with his fiancée. When Garrett and I had first met, I'd harbored secret hopes, but as always, my "gaydar" was malfunctioning terribly. We'd become friends instead, and I was delighted when he'd fallen head over heels in love in his late forties. Garrett had heard all about Tiffany, of course, and he was thrilled to meet her. We all spoke in hushed whispers, so as not to break the spell, and I made no effort to hide how proud I was of my beautiful, poised niece. Truth be told, I often imagined people on the streets thinking, "What a gorgeous daughter he has, and they seem to be so close!" I knew my desire to inspire admiration, even envy, in strangers was nothing to be proud of, but I couldn't help it. I loved walking around New York City with Tiffany.

The sun was inches from the horizon and the sky over New Jersey was just taking on a pinkish hue as we said goodbye to Garrett and his soon-to-be wife.

"Why don't we walk out on the pier?" I suggested. "That way we'll see the sunset straight on, without craning our necks."

"Sure," she agreed. "I don't think my feet are bleeding yet."

"Ah, the perils of new shoes," I teased. "Let's not have a repeat of our night at Carnegie Hall, okay?" She'd worn a new pair of sandals to attend a friend's choral concert with me, and when the pain of her fresh blisters got bad, I'd had to carry her on my back through what felt like two miles of subway tunnels.

"Well, at least here I could go barefoot if

I have to. Not like in the subway. Will you put Band-Aids on the blisters when we get home?"

"Of course," I said as we walked farther out, surrounded now by purple, sparkling water. "You know what I'd like to do?" I asked.

"What?"

"I'd like to take you to Paris when you graduate from high school. Venice is my favorite city in the world so far, but Paris should be everyone's first foreign city."

"That would be so ill," Tiffany responded, smiling. "Oh, look!" she said. On the grass to our left a group of teenagers laughed as their token gay friend vogued to a Madonna CD. I wondered if Tiffany was thinking how much she'd rather be with her friends than with me; there was no one else I'd have rather been with.

"Two drifters, off to see the world," I sang softly. "There's such a lot of world to see."

"What's that song?" Tiffany asked.

"Oh, it's from an old movie that was made from my favorite novella. Do you want me to stop?"

"No, it's pretty," she replied — a first.

"We're after the same rainbow's end, waitin' round the bend, my huckleberry friend, Moon River and me." (I have an awful voice, but by talk-singing in a stage whisper like a male Marilyn Monroe, I'd managed not to mangle the lyric.)

"What's a 'huckleberry friend'?" Tiffany asked.

"Well, I guess it's, like, your best adventurer-friend, someone you want to do memorable things with."

Tiffany smiled and took my hand in hers as we walked, probably for the first time since she was ten.

"Uncle Eddy," she said as we approached the end of the pier, the Jersey City sky now a masterpiece of psychedelic spin art. "This summer I'm going to need to go on the pill."

Oh, Lord have mercy, I thought, taking a big salty gulp of the brackish river's air. That's right, Ed. Never, *ever,* forget to breathe.

# Acknowledgments

First and foremost, I would like to thank my family — my mom, dad, sisters, brother-in-law, and niece J.J. — for their love, encouragement, and support (despite what I might — and did — write about them).

I couldn't have lived through the year described in this book, never mind have written about it, without the following people: Charlotte Deaver, Michael Serrapica, Brian Belovitch, and Ana de Orbegoso. Additional emotional backup was provided by Gilbert Rios, Liz Fender, Laura Sabatell, Cheryl Sucher, Gene Reilly, Sue Crystal, and Hank Flacks. *Namaste,* Kathy Resner Clobridge. And most special, eternal thanks to my beloved "heavy lifter," Dafna Yoran, and to my fellow traveler, Susan Lazarus.

At Miramax Books, much gratitude to Jonathan Burnham and Kathy Schneider for giving me the opportunity to tell this story, to JillEllyn Riley for her invaluable editorial input and moral support, to Claire McKinney for her savvy promotional skills, and to Kristin Powers for pulling it all together (and for putting up with me).

Brevity prohibits me from expressing here the depth of my appreciation for my agent and treasured friend, Mitchell Waters. Besides his brilliant advocacy and editorial prowess, Mitchell provided a near-daily shoulder throughout my two years of living and writing this book; without him, it would not exist. Heartfelt thanks to all of the Curtis Brown, Ltd. family, and in particular to Timothy Knowlton, Dave Barbor, Peter Ginsberg, Rob Pellecchia, Robby O'Connor, and Jonathan Lyons. Also thanks to my London agent Shirley Stewart, Amy Schiffman of the Gersh Agency, publicist Scott Manning, and my dear friend and website designer, Mark Frankel of Arroyo Design.

Last, and the opposite of least, I would like to acknowledge my niece Brittany, who brought fire back into my world — the kind of fire that can only be contained by an embrace. May she burn bright and long, and may she find the courage to grace the world with her talents. I am forever in her debt.

We hope you have enjoyed this Large Print book. Other Thorndike, Wheeler or Chivers Press Large Print books are available at your library or directly from the publishers.

For more information about current and upcoming titles, please call or write, without obligation, to:

Publisher
Thorndike Press
295 Kennedy Memorial Drive
Waterville, ME  04901
Tel. (800) 223-1244

Or visit our Web site at:
www.gale.com/thorndike
www.gale.com/wheeler

OR

Chivers Large Print
published by BBC Audiobooks Ltd
St James House, The Square
Lower Bristol Road
Bath BA2 3BH
England
Tel. +44(0) 800 136919
email: bbcaudiobooks@bbc.co.uk
www.bbcaudiobooks.co.uk

All our Large Print titles are designed for easy reading, and all our books are made to last.